ATHENAZE

ATHENAZE

An Introduction to Ancient Greek

Revised Edition
Book II

Teacher's Handbook

Maurice Balme
and
Gilbert Lawall

New York   Oxford
OXFORD UNIVERSITY PRESS
1991

Oxford University Press

Oxford   New York   Toronto
Delhi   Bombay   Calcutta   Madras   Karachi
Petaling Jaya   Singapore   Hong Kong   Tokyo
Nairobi   Dar es Salaam   Cape Town
Melbourne   Auckland

and associated companies in
Berlin   Ibadan

Copyright © 1991 by Oxford University Press, Inc.

Published by Oxford University Press, Inc.,
200 Madison Avenue, New York, New York 10016

Oxford is a registered trademark of Oxford University Press

Library of Congress Cataloging-in-Publication Data
(Revised for volume 2)
Balme, M. G.
Athenaze.
English and Ancient Greek. Includes index.
1. Greek language—Grammar—1950– .
2. Greek language—Readers. I. Lawall, Gilbert.
PA258.B325 1990 488.82'421 89-22967
ISBN 0-19-505621-3 (v. 1 : pbk.)
ISBN 0-19-506384-8 (teacher's handbook, v. 1)
ISBN 0-19-505622-1 (v. 2)
ISBN 0-19-506390-7 (teacher's handbook, v. 2)

4   6   8   9   7   5   3

Printed in the United States of America
on acid-free paper

Contents

ATHENAZE: SCOPE AND SEQUENCE
Book II: Chapters 17–31

CHAPTER	READINGS Daily Life	History	WORD STUDY	ESSAYS	WORD BUILDING	GRAMMAR Nouns and Pronouns	Adjectives and Participles	Verbs	Syntax	Miscellaneous
17	Journey to and arrival at Epidaurus. Sanctuary of Ascelpius.	Persians take Athens a second time.	Derivatives (psych-, analy-).	Healing sanctuaries: Asclepius and Epidaurus.	Nouns and adjectives from verbs.		future participle.	Future tense. Irregular verb εἰμι.	Purpose: ὡς + future participle. Article + participle.	
18	Philip's cure. Sacrifice to Asclepius.	Rumblings of war between Athens and Sparta. Athenian victory at Plataea.	Derivatives (auto-).	Sparta and Corinth.	Words from δίδωμι and τίθημι.	ταχύς.		δίδωμι and τίθημι.	Uses of αὐτός.	
19	Beginning of return trip to Attica.	Battle of Mycale.	Derivatives (-cracy).	Mycenae.	Adverbs from prepositions.		Attributive and predicate position.		Genitive absolute.	Further uses of the article.
20	Visit to Mycenae. Encounter in Corinth. Arrival at Eleusis.	Athenians remind Spartans of Athenian services.	Derivatives (-graph).	Events leading to Peloponnesian War.	Nouns and Verbs from same stem.			ἵστημι and καθ-ίστημι.	Verbs with supplementary participles.	
21	Arrival at Athens and Assembly.	Pericles' speech to Assembly. Farmers move to city.	Derivatives (anthro-).	Athenian Democracy.	Verbs, nouns, and adjectives from δίκη and βουλή.			Subjunctive. ἵημι.	Subjunctive: hortatory, deliberative, prohibitions, purpose.	
22	Return home. Preparation and journey to city.	Embassy before invasion of Attica. Plague.	Derivatives (academic subjects).	Athenian democracy in action.	Nouns and adjectives from verbs with stems ending in gutturals.			δείκνυμι.	Clauses of fearing. Indefinite or general clauses. Indirect statements and questions.	
23		Invasion of Attica. Achievements of Pericles.	Derivatives (political terms).	Peloponnesian War (first phase).	Verbs and nouns formed by adding suffixes to roots.		Passive voice (present and imperfect). φημί.		Indirect statements with infinitives and participles. Attraction of relative pronoun to case of antecedent.	Prepositional prefixes and euphony.

CHAPTER

CHAPTER	READINGS		WORD STUDY	ESSAYS	WORD BUILDING	GRAMMAR				Miscellaneous
	Daily Life	History				Nouns and Pronouns	Adjectives and Participles	Verbs	Syntax	
24	Philip's education.	Prologue to Herodotus' history.	Derivatives (musical terms).	Greek education.	Denominative verbs.		Comparison of adjectives.	Passive voice: aorist and future. Aorist of deponent verbs.	ὅπως + future indicative with verbs of care or effort.	
25		Croesus and Solon.	Derivatives (words in study of history).	Herodotus.	Denominative Nouns.			Optative.	Optative: wish, in subordinate clauses, in indirect speech.	
26		Adrastus kills Atys and himself.	Derivatives (literary terms).	Shame and guilt.	Adjectives from verb or noun stems.				Uses of gen., dat., and acc. cases.	Correlatives.
27		Croesus versus Cyrus.	Derivatives (philosophical terms).	Signs, dreams, and oracles.	Compound words.			Perfect and pluperfect, middle and passive.	Uses of πρίν. Articular infinitive.	
28		Apollo saves Croesus. Croesus sends envoys to Delphi.	Derivatives (medical specialists).	Rationalism and mysticism.	Nouns and adjectives from verbs with present reduplication			Perfect and pluperfect active.	Verbs mostly in perfect tense. Uses of ὡς.	
29		Naval victory of Phormio (1).	Derivatives (theological terms).	Thucydides.	Words from δίκη.	οὐ and σφῶν		οἶδα	Result clauses with ὥστε. Potential optative.	
30		Naval vistory of Phormio (2).	Derivatives in English paragraph.	Downfall of Athens.	Words from καιδ- and λεγ-/λογ-.				Conditional sentences. Complex sentences in indirect speech.	
31	Family celebrating peace and Rural Dionysia.	Old Comedy: Acharnians.		Aristophanes and Old Comedy.			Verbal Adjective in -τέος. Uses of the participle.	3rd person imperatives.	Uses of the negative.	Crasis. Elision. Prodelision or aphaeresis.

INTRODUCTION

For general information about the course, the student's books, and the teacher's handbooks, teachers should consult the Introduction to the teacher's handbook for Book I.

Some of the words that are glossed in the reading passages in the student's book are not words that students will be expected to learn while studying from this course, and these words do not appear in the chapter vocabulary lists or in the Greek to English Vocabulary at the end of the book. If students wish to learn more about these words, they will have to consult a standard Greek dictionary. In the glosses of verb forms that occur in the readings we often include the dictionary form of the verb in parentheses. For example, on page 41, the word ἐκρέματο in line 22 is glossed as follows:

ἐκρέματο (*from* κρεμάννῡμι) were hanging

If students wish to learn more about the verb κρεμάννῡμι, they will have to look it up in a standard Greek dictionary, since it does not occur in the vocabularies in *Athenaze*. We do usually provide the dictionary form for such verbs to make it easier for students to look up the words if they wish to.

References in this teacher's handbook to a chapter, grammar section, and page(s) refer to the student's book; e.g., Chapter 29, Grammar 4, pages 187–188, refers to the student's book.

Cultural and Historical Background:

We cite passages from the following books in conjunction with the teacher's notes on the cultural and historical background essays in each chapter of this second book of the course:

Boardman, John, Jasper Griffin, and Oswyn Murray, eds. *The Oxford History of the Classical World.* New York: Oxford University Press, 1986.

Easterling, P. E., and B. M. W. Knox, eds. *The Cambridge History of Classical Literature: I: Greek Literature.* New York: Cambridge University Press, 1985.

Grant, Michael and Rachel Kitzinger, eds. *Civilization of the Ancient Mediterranean: Greece and Rome.* New York: Charles Scribner's Sons, 1988.

Luce, T. James, ed. *Ancient Writers: Greece and Rome.* New York: Charles Scribner's Sons, 1982.

The World of Athens: An Introduction to Classical Athenian Culture. New York: Cambridge University Press, 1984.

References to other books are given in the notes to each chapter.

ATHENAZE

OVERVIEW OF THE GREEK VERB

This section is offered not as a body of material to be learned at this stage in the course but as an aid that should be consulted and to which reference should be made frequently during the study and teaching of Book II. Students should be assured that they are not expected to learn everything contained in this section now but that they should use it as a framework of reference throughout their study of Greek in Book II.

One of the most troublesome matters for most students is the distinction between active and passive voice, and in Greek the problem is compounded with the addition of the middle voice. We therefore believe that it is useful to spell out the distinctions as clearly and simply as possible (pages 1–2), reminding students of what they have already learned about the middle voice. The charts on pages 4–5 are arranged in such a way as to emphasize the categories of active, middle, and passive.

We include in the charts all of the categories of forms that students will be expected to learn in the course of Book II, including subjunctives, optatives, imperatives (both second and third person), infinitives, and participles. Brief explanation of the third person imperative is included on page 2, but it need not be emphasized at this stage since these forms will not be introduced until Chapter 31. A brief explanation of sequence of *moods* is included on page 2 to alert students to this important feature of the Greek language; those who have studied Latin will see the parallel with primary and secondary sequences of *tenses* in that language. Further discussion of the sequence of moods in Greek should obviously be left to the chapters in which these matters are formally discussed.

Because of limitations of space, we give only the periphrastic forms of the perfect active subjunctive and optative; the alternative forms are given in Chapter 28.

Note that we do not mention or include the dual forms of nouns or verbs. We believe that these are best left until students begin to encounter them in their reading of Greek authors after completion of this course.

The presentation of the two stems of λύω on page 3 may be a good opportunity to remind students of the distinctions in pronunciation between long and short vowels and of the conventions of marking long vowels with macrons. It should be remembered that the circumflex accent implies a long vowel or diphthong and that alpha with iota subscript is long but is usually not marked with a macron, e.g., νεᾱνίᾳ, in which the final alpha is long.

17
Η ΕΠΙΔΑΥΡΟΣ (α)

Title: "Epidaurus"

The purposes of this chapter are:

1. Reading: (α) to record a brief stopover at Salamis on the voyage to Epidaurus and to describe how Dicaeopolis and Philip meet a woman there with a stomach ailment, who is also going to Epidaurus; (β) to describe the arrival at Epidaurus, where the woman with the stomach ailment lodges at an inn while Dicaeopolis and Philip make their way in the evening to the sanctuary of Asclepius, where they rouse the doorkeeper and are introduced to the priest, who gives them instructions to return the next day; to record Philip's preparations at the sanctuary the next day and his vigil in the *abaton* at night; to continue the story of the Persian Wars in the reading at the end of the chapter adapted from Herodotus, with the story of the second taking of Athens, after the battle of Salamis
2. Grammar: (α) to introduce the future tense, including that of the verb "to be"; (β) to present the irregular verb εἶμι, the use of the future participle to express purpose, and uses of the participle with the definite article
3. Background: to present a discussion of healing sanctuaries, Asclepius, and Epidaurus

Illustration

A marble relief from the Piraeus (fourth century B.C., Piraeus Museum). It shows Asclepius healing a woman. Behind him stands Hera (?), the patron goddess of women; to the left members of the sick woman's family are praying for her.

Caption under Illustration

"The doctors order me to go to Asclepius; perhaps the god will help me": students should have no trouble with the Greek; ἴσως is given in the vocabulary list, and students will recognize the future tense from examples in Book I, the Preview of New Verb Forms in Book I, and the Overview of the Greek Verb in Book II. Draw attention to the σ as sign of the future tense, and alert students to the fact that the future tense will be formally presented in this chapter.

Vocabulary

Remind students that in Book II we will give in the chapter vocabulary lists full sets of principal parts for most verbs. We will not give the principal parts of regular contract verbs that follow the patterns of the model contract verbs φιλέω, τῑμάω, and δηλόω; for the principal parts of these model verbs and of simple verbs that appear in the vocabulary lists compounded with prefixes, students should consult the Greek to English vocabulary list at the end of their books. Also, remind students that after the α and β readings we will give full sets of principal parts of verbs that they met in Book I. These sets are arranged according to certain linguistic principles (see Reference Grammar, paragraph 35) to help students see similarities among verbs and organize them into meaningful groupings.

We include here some verbs that students have already met (ἀφικνέομαι, γιγνώσκω, ἕπομαι, and πλέω) in order to show the formation of the future tense of these verbs and their other principal parts. We give the principal parts of the compound verb ἀπέχω to show the principal parts of the uncompounded verb ἔχω. It should be pointed out that the uncompounded verb ἔχω has two future formations, ἕξω and σχήσω, but that the compound ἀπέχω has only ἀφέξω (remind students of how ἀπο- + ἕξω becomes ἀφέξω).

Brief discussion of the formation of the future while going over the vocabulary list will prepare students to recognize the future tenses in the reading more easily. Show how the σ tense sign has combined with the final consonant of the stem in ἀφίξομαι (stem ἀφικ-), ἕψομαι (stem ἑπ-), and τεύξομαι (stem τευχ-).

πότερον . . . ἤ: students may be warned that πότερον often need not be translated; when used in direct questions it simply indicates that what follows will be a double question and it need not be translated itself.

Verbs

Reading passage α contains the following verbs in the future tense: ἕψομαι (4), ὠφελήσει (10), ἀποπλεύσεται (11), ἀφιξόμεθα (12 and 13), γνωσόμεθα (14), ἐπάνιμεν (15), ὁρμησόμεθα (19), ἀφιξόμεθα (20), πλευσόμεθα (22), παρεσόμεθα (22), and λύσομεν (23). We gloss ἐπάνιμεν and παρεσόμεθα, and we recommend that teachers not discuss these forms until after εἶμι is studied in Grammar 2 and the future of εἰμί in Grammar 1. The other forms will be easily recognized as futures after brief discussion of the formation of the future conducted in conjunction with examination of the verbs in the vocabulary list (see above). The three verbs not included in that list (ὠφελήσει, ὁρμησόμεθα, and λύσομεν) will be easily recognized as futures because of the σ tense sign.

Translation

Lines 1–16
Meanwhile Dicaeopolis, leading Philip, disembarked from the ship and said, "Come on, son, what should we do? Do you want to look for a wine-shop and take some dinner?" And Philip (replied), "Yes, certainly, father. You lead then, and I will follow." After finding a wine-shop near the harbor, they sat down drinking wine and talk-

ing to the people there (those present). Of those present, a certain woman asked Dicaeopolis where he was going, and learning that he was going to Epidaurus she said, "I also am going to Epidaurus. For I am sick in the stomach, and the doctors cannot help me at all; and so they tell me to go to Asclepius; for perhaps the god will help me. But tell me, when will the boat sail off? Will we arrive at Epidaurus today or not?" And Dicaeopolis (replied), "I don't know. But they say that Epidaurus is not far off. Perhaps we will arrive before night or even earlier. But listen; for we shall learn soon; for I hear the captain calling us. Shall we not return to the ship quickly?"
[Help students as necessary with the aorist middle infinitive ἑλέσθαι (3) and the present imperative ἡγοῦ (4).]
Lines 17–23
And so standing up they hurried to the ship. And the captain seeing them approaching, shouted (shouting said), "Get in quickly; for we will start at once. For we must arrive at Epidaurus before night." And Dicaeopolis said, "When will we arrive there?" And the captain (replied), "If we get (having got) a favorable wind, with luck, we will sail quickly and be there toward evening. But hurry; for we are going to cast off (loose) the ship at once."
[πρὸς ἑσπέραν (22): in Book I students met πρός + acc. of motion (πρὸς τὸ ἔρμα, 1β:3); here it is used of time ("toward evening").]
Lines 24–26
And so they quickly went on board, and the sailors, after casting off the ship and rowing forward toward the sea, raised the sails. And a favorable wind filled the sails, so that the ship ran (sailed) quickly through the waves.

Principal Parts

The verbs that are given in most of the sections titled Principal Parts that follow the reading passages are verbs that were introduced in Book I, where only the present and aorist tenses were given. Full principal parts are given in these sections in Book II, and students should memorize them carefully. More information on principal parts and the ways in which they are grouped for study in these sections after the reading passages will be found in the Reference Grammar, Section 35 and in the appendix to this handbook, titled "Principal Parts."

We give λύω before δακρύω because it is the model verb *par excellence*. Note that in the perfect and the aorist passive of λύω the stem vowel is short; in δακρύω it remains long throughout.

Word Study

1. *psychologist:* from the Greek words, ἡ ψῡχή + ὁ λόγος (ὁ λογιστής = one who calculates or studies). One who studies the soul or personality.
2. *psychiatrist:* from ἡ ψῡχή + ὁ ἰᾱτρός. One who heals the soul or treats psychic disorders.
3. *analysis:* from ἀναλύω = I unloose; I resolve into elements, investigate analytically; ἡ ἀνάλυσις = resolution of a problem by analysis (especially in mathematics); analysis.
4. *psychoanalyst:* from ἡ ψῡχή + ἀνάλυσις; one who analyzes the soul or personality into its constituent elements of the conscious and unconscious mind (especially used of Freudian psychology).
5. *psychic phenomena:* from ἡ ψῡχή (ψῡχικός, -ή, -όν) + τὰ φαινόμενα (appearances); manifestations of the soul or spirit as opposed to material phenomena.

Grammar 1

Review the formation of the first aorist (Book I, pages 140–141) and of the aorist of liquid verbs (Book I, page 149) while teaching the formation of the future.

Some teachers may find it useful when teaching the verbs at the bottom of page 9 to give students the stems, e.g., βα- (for βαίνω), γνω- (for γιγνώσκω), πενθ- (for πάσχω), and δραμε- (for τρέχω).

When teaching the future of εἰμί, review the present forms (Reference Grammar, paragraph 47) and show students that the stem of this verb is ἐσ- (as in Latin *es-se*), which is seen in the present forms ἐστί, ἐσμέν, and ἐστέ.

Exercise 17a

Have students review Book I, pages 129, 141, 149, and 184 before doing this and the following exercise.

1. αἰτήσω, ᾔτησα
2. ἀναγκάσω, ἠνάγκασα
3. ἄρξω, ἦρξα
4. βλέψω, ἔβλεψα
5. νῑκήσω, ἐνίκησα
6. νομιῶ, ἐνόμισα
7. ὠφελήσω, ὠφέλησα
8. δουλώσω, ἐδούλωσα
9. ζητήσω, ἐζήτησα
10. γράψω, ἔγραψα
11. σώσω, ἔσωσα
12. φυλάξω, ἐφύλαξα
13. ἀποκρῑνοῦμαι, ἀπεκρῑνάμην
14. πιστεύσω, ἐπίστευσα
15. νεμῶ, ἔνειμα

Note on no. 11: in this book we write the future and aorist of σῴζω as σώσω and ἔσωσα, although the iota subscript is found in the aorist in some inscriptions.

Note on no. 15: students should deduce the aorist of νέμω by analogy with that of μένω (see Book I, page 149).

Exercise 17b

1. πέμψει, ἔπεμψε(ν)
2. λῡσόμενοι, λῡσάμενοι
3. τῑμήσομεν, ἐτῑμήσαμεν
4. φιλήσετε, ἐφιλήσατε
5. μενοῦμεν, ἐμείναμεν
6. ἀποκρῑνεῖται, ἀπεκρῑνατο
7. δηλώσειν, δηλῶσαι

8. βοήσουσι(ν), ἐβόησαν
9. γνώσεται, ἔγνω
10. πλευσόμεθα, ἐπλεύσαμεν
11. πράξουσι(ν), ἔπραξαν
12. κομιεῖ, ἐκόμισε(ν)
13. βήσεσθαι, βῆναι
14. μαθήσεσθε, ἐμάθετε
15. βοήσεις, ἐβόησας

Exercise 17c

1. What will you do, boy? Will you return home or stay here?
2. When will we arrive at the harbor? Will we sail there quickly?
3. This young man will win in the contest and receive a crown.
4. Will you stay all day in the city or hurry home?
5. We will soon learn what happened.
6. We will hurry to the city and wait for you in the agora.
7. The doctor will send the boy to Epidaurus; for perhaps Asclepius will help him.
8. When he learns this, the general will immediately send us help.
9. We will wait for you two days on the island.
10. If you return home (returning home), you will learn what the women are suffering (what is happening to the women).

Exercise 17d

1. ἀνάστηθι καὶ πόνει· ὁ γὰρ δεσπότης δι' ὀλίγου πάρεσται.
2. ἆρ' οὐ σιγήσεις, ὦ νεᾱνίᾱ, καὶ τοῦ στρατηγοῦ ἀκούσῃ;
3. οἱ ἔμποροι οἳ ἐν ἐκείνῃ τῇ νηὶ πλέουσιν εἰς τὴν Κόρινθον τριῶν ἡμερῶν ἀφίξονται.
4. ἴσως πρὸ νυκτὸς οἴκαδε ἀφιξόμεθα.
5. ὁ ἰᾱτρὸς οὐ δυνήσεταί σε ὠφελεῖν ἀλλὰ κελεύσει σε πρὸς τὴν Ἐπίδαυρον ἰέναι.

Healing Sanctuaries: Asclepius and Epidaurus

Illustration (page 11)

The theater at Epidaurus was built in the fourth century B.C. It is the best preserved of all Greek theaters and has remained unaltered since its building. Despite its huge size (it holds 14,000 spectators), its acoustics are perfect. It is still used today for performances of Greek dramas.

Illustration (page 13)

This votive offering is from the sanctuary of Asclepius on the island of Melos, Roman period (London, British Museum). Note that in the inscription the iota subscripts are omitted in the dative forms ΑΣΚΛΗΠΙΩ and ΥΓΕΙΑ (= ΥΓΙΕΙΑ). Ὑγίεια (Health) is personified as a goddess.

For further reading, see *Civilization of the Ancient Mediterranean*, Vol. II, pp. 901–904; *The Oxford History of the Classical World*, p. 267; and E. J. and L. Edelstein, *Asclepius* (Baltimore, Johns Hopkins University Press, 1945).

Η ΕΠΙΔΑΥΡΟΣ (β)

Vocabulary

We give the principal parts of ἐπιτρέπω to show the principal parts of the uncompounded verb τρέπω "I turn."

We give εἶμι as the future of ἔρχομαι, and we list all of the compounds of ἔρχομαι that occur in passage α. Students have seen certain forms of most of these verbs before, but they should now learn the principal parts carefully, using the principal parts of ἔρχομαι as a model. It may be useful to discuss εἶμι as the future of ἔρχομαι and to look at the forms on page 17 before reading passage β. Explain right off that the indicative forms of εἶμι refer to future time but that the infinitive and participle usually re-

fer to present time and are used in Attic
Greek in place of the corresponding
forms of ἔρχομαι. It is essential that students grasp this point. Thus, the infinitive ἰέναι, and the participle ἰών, ἰοῦσα,
ἰόν are present in meaning. The imperatives ἴθι and ἴτε, of course, refer to
future time, as do all imperatives.

The impersonal verb χρή is used in
the same way as the impersonal δεῖ (see
Book I, page 118), with accusative subject
and infinitive (sometimes χρή is used
with infinitive alone). Χρή is properly
used of moral obligation, δεῖ of necessity, but the latter came to be used in the
sense of the former.

New usage of preposition: κατά (+
acc.) = according to: κατὰ νόμον (45–
46). For a list of prepositional usages in
Books I and II, see Reference Grammar,
paragraph 28. Each new usage of prepo-
sitions will be noted, as is done here, in
subsequent vocabulary notes in this
teacher's handbook.

Verbs

It may be convenient to sort out the
forms of ἔρχομαι and its compounds that
occur in this passage, as follows:

Present: ἰέναι (3, 5; already familiar to students from Book I) and
προσιόντας (24, glossed here),

Future: ἐπάνιμεν (9, glossed in passage α), εἶμι (18), εἴσιτε (20;
glossed here), and ἄπιτε (29,
glossed here).

Aorist (familiar from Book I):
ἐξελθών (11), ἤλθετε (13),
ἐπανελθών (19), εἰσῆλθον (22),
ἀπελθόντες (31), παρελθών (33),
and ἐπανελθών (43).

Here is a complete list of verbs and
participles in the future tense in this
passage: κόψω (8), ἐπάνιμεν (9),
ἀκούσεται (10), ἡγήσεται (10), ἡγήσῃ
(16), εἶμι (18), ζητήσων (18), ἐρωτήσω
(18), δέξεται (20), ἐπιτρέψεις (26),
δυνήσεται (27), ἐπιτρέψω (29), πάρεσται

(30), and ἡγησόμενος (30).

The future participles (18, 30) are
used with ὡς to express purpose (see
Grammar 3).

Translation

Lines 1–16

And so sailing all day, when
evening was falling, they arrived at
Epidaurus, having suffered nothing bad
(i.e., without trouble). And when they
had disembarked onto land, Dicaeopolis
decided to go straight to the sanctuary of
Asclepius; for it was not far away. But
the woman who was sick in the stomach
was so tired that she did not want to go
that day but stayed in an inn near the
harbor. But they (i.e., Dicaeopolis and
Philip) set out, and, arriving soon, they
found the gates shut. And so Dicaeopolis
said, "The gates are shut; so what should
we do? Shall I knock on the gates or
shall we return to the harbor? For it is
late." And Philip said, "But knock, father, if you will (if it seems good). For
perhaps someone will hear and lead us
to the priest." And so Dicaeopolis
knocked, and an attendant soon came
out and said, "Who are you that knock
(being who do you knock) on the gates at
this time of day? Where have you come
from and what do you want here
(wanting what are you present)?" And
Dicaeopolis (replied), "I am Dicaeopolis,
(being) an Athenian, and I bring my
son, in the hope that (if in any way) the
god may be willing to heal his eyes (the
eyes for him). For he has become (is)
blind. Won't you lead us to your master?"
[We gloss the perfect passive participle
κεκλεισμένᾱς "shut" (7), and students
will understand the immediately following phrase κεκλεισμέναι εἰσίν (7)
without any need for explanation of the
perfect passive indicative form (= "have
been closed and are now closed" or more
simply "are closed").

κόψον (9): help students if they have
trouble with the aorist imperative form.

ἐάν πως. . . ἐθέλῃ (14–15): the form may be identified as subjunctive, but no elaborate discussion of conditions is needed at this stage. Students should begin to identify long vowel endings, e.g., ἐθέλῃ (as opposed to ἐθέλει) as subjunctive. The idiom ἐάν πως + subjunctive (= literally, "if in any way. . . .") is often used to mean "in the hope that. . . . "

Words glossed earlier in chapter: τὴν γαστέρα with respect to her stomach   ἐπάνιμεν shall we return?]

Lines 17–21

And the attendant said, "It is late, but still, stay here; for I will go to look for the master, and I will ask whether he is willing to receive you." And so they waited at the gates; and not much later the attendant returned and said, "Come in; for the master will receive you." So saying (having said these things) he led them into the sanctuary.
[εἶμι (18): students will have no problem with this form if the future tense of ἔρχομαι is discussed prior to the reading.]

Lines 22–32

After passing through the gates, they entered a great courtyard; and there near the temple sat an old man, who, seeing them approaching, said, "Greetings, friends. What have you come for (wanting what have you come)?" And so Dicaeopolis told everything, and the priest, looking kindly at the boy, said, "Tell me, boy, will you entrust yourself to Asclepius? Do you believe this, that the god will be able to help you?" And Philip (replied), "Yes, certainly; for all things are possible for the gods; I trust the god and will entrust myself to him." And the old man (said), "Good, boy. Now go away to the inn, and tomorrow my attendant will come to you to lead the child to me." And so father and son went away and spent the night in the inn.
[τοῦτο πιστεύεις (27): note that a neuter pronoun with πιστεύω is accusative rather than dative. Compare τῷ θεῷ

πιστεύω (28). The verb πιστεύω, like other verbs of believing, is regularly followed by an infinitive in indirect statement (see Chapter 24, page 96), but here the ὅτι clause expands the pronoun τοῦτο; this is the usual idiom.

ὑμῖν πάρεσται (30): help students as necessary to arrive at the sense "will be with you," "will come to you."]

Lines 33–42

And the next day when day first dawned, the attendant came and led Philip to the priest. And he received the boy kindly and said, "Come, boy, now you must prepare yourself. For you must have holy thoughts and be pure in soul. But have no fear; for Asclepius is the most benevolent (man-loving) of the gods and is always gracious to those who are pure in soul. Cheer up!" So saying he led the boy into the temple. And there Philip first purified himself, and then he waited the whole day in the temple, having holy thoughts and praying the god to appear in (his) sleep.
[παρασκευάζεσθαι (36): note the use of the middle voice, "to prepare yourself."

ὅσια . . . φρονεῖν (36): neuter plural adjective used as internal accusative, "to have holy thoughts."

τὴν ψῡχήν (36–37): accusative of respect.

φοβοῦ (37): help students as needed with the imperative form.

τῶν θεῶν (38): partitive genitive with the superlative adjective φιλανθρωπότατος. Proper oral phrasing of the sentence will indicate the relationship between the words.

ἐκαθήρατο (40): "purified himself " (middle voice). Greek religion attached great importance to purification; this might involve merely a ritual washing but might also involve sacrifice.]

Lines 43–50

Finally, when evening was coming, the priest returned and said, "Come, boy; for all is ready; follow me." And he led the boy out of the temple to the altar and told him to make a libation according to custom. And he took the bowl in his hands and made a libation, and, raising his hands toward heaven, he said, "Asclepius, savior, most kindly of the gods, hear my prayer (me praying), who thinking holy thoughts and being pure in soul am here (as) your suppliant. Be gracious to me who have become blind, and, if it seems good to you, heal my eyes."

[ταῖς χερσί (46): the declension of this noun is as follows: χείρ, χειρός, χειρί, χεῖρα, χεῖρες, χερῶν, χερσί, χεῖρας.]

Lines 51–56

Then the priest led the boy to the holy place and told him to lie on the ground and sleep. And so Philip lay down, but for a long time he could not sleep; for being alone in the holy place he was very afraid; for it was night and everywhere there was darkness and silence, except that occasionally he heard the sacred snakes hissing gently.

[τὸ ἄβατον (51): "the holy place." See essay (pages 12–13) for a description of this; it means literally "the not-to-be-trodden" (place), i.e., a place sacred to the god where none but the ritually purified might walk.]

Principal Parts

The verb πιστεύω provides the regular pattern, and we accordingly put it first.

Note the σ in the perfect middle/passive and the aorist passive of κελεύω. No other verb with stem in -ευ- has this.

Note that πορεύομαι has a deponent aorist passive = I marched, went. The aorist middle -επορευσάμην occurs rarely in compounds.

Word Building

Note that adjectives formed by adding the suffix -τός to the verb stem are either passive in meaning, e.g., γραπτός, -ή, -όν = "written," or they denote possibility, e.g., γνωστός, -ή, -όν = "known" or "knowable."

1. I hit, hit upon, get, happen; chance, luck; lucky; unlucky; luckless (the prefix δυσ- is the opposite of εὐ-, whereas the prefix ἀ- simply negates; thus, εὐτυχής = blessed with good luck, lucky; δυστυχής = cursed with bad luck, unlucky; and ἀτυχής = without luck, luckless)

2. I believe, trust; faith, trust; faithful, trusty; faithless, untrustworthy; I disbelieve, mistrust

3. I am able, powerful; ability, power; possible, capable; impossible, incapable

4. I learn, get to know; judgment, opinion; understood, known; unknown (cf. Paul's famous words to the Athenians (Acts 17:23) εὗρον καὶ βωμὸν ἐν ᾧ ἐπεγέγραπτο ᾽Αγνώστῳ Θεῷ. "I found even an altar on which had been inscribed 'To an Unknown God.'")
(Also δύσγνωστος, -ον hard to understand, hard to recognize.)

5. I draw, write; drawing, writing; written; unwritten

Grammar 2

The following supplementary exercises may be used after students have studied the forms of εἶμι and reviewed the forms of εἰμί (Reference Grammar, paragraph 47):

(a) Identify and translate the following forms:

1.	ἴθι	6.	ἰών
2.	ἴσθι	7.	εἰσι(ν)
3.	εἶναι	8.	ἦμεν
4.	ἰέναι	9.	ἦμεν
5.	ὤν	10.	ἦσαν

Answers:

1. imperative singular of εἶμι = go!
2. imperative singular of εἰμί = be!
3. infinitive of εἰμί = to be
4. infinitive of εἶμι = to go
5. participle of εἰμί = being
6. participle of εἶμι = going

7. 3rd singular of εἶμι = he/she will go
8. 1st plural imperfect of εἶμι = we were going
9. 1st plural imperfect of εἰμί = we were
10. 3rd plural imperfect of εἶμι = they were going

(b) Give the Greek for:

1. Go! (*plural*)
2. Be brave! (*plural*)
3. He/she was going.
4. He was brave.
5. They will go.
6. We will be brave.
7. to be
8. to go
9. They will be.
10. going

Answers:

1. ἴτε.
2. ἀνδρεῖοι ἔστε.
3. ᾔει.
4. ἀνδρεῖος ἦν.
5. ἴᾱσι(ν)
6. ἀνδρεῖοι ἐσόμεθα.
7. εἶναι
8. ἰέναι
9. ἔσονται.
10. ἰών

Grammar 3

Notes:

Grammar 4

Notes:

Exercise 17e

1. Go, boy, and tell your mother that I am waiting by the door.
2. Will you not go to the agora to learn what has happened?

3. The slave went out to look for his master.
4. You must send a messenger to tell all to the king.
5. Xerxes was preparing a very large navy to enslave the Greeks.
6. The Greeks were preparing to fight bravely.
7. We will always honor those who died in this battle.
8. I will tell the girls to go home immediately.
9. Those who do all in accordance with the law will become dear to the gods.
10. The boys were returning home to relate to their mother what had happened.

Exercise 17f

1. πρὸς τὸ ἄστυ ἴμεν ὡς μαθησόμενοι τί ἐγένετο/τὰ γενόμενα.
2. ὁ στρατηγὸς ἄγγελον πέμψει ὡς λέξοντα τοῖς πολίταις τί χρὴ (αὐτοὺς) ποιεῖν/ποιῆσαι.
3. οἱ ἄνδρες τὰς γυναῖκας πρὸς τὸ ἄστυ ἄγουσιν ὡς θεᾱσομένᾱς τοὺς χορούς.
4. ὁ ἱερεὺς ἐπάνεισιν εἰς τὸ ἱερὸν ὡς σπονδὴν ποιησόμενος.
5. οἱ ἐν τῇ ἀγορᾷ μένοντες βούλονται τοῦ ἀγγέλου ἀκούειν.

ΟΙ ΠΕΡΣΑΙ ΤΑΣ ΑΘΗΝΑΣ ΔΕΥΤΕΡΟΝ ΑΙΡΟΥΣΙΝ

Title: "The Persians Take Athens a Second Time"

Students have had δεύτερος as an adjective but will have to deduce its use here in the accusative case as an adverb.

Translation

Lines 1–9
With the beginning of spring Mardonius set out from Thessaly and led his army with haste against Athens. And as he advanced, none of the Boeotians resisted him, nor did the Spartans come to help the Athenians. When he arrived

in Attica, he did not find the Athenians, but he learned that most were in Salamis and in the ships; and he took the city deserted. But when he was in Athens he sent a messenger to Salamis, bearing a friendly message (friendly words); for he said that the king would give Attica back to the Athenians and make an alliance (with them), if they stopped fighting (ceased from war). But the Athenians did not accept the proposal (the words) but sent the messenger away.

Lines 10–19

The Athenians crossed to Salamis as follows; as long as they hoped that the Spartans would send an army to help, they stayed in Attica; but when the Spartans did not come to help and Mardonius advanced and arrived in Boeotia, then they evacuated everything from Attica and themselves crossed to Salamis. And they sent messengers to Sparta to blame the Spartans because they were not coming to help. And when the messengers arrived in Sparta, they said this: "The Athenians sent us to say that the king of the Persians is willing to give back Attica and make an alliance; but we, although wronged by you, did not accept the proposal. But now we tell you to send an army as quickly as possible to ward off the barbarians from Attica."
[στρατὸν πέμψειν τοὺς Λακεδαιμονίους (10–11): help with the indirect statement is provided in the gloss; the construction will not be formally taught until Chapter 23, Grammar 3, but students should become accustomed to it well before then.]

Exercise 17g

1. οἱ Λακεδαιμόνιοι, οἳ τούτῳ τῷ χρόνῳ ἑορτὴν ἐποιοῦντο, οὐκ ἤθελον ἐπεξιέναι ἐπὶ τοὺς Πέρσας ἀλλ' ἔτι ἔμελλον.

2. τέλος δὲ οἱ τῶν Ἀθηναίων ἄγγελοι εἶπον· "ὑμεῖς μὲν Λακεδαιμόνιοι τοὺς συμμάχους προδίδοτε, οἱ δὲ Ἀθηναῖοι ἀδικούμενοι ὑφ' ὑμῶν σπονδὰς ποιήσονται πρὸς τοὺς Πέρσας.

3. "σπονδὰς οὖν ποιησάμενοι καὶ σύμμαχοι γενόμενοι τοῖς Πέρσαις, στρατευσόμεθα μετὰ αὐτῶν/σὺν αὐτοῖς ἐπὶ τὴν Πελοπόννησον.

4. "τότε δὴ παθόντες μαθήσεσθε ὅτι οὐ χρὴ τοὺς συμμάχους προδοῦναι."

5. τέλος δὴ τούτους τοὺς λόγους φοβούμενοι οἱ Λακεδαιμόνιοι τὴν στρατιὰν ἔπεμψαν πρὸς τὴν Ἀττικήν.

For no. 2, students will find the Greek for "wronged by you" in line 17 of the tail reading.

18
Ο ΑΣΚΛΗΠΙΟΣ (α)

Title: "Asclepius"

The purposes of this chapter are:

1. Reading: (α) to recount the cure of Philip; (β) to tell of the arrangements for a sacrifice and memorial in honor of the cure and to introduce the theme of impending war between Athens and Sparta in a conversation between Dicaeopolis and the priest of Asclepius; to recount in the narrative adapted from Herodotus the story of the Athenian victory over the Persian land forces at Plataea
2. Grammar: (α) to introduce the forms of the verbs δίδωμι and τίθημι; (β) to review the uses of αὐτός and to present the declension of adjectives like ταχύς
3. Background: to sketch the history of Sparta and Corinth as background for an understanding of the political map of Greece at the outbreak of the Peloponnesian Wars

Illustration

Statue from the sanctuary of Asclepius, fourth century B.C. (Epidaurus Museum).

Caption under Illustration

"Asclepius was august and tall": students will find σεμνός in the vocabulary list.

Vocabulary

We include τίθημι in the vocabulary list to show its principal parts even though it does not occur in uncompounded form in the reading. We include the aorist infinitives and participles of δίδωμι and τίθημι because they are so different from the aorist indicative forms and therefore difficult to recognize.

The declension of χάρις is: ἡ χάρις, τῆς χάριτος, τῇ χάριτι, τὴν χάριν; αἱ χάριτες, τῶν χαρίτων, ταῖς χάρισι(ν), τὰς χάριτας.

New usage of preposition: περί (+ *gen.*) = around: περὶ οὗ (3).

New usage of preposition: ὑπέρ (+ *acc.*) = over, above: ὑπὲρ τοὺς λόφους (14).

Verbs

Passage α contains the following forms of δίδωμι and τίθημι or their compounds: δώσεις (8), δώσω (10), ἐπέθηκε (11), and ἀπόδος (18).

Translation

Lines 1–12
But finally Philip was so tired that he fell into a deep sleep. And the god appeared to him as he slept; he was august and tall, and in his right hand he carried a staff, around which curled the sacred serpent. He stood by the boy and with a kindly look (looking kindly) he said this, "What is the matter with you, boy? Why are you sleeping in my holy place?" And he, not at all afraid—for the god seemed kindly—said, "I am blind, Asclepius; and so I have come to ask you to heal my eyes (the eyes for me)." And the god said, "And if I heal your eyes, what will you give me?" And the boy for a long time was at a loss what he ought to say, but finally he said, "I don't have much, but I will give you my knucklebones." And the god laughed and came to him and put his hands on his eyes. And after doing this he went away.
[τοὺς . . . ἀστραγάλους (10): knucklebones were used as dice: "the four faces of the knucklebones were of different shapes, one flat, one irregular, one concave, one convex, and in dicing these had the value respectively of 1, 6, 3, 4" (*Oxford Classical Dictionary*, "Astragalus," p. 110). See illustration.]

Lines 13–19

On the next day when day first dawned, Philip woke up and, behold, he could see; for he saw the sky and the sun rising above the hills and the trees moving in the wind; and he enjoyed looking; for everything seemed to him most beautiful. And so he hurried to find the priest. And he, seeing him approaching, said, "Greetings, boy; it is clear that the god has come to you in kindness (kindly). And so give thanks to the god. But go to look for your father."
[ἀπόδος (19): note the accent (normally recessive in imperatives; the accent cannot precede the last syllable of the preposition before the simple verb; compare παράδος (18β:9) and ἀνάθες (18β:22).]

Principal Parts

We list φιλέω first because it serves as the model for most -ε- contract verbs. Students should be warned that δοκέω (δοκ-/δοκε-), πλέω (πλευ-/πλεϝ-/πλυ-), and σκοπέω (σκεπ-) are irregular (see English to Greek Vocabulary for their principal parts).

Call attention to the irregular future of καλέω, which is identical to the present (Attic future). In the aorist καλέω keeps ε, instead of changing to η, and in both perfects and the aorist passive the short α of the stem drops out (syncope).

Students should be reminded that most -α- contract verbs have principal parts like those of τῑμάω. More examples of -α- contract verbs will be given after reading passage β.

Word Study

1. *autobiography*: from αὐτός (self) + ὁ βίος (life) + γράφω. Writing one's own life. In late Greek we find βιογραφίᾱ but not αὐτοβιογραφίᾱ.
2. *autograph*: from αὐτός + γράφω. αὐτόγραφος, -ον = written with one's own hand occurs twice in Plutarch (1st century A.D.)

3. *automatic*: from αὐτός + μα- + -τος. αὐτόματος, -ον = self-moved, of one's own accord; (of things) spontaneous, automatic. the word first occurs in Homer (*Iliad* 2.408) and is common in later Greek; the root μα-, found only in Homer in the perfect form, e.g., μέμαᾱσι, means to be eager or to rush.
4. *autonomous*: from αὐτός + νόμος. αὐτόνομος, -ον = having one's own laws, independent (of persons and states).
5. *autistic*: from αὐτός + ίστης (a termination which expresses the agent), (Aristotle, fragment 669 has the form ὁ αὐτίτης = one who is by himself). *Autistic* is a recent medical coinage, used to describe children who are imprisoned in themselves.

Illustration (page 21)

Drawn from a first century B.C. or A.D. copy on marble by Alexander of Athens of a Greek painting of about 430 B.C. (Naples, Museo Nazionale).

Grammar 1

Notes:

Exercise 18a

δώσεις (8); 2nd sing. future indicative active

δώσω (10); 1st sing. future indicative active

ἐπέθηκε (11); 3rd sing. aorist indicative active

ἀπόδος (18); aorist active imperative singular

Exercise 18b

1. 3rd sing. imperfect indicative active of δίδωμι; he/she was giving

2. 3rd sing. present indicative middle of τίθημι; he/she is placing for himself/herself
3. present infinitive middle of δίδωμι; to give (for oneself)
   [The middle of δίδωμι is, in fact, only found in compounds, e.g., ἀποδίδομαι = I sell.]
4. aorist infinitive active of τίθημι; to put
5. nom. fem. sing. present participle active of δίδωμι; giving
6. 2nd sing. present indicative active of δίδωμι; you give
7. 2nd pl. imperfect indicative active of δίδωμι; you were giving
8. nom. sing. masc. present participle active of τίθημι; putting, placing
9. 2nd sing. aorist indicative active of δίδωμι; you gave
10. 3rd pl. aorist indicative active of τίθημι; they placed, put
11. 3rd pl. imperfect indicative middle of τίθημι; they were placing for themselves
12. 2nd sing. aorist imperative middle of δίδωμι; give (for yourself)
13. 3rd pl. present indicative active of δίδωμι; they give
14. 2nd sing. present indicative active of τίθημι; you place
15. 3rd pl. imperfect indicative middle of δίδωμι; they were giving (for themselves)

Exercise 18c

1. δός
2. θοῦ
3. δόντα
4. θέμενος
5. δοῦναι
6. τιθέασι
7. τιθέναι
8. δίδοσθαι
9. διδούς
10. τίθενται
11. δίδονται
12. ἔδοντο
13. θοῦ
14. δόμενοι

15. ἔθετο

Exercise 18d

1. The old man refused to give the money to the foreigner.
2. When their mother gave (them) food, the children immediately began to eat.
3. The master sent the slave to pay us (give us back the money).
4. We will go to ask the king to help you.
5. Give thanks to god; for he saved us.
6. The farmer asked his friend to give back the dog.
7. You give me the wine, and I will give you the food.
8. The father laughed kindly and gave the dog to the boy. (or) The father, laughing kindly, gave the dog to the boy.
9. The suppliants, sitting by the altar, gave thanks to god.
10. The god, after putting his hands on the boy's eyes, went away.

In no. 1, οὐκ ἠθέλησε by rules of aspect can only be properly translated as "refused"; "was not willing" would imply continuity and would be a translation of οὐκ ἤθελε.

In no. 2, help students with translation of the imperfect as inchoative, "they began to eat."

Exercise 18e

1. ὁ ναύκληρος τὸ ἀργύριον τῷ ναύτῃ ἔδωκεν.
2. χάριν τῷ θεῷ ἀποδοῦσαι, αἱ γυναῖκες οἴκαδε ἐπανῆλθον.
3. ἐκέλευσά σε τό τε ἄροτρον ἐν τῷ ἀγρῷ θεῖναι καὶ σῖτον τοῖς βουσὶ δοῦναι.
4. σὺ μὲν τὰ ἱστία εἰς τὴν ναῦν εἴσθες, ἐγὼ δὲ τὰς κώπας εἰσήσω.
5. δῆλόν ἐστιν ὅτι αὗται αἱ γυναῖκες οὐδὲν ἀργύριον τούτῳ τῷ γέροντι ἔδοσαν.
6. τῷ ναυκλήρῳ τρεῖς δραχμὰς ἀποδόντες, οἱ ξένοι εἰς τὴν ναῦν εἰσέβησαν.

Sparta and Corinth

For further reading, see *Civilization of the Ancient Mediterranean*, Vol. I, pp. 18–19, 19–21, and 27–30; *The Oxford History of the Classical World*, pp. 26–31; and Oswyn Murray, *Early Greece*, chapters 9 and 10 (Fontana, 1980).

Draw to the attention of students the illustrations on page 226 (the Eurotas valley) and 227 (ancient Corinth).

Ο ΑΣΚΛΗΠΙΟΣ (β)

Vocabulary

We give the principal parts of προστρέχω to show the principal parts of the uncompounded verb τρέχω "I run."

New usage of preposition: διά (+ *acc.*) = because of: διὰ τοῦτο (46). Note that διά + *acc.* has been used since Chapter 2 in the phrase διὰ τί; = Why? (= Because of what?), but that the preposition was not introduced as a vocabulary item in its own right with the accusative in Book I.

New usage of preposition: ἐπί (+ *dat.*) = for (of price): ἐπὶ μιᾷ δραχμῇ (13).

Verbs

Passage β contains the following forms of δίδωμι and τίθημι or their compounds: ἀποδοῦναι (5), ἀναθεῖναι (7, 8), παράδος (9), ἀναθήσω (10, 13), δός (13), παρέδωκεν (17), δοῦναι (20), δώσω (21), ἀνάθες (22), ἀνέθηκε (23), and διδόναι (33).

Translation

Lines 1–19

They found Dicaeopolis sitting in front of the inn. And when he saw the boy walking firmly and seeing, he stood up, and running toward him he embraced him and said, "Dearest child, do I really see you (being) cured (healthy, sound)? Did the god really heal your eyes? We must pay hearty thanks to Asclepius." And turning to the priest, he said, "Am I allowed to make a sacrifice? Am I allowed to put up an offering to the god as well?" And the priest (replied), "Of course (how not?). You may. Do you also want to put up a memorial of the cure in the temple? (For) you give me three drachmas, and I will make the sacrifice and put up the memorial for you." But Dicaeopolis groaning said, "Three drachmas do you say? Oh, what an expense!" But the priest (answered), "You are talking nonsense (saying nothing), man; for the expense is not large. For I will make the sacrifice for one drachma, and I will put up the memorial for two. And so give me three drachmas, if you want me to do this." But Dicaeopolis said, "But I haven't got three drachmas; for I am a poor man. Are two enough for you?" And the priest (replied), "All right (let it be so); two are enough, if you don't have more." And so Dicaeopolis handed over two drachmas, and the priest, calling the attendant, told him to bring a cock and leading them to the altar made the sacrifice. [ἀλεκτρυόνα (18): cocks were commonly sacrificed to Asclepius as an offering to secure his help. Socrates' last words were, "Crito, we owe a cock to Asclepius; please pay the debt and don't forget" (Plato, *Phaedo* 118a). Burnet (*Plato's Phaedo* [Oxford University Press], p. 118) says, "He hoped to awake (from death) cured like those who are healed by sleeping in the Asclepieion at Epidaurus."]

Lines 20–26

And Philip said, "I too must make a gift (give something). For I said to the god that I would give my knucklebones. Look, take these and dedicate them to the god and write on the memorial (tablet), if you approve (if it seems good to you), that Philip dedicated these knucklebones to Asclepius with (having) the greatest gratitude." And the priest replied, "But I will gladly do this; for the god will rejoice to receive (receiving) them. But now you must journey home.

Come on, I will accompany you to the gates."
[Word glossed earlier in chapter: τοὺς . . . ἀστραγάλους knucklebones.]

Lines 27–34

While they were walking to the gates, the priest said to Dicaeopolis, "You were in Athens recently; tell me, then, how are things? Will there be war against the Peloponnesians, or will you be able to preserve the peace? For it is clear that the Corinthians are urging the Spartans on to war, since they are (being) hostile to the Athenians. So what do you think? Will they be willing to allow arbitration of their differences or will they resolve their differences by war rather than words?"
[εἰρήνην (30): the First Peloponnesian War was ended by the Thirty Years' Peace between Athens and Sparta (446 B.C.); under the terms of this peace any disputes were to be referred to arbitration by a third party. The priest's words are based on Thucydides 1.140, Pericles' speech to the Assembly, which is quoted in adapted form in passage 21β.]

Lines 35–50

And Dicaeopolis said, "The Corinthians have been hostile for a long time now and are plotting against us, but nevertheless the Spartans will not make war; for they always avoid action (keep quiet), fearing the power of the Athenians." And the priest said, "But surely the Spartans do not fear the Athenians; for they and their allies have a vast army, which the Athenians will not dare stand up to by land." And Dicaeopolis said in reply (answering), "But we rule the sea, so that we have more resources of war; for we have masses of money and masses of ships; and so they will not be able to harm us and will not be able to win a long war, nor indeed will they dare attack us." And the old man said, "You clearly have great confidence (you are clear trusting much) in your city and her power. But (it is), for this reason, in my opinion (as it seems to me)

that the Spartans will make war, for, fearing the power of the Athenians, they will not be willing to disregard its increase (it increasing). But nevertheless I will rejoice if you are proved right and I wrong."
[πάλαι . . . εἰσιν (35): literally "are long ago," but this idiom is best translated "have been for a long time now."

ἀποκρῑνάμενος εἶπεν (41): "they said in reply," a common phrase, which illustrates the aorist aspect of the participle, here of simple action with no reference to past time; it does not mean "having answered, he said."

δῆλος εἶ. . . . πιστεύων (45–46): = δῆλόν ἐστιν ὅτι πιστεύεις. Both constructions are common; the personal construction (δῆλος εἶ) is perhaps more common.

The priest is right (45–48); Thucydides (1.23) says that the real reason for the war was the following: "the Athenians becoming great and causing fear to the Spartans compelled them to make war"—τὴν γὰρ ἀληθεστάτην πρόφασιν τοὺς Ἀθηναίους ἡγοῦμαι μεγάλους γενομένους καὶ φόβον παρέχοντας τοῖς Λακεδαιμονίοις ἀναγκάσαι ἐς τὸ πολεμεῖν.]

Lines 51–52

By now they were at the gates. And so, bidding the old man farewell, Dicaeopolis and the boy began their journey.
[ἐπορεύοντο: inchoative imperfect, denoting the beginning of an action.]

Principal Parts

If ε, ι, or ρ precedes the final α of the stem of -α- contract verbs, the future, aorist, perfect, and aorist passive have ᾱ instead of η. This is shown in πειράω in the list and in θεάομαι, θεάσομαι, ἐθεᾱσάμην, τεθέᾱμαι I see, watch, look at. This rule is broken by χράομαι, which has η even though the α of the stem is preceded by ρ (note also the insertion of σ in the aorist passive).

Students should be reminded that

most -o- contract verbs have principal parts like those of δηλόω.

Word Building

1. I give; ἡ δό-σις = the act of giving, gift (cf. ἡ ποίη-σις = the act of composing, poetry, poem); I give back; I give in; I give, I hand over
2. I give up, betray; ὁ προ-δό-της = traitor (cf. ὁ ποιητής = maker, poet); ἡ προ-δο-σίᾱ = treachery (the suffix -σίᾱ attached to a verb stem gives an abstract noun)
3. I put, place; I put up; I put on (i.e., I put something on top of something else); I put together

Grammar 2

Notes:

Grammar 3

In the masculine and neuter the stems of these adjectives end in -υ (cf. ἄστυ). In the case of the adjectives, however, the genitive singular masculine and neuter is ταχέος (contrast ἄστεως), and the neuter plural nominative and accusative -εα does not contract (contrast ἄστη).

Exercise 18f

1. The enemy will not dare to do the same things again.
2. The woman, after handing over the money to the doctor, returned home by the same road.
3. The king himself will go to the agora to announce this to the people.
4. You must give thanks to the god himself.

Exercise 18g

1. οἱ ναῦται αὐτοὶ τὸν χειμῶνα ἐφοβοῦντο.
2. οἴκαδε ἐπλέομεν/ἐπλεύσαμεν ἐν τῇ αὐτῇ νηί, ἣ ταχεῖά τε ἦν καὶ

μεγάλη.
3. ὁ αὐτουργὸς ἐλαύνει τοὺς αὐτοὺς βοῦς ἀνὰ τὴν τραχεῖαν ὁδόν.
4. αὐτὸν τὸν ἄγγελον παρά σε πέμψω ὡς λέξοντά σοι τί χρή/δεῖ σε πράττειν/πρᾶξαι (ποιεῖν/ποιῆσαι).

Η ΕΝ ΤΑΙΣ ΠΛΑΤΑΙΑΙΣ ΝΙΚΗ

Title: "The Victory at Plataea"

Translation

Lines 1–4

When Mardonius learned that the Spartans were now on the march, he set fire to Athens and destroyed all the houses and temples and withdrew into Boeotia. And so the Spartans advancing arrived in Attica, and the Athenians crossing from Salamis joined with the Peloponnesians.
[Students are to deduce τοῖς Πελοποννησίοις (4) from ἡ Πελοπόννησος, which they have had.]

Lines 5–11

When they arrived in Boeotia, they learned that the barbarians were encamped on the river Asopus; and so they positioned themselves opposite (them) on a certain hill. And when the Greeks did not come down into the plain, Mardonius sent out all his cavalry against them. And the Greeks pushed back the cavalry and killed the general himself, so that they were much more confident. And after this they decided to go down toward Plataea. And the barbarians, learning that the Greeks were in Plataea, marched there themselves also. And Mardonius drew up his army for battle (to fight).
[πολλῷ (9): dative of degree of difference.]

Lines 12–20

And for eleven days they waited, neither side wanting to start the battle; but on the twelfth day Pausanias decided to change position again; for at the same time they were short of water and they were suffering (bad things) at the hands of the cavalry (who were) always attacking (them). And so after waiting for night they set out. But when day dawned, Mardonius saw that the Greek camp (the camp of the Greeks) was deserted (he saw the camp being deserted); and so he pursued the Greeks at full speed (at a run). And first the barbarians caught the Athenians, who fighting very bravely pushed back the cavalry. Then Mardonius fell on the Spartans, and a mighty battle developed. But when Mardonius himself was killed, the barbarians turned and fled in disorder (in no order) into their camp.

[τῷ Παυσανίᾳ (12): Pausanias, regent for the Spartan king, who was a minor, was commander-in-chief of the Greek army.

ἀπέθανεν (19): "was killed"; ἀποθνῄσκω is regularly used instead of the passive of ἀποκτείνω.]

Exercise 18h

1. οἱ Λακεδαιμόνιοι τοὺς βαρβάρους πρὸς τὸ στρατόπεδον διώκοντες τῷ τείχει προσέβαλον ἀλλ' οὐκ ἐδύναντο αὐτὸ ἑλεῖν.
2. ἐπεὶ οἱ Ἀθηναῖοι ἐβοήθησαν, οἱ βάρβαροι οὐκ ἔφυγον ἀλλ' ἀνδρείως ἐμάχοντο.

3. τέλος δὲ οἱ μὲν Ἕλληνες ἐπὶ τὸ τεῖχος ἀνέβησαν, οἱ δὲ βάρβαροι οὐδενὶ κόσμῳ ἔφυγον.
4. μετὰ τὴν μάχην ὁ Παυσανίας, στρατηγὸς ὢν τῶν Λακεδαιμονίων, αὐτὸς μνημεῖον ἀνέθηκεν ἐν Δελφοῖς·

> When (as) leader of the Greeks
> he had destroyed the army of
> the Medes,
> Pausanias dedicated this
> memorial to Apollo.

This dedication of Pausanias, the first sign of the megalomania that resulted in his downfall the following year, caused a diplomatic rumpus (see Thucydides 1.132). The inscription was carved on a golden tripod supported by three intertwined snakes of bronze. The inscription was obliterated by the Spartan authorities, who put in its place the names of the cities that had taken part in the war. The gold tripod was melted down in the fourth century, but part of the serpent column survives with the names of thirty-one cities inscribed on it; the beginning of the inscription reads: τοίδε (= οἴδε) τὸν πόλεμον ἐπολέμεον· Λακεδαιμόνιοι, Ἀθηναῖοι, Κορίνθιοι. . . .

19
Ο ΝΟΣΤΟΣ (α)

Title: "The Return"

The noun is given in the vocabulary list; students have encountered the verb νοστέω in Book I, e.g., page 147, line 31.

The purposes of this chapter are:

1. Reading: (α and β) to recount the first part of Dicaeopolis' and Philip's return journey (by land) to Attica, including viewing of the farms as they pass by, an encounter with a young hunter, who gives them a hare, and an encounter with a shepherd, who takes them in for the night; to conclude the series of stories adapted from Herodotus with that of the battle of Mycale
2. Grammar: (α) to introduce the genitive absolute; (β) to present further discussion of the attributive and predicate position of adjectives, the placement of other attributives, and some further uses of the article
3. Background: to present a brief history of Mycenae in anticipation of Dicaeopolis' and Philip's visit to the site on the next part of their return home in Chapter 20

Illustration

Attic black figure neck amphora by the Antimenes Painter, ca. 575 B.C. (London, British Museum).

Caption under Illustration

"While men are collecting olives, a boy is climbing into the tree": ἐλάᾱς and συλλεγόντων are new words, which students will find in the vocabulary list below the illustration. The genitive absolute, τῶν ἀνθρώπων . . . συλλεγόντων, is a new construction, treated formally in Grammar 1; it will be useful to give some explanation of it when reading the caption and thereby prepare students for the two genitive absolutes in the reading passage.

Vocabulary

We give the verb ἐσθίω, which students have already had in the vocabulary list in Chapter 9, in order to show its principal parts.

The word ἐλάᾱ is Attic for ἐλαίᾱ, hence the ending in -ᾱ (as always after ε, ι, or ρ).

Genitive absolutes

Two genitive absolutes occur in this passage: ἤδη θάλποντος τοῦ ἡλίου (1–2) and οὐδενὸς γὰρ ὄντος ἡμῖν ἀργυρίου (3–4). Let students discover these and work out their meanings by analogy with the genitive absolute in the caption under the illustration.

Translation

Lines 1–10
When they arrived at the harbor, they were very tired and, as the sun was already hot, they sat under an olive tree and drank wine and ate some food. But soon Dicaeopolis said, "What should we do, son? For as we have no money, we cannot return home by sea. And so we must go on foot." But Philip said, "Don't worry about that, father. For I will be glad to go on foot and to see the tilled fields and the mountains. But how will we find the way that leads to Athens?" And he (replied), "Don't worry about this, (my) boy, for we will easily find it. So stand up; for if you agree (if it seems good to you), it is time to start."

Lines 11–18
And so standing up they set off, and first they went through a plain, in which there were many tilled fields of men; and they saw lots of people working in the fields, of whom some were driving oxen and plowing the plowland and others were climbing into the trees and gathering olives. And when they approached the hills, they saw vineyards,

in which people were collecting grapes; and some of the grapes donkeys were carrying home in great baskets, and others the women put on the ground to dry in the sun.
[ἐπορεύοντο (11): inchoative imperfect, denoting the beginning of an action.

ἦσαν (11): provide help as needed with this imperfect of εἰμι.

It may be useful to give the full set of forms of the imperfect of ὁράω (12): ἑώρων, ἑώρᾱς, ἑώρᾱ, ἑωρῶμεν, ἑωρᾶτε, ἑώρων.

Lines 17–18: grapes were dried in the sun to make raisins; the practice continues today.]

Principal Parts

Verbs with labial stems (ending in β, π, or φ) are given in this and the next group of principal parts.

Note that τ is added to the stem βλαβ- in the first principal part and that βλαβ- changes to βλαπ- before the τ. Note the aspiration of the final consonant of the stem in the second perfect active. This aspiration occurs also in the perfect active and aorist passive of πέμπω; the perfect active of πέμπω also shows a change in the stem vowel from ε to ο, as does λείπω. Note the assimilation of the final β of the stem βλαβ- in the perfect middle/passive, and note the disappearance of the final π of the stem πεμπ- in the perfect middle/passive πέπεμμαι. The extent to which these linguistic phenomena are to be explained to the students at this stage is left up to the teacher, but the principal parts themselves should be carefully memorized by the students.

Word Study

1. *aristocracy*: ἡ ἀριστοκρατίᾱ (ἄριστος, -η, -ον + τὸ κράτος) = the rule of the best , i.e., the best by birth, the nobles.
2. *autocracy*: αὐτός, -ή, -ό + τὸ κράτος = rule by oneself, absolute power. Compare αὐτοκρατής, -ές = ruling by oneself, absolute.

3. *plutocracy*: ἡ πλουτοκρατίᾱ (ὁ πλοῦτος + τὸ κράτος) = government by an oligarchy of the wealthy.
4. *theocracy*: ἡ θεοκρατίᾱ (ὁ θεός + τὸ κράτος) (Josephus, first century A.D.) = rule by a god/God or by a priesthood.
5. *bureaucracy*: French *bureau* + τὸ κράτος (hybrid coinage, 1848).
6. *technocracy*: ἡ τέχνη + τὸ κράτος; (coined 1932) = the organization and management of society by technical experts.

Grammar 1

This is a good time to discuss some of the common expressions of time, such as the genitive absolutes ἡμέρᾱς/ἑσπέρᾱς/ νυκτὸς γιγνομένης/γενομένης, translated "when day was dawning/at daybreak," "when evening was falling/fell," and "when night was falling/fell," etc. Students should be alerted to the use of the verb γίγνομαι in such expressions and warned against using the verb πίπτω. For specific references to sunrise and sunset, we use τοῦ ἡλίου ἀνατέλλοντος of the rising sun and τοῦ ἡλίου καταδύντος of the setting sun.

In such temporal expressions the present participle with its imperfective aspect will view the action as a process, e.g., "when/as day was dawning," while the aorist will view it as a simple event or fact, e.g.,"when day dawned/ had dawned," "at daybreak." Students should be alerted to alternative translations such as "at daybreak" and told to use them when appropriate in translating from Greek to English and to be on the lookout for them in the English to Greek translation exercises, such as Exercise 19b, no. 1, where "at daybreak" should be translated with a genitive absolute and not a prepositional phrase.

In Exercise 19a, students are asked to pay particular attention to aspect in the Greek and to tense in English when translating participles. It may be useful

at this point to refer students to Reference
Grammar, paragraph 36, Aspect, and to
have them study what is said there about
the imperfective and the aorist and to
examine the sentences using present
and aorist imperatives, infinitives, and
participles on pages 247–248. After each
of the translations of sentences in Exercise 19a below, we offer brief comments
that may help clarify matters of aspect
in Greek and of tense usage in English.

Exercise 19a

1. When/As evening was falling, the
    foreigners arrived in the city.
    (Present participle = imperfective
    aspect or process, "was falling";
    the present participle describes an
    action taking place simultane-
    ously with that of the main verb,
    which is past tense, and so it is
    translated into English with a past
    tense, "was falling." In translat-
    ing from English into Greek stu-
    dents must be warned not to try to
    use a past tense of the Greek par-
    ticiple in situations such as this.)
2. Since the old man was getting an-
    gry, the boy was afraid.
    (Same as no. 1 above.)
3. When all was ready, the priest
    made the sacrifice.
    (The present participle of εἰμί indi-
    cates a continuous state rather than
    a process; since ἐποιήσατο, the verb
    of the main clause, is in a past
    tense, we translate ἑτοίμων ὄντων
    "was ready.")
4. When the wind became/had be-
    come stronger (greater), the ship,
    being small (since it was small),
    was in danger.
    (Aorist participle = simple event;
    the aorist participle is often used, as
    here, of an action that took place
    prior to that of the main verb, and so
    it is translated into English with
    "became" or–to be more specific
    about the temporal relationship–
    "had become." Again, students

should be alerted to look out for such
temporal relationships when translating from English into Greek;
often an English pluperfect will be
translated with an aorist in Greek,
namely, when the action is viewed
as a *simple event* as opposed to an
action that had been *completed* at
some time prior to another action in
the past = pluperfect. Students
should also take note that the present participle οὖσα may in this
sentence be translated with an imperfect in English, "since it was
small.")

5. Although the city was far away, we
    did not hurry.
    (Present participle = a continuous
    state–cf. no. 3 above–simultaneous
    with the action of the main verb,
    and so it is here translated with
    "was.")
6. Since night fell/had fallen (At
    nightfall), we decided to stay in the
    city.
    (Same as no. 4 above.)
7. Since the farmers became/had be-
    come hostile, the young men left the
    plain and went up onto the moun-
    tain.
    (Same as no. 4 above.)
8. Although his wife was tired, the
    man went quickly down the hill.
    (Same as no. 5 above.)
9. Since his daughter was asking, the
    father walked more slowly.
    (Same as no. 1 above.)
10. When/Since the priest made/had
    made the request (At the priest's re-
    quest), the suppliants put up an of-
    fering.
    (Same as no. 4 above.)
11. When/Since the suppliants
    paid/had paid much money, the
    priest put up an offering.
    (Same as no. 4 above.)
12. When/As the sun was rising, the
    boy was already going to the field.
    (Same as no. 1 above.)
13. When the sun set/had set (At sun-

set), after working all day, the boy wanted to return home.
(Here the aorist participle in the genitive absolute could indicate action either *simultaneous with* or *prior* to that of the verb in the main clause. Students should be informed that aorist participles can indicate action either simultaneous with or prior to that of the main clause. The aorist participle ἐργασάμενος clearly indicates action prior to that of the main verb, thus "after working" or "having worked.")

In No. 5, provide help if necessary with πολύ (adverbial) "far."

Exercise 19b

1. ἡμέρᾱς γενομένης, πεζοὶ ἦμεν/ἤλθομεν πρὸς τὸν λιμένα.
2. τοῦ ναύτου αἰτήσαντος, ἔδοξεν ἡμῖν εἰς τὴν ναῦν εὐθὺς εἰσβῆναι.
3. τοῦ ναυκλήρου κελεύσαντος, οἱ ναῦται τὴν ναῦν ἔλῡσαν.
4. καίπερ μεγάλου ὄντος τοῦ ἀνέμου καὶ μεγάλων τῶν κῡμάτων, οὐδεὶς ἐφοβεῖτο.
5. τῆς νεὼς ἐν κινδύνῳ οὔσης, ὁ ναύκληρος τοὺς ναύτᾱς ἐκέλευσε τὰ ἱστία στεῖλαι.

Mycenae

Illustration (page 37)

The massive defenses surrounding the citadel of Mycenae were built about 1250 B.C. The gate is built of huge limestone blocks, and the triangular space above the lintel is filled with the earliest European monumental sculpture; two rampant lions confront each other across an architectural column, and their feet rest on altars. The heads, which were made separately, are missing.

Illustration (page 38)

From about 1500 B.C. the kings of Mycenae were buried in great chamber tombs built into hillsides (tholos tombs). The Treasury of Atreus, also called the Tomb of Agamemnon, is the latest of these (about 1250 B.C.) and the most splendid. The tomb is approached by a passage about twenty feet wide and 120 feet long. The doorway was flanked by half columns of green marble, and the space above the lintels, by a skin of red marble. The chamber is in the shape of an enormous dome, forty-three feet high and forty-seven feet in diameter.

For further reading, see the *The Oxford Classical Dictionary,* "Mycenae" and "Mycenaean Civilization," and E. Vermeule, *Greece in the Bronze Age* (University of Chicago Press, 1964).

Ο ΝΟΣΤΟΣ (β)

Vocabulary

Notes:

Lines 1–10

But not much later they left behind the tilled fields of men and began to climb (*ingressive aorist*) onto the mountains; and now they rarely met any men, but they did see a few shepherds who were grazing their sheep. And they went through great woods, in which there were many oaks and many pines. But when the road became steep and not easy to find, Dicaeopolis got into difficulty, not knowing the way; but Philip, seeing a man aproaching, said, "Look, father; do you see that man coming down toward us?" And Dicaeopolis (answered) "But where is he? For I don't see him." And Philip replied, "There, near that oak. And he is clearly a hunter; for a Spartan dog is following him."
[οὐ ... διὰ πολλοῦ (1): help students as necessary to see that this phrase means the same as δι' ὀλίγου "soon," which they have seen since Chapter 5.

Word glossed earlier in chapter:
τὰ . . . ἔργα tilled fields.

εἰς ἀπορίαν κατέστη (5–6): this expression (". . . got into . . . ") is pre-
viewed in this chapter (see lines 18 and
29 of this reading passage for other examples). The verb καθίστημι will be
treated formally in Chapter 20 (see
Grammar 2, pages 50–51).

κατιόντα (8): compound verb to be
deduced.

φαίνεται . . . ὤν (9–10): "he is
clearly"; contrast this use of φαίνεται
with the participle with its use with the
infinitive: φαίνεται . . . εἶναι = "he ap-
pears/seems to be." (See Chapter 20,
Grammar 3c, page 55.)

κύων . . . Λάκαινα (10): Spartan
hounds were the best hunting dogs.]

Lines 11–27

But as the young man was drawing
near, the dog barked (barks) fiercely
and rushed (rushes) at them; but the
young man stopped and shouted (said
shouting), "Stop, Arge, and be quiet."
And so Dicaeopolis approached and
said, "Greetings, young man. Do you
know if this road leads to Corinth?"
And he (replied), "Yes, certainly it
leads there. Look, you can see it leading
over the mountain. And you will easily
recognize it, since the stone heaps
(cairns) show (the way). But Corinth is
a long way off, and it will soon be night;
and perhaps you will get into danger
spending the night alone in the mountains; for the mountains are deserted
and (the mountains being deserted) you
will not meet anyone except a shepherd.
But come, how are you off for food? But
wait; I will give you a hare. Look!"
And so saying, he put down the pole that
he was carrying on his shoulders; for
two beasts were hanging from the pole,
one of which he untied and gave to Dicaeopolis. And he accepted it and
thanked him heartily (paid very great
thanks). But the young man said, "It is
nothing. For there are very many hares
in the mountains, and I easily catch

them; for I am very clever at hunting.
And so farewell and good luck to you."
So saying, he went on down the path, and
they slowly went up.
[λαγών (21): for the declension of this
word (Attic declension), see the first
teacher's handbook, page 22.

κατέθηκεν (22): compound verb to be
deduced.

δεινότατος . . . εἰμι κυνηγετεῖν (25–
26): "I am very skilled at hunting";
δεινός can mean "skilled" and can be
followed by an infinitive, literally,
"very skilled to hunt."

εὐτυχοῖτε (26): the form is glossed,
and no explanation of the optative need
be given at this time.

ἀνῆσαν (27): compound verb to be
deduced.]

Lines 28–38

When evening was falling, they
met a shepherd, who was driving his
flocks down the road. And he, seeing
them approaching, got into a panic and
shouted (said shouting), "Who are you
who journey through the night? Where
have you come from and where are you
going?" And Dicaeopolis approached
and told him everything, and the shepherd, receiving them kindly, said, "But
all beggars and strangers are under the
protection of Zeus. But as night is already falling, I advise you not to spend
the night alone on the mountains. Come
now, come with me to my hut, in which
you may spend the night." And so they
gladly accepted the shepherd's words
and followed him to a little hut. And the
shepherd (said), "Look; you go in. I will
milk my goats and ewes, and you put
down your baggage and light a fire and
sit down."
[πάντες . . . πρὸς Διός εἰσι πτωχοί τε
ξεῖνοί τε (32–33): "all beggars and
strangers are under the protection of
Zeus": the shepherd quotes from Homer,
Odyssey 6.208–209: πρὸς γὰρ Διός εἰσιν
ἅπαντες / ξεῖνοί τε πτωχοί τε (although
he does not quite get it right); most
Greeks knew large portions of Homer by

heart. Hospitality to beggars and strangers was a moral obligation generally accepted throughout Greek history.

37–38: the shepherd, like Polyphemus, milks his ewes; cows were not kept for milk.]

Lines 39–48

And so Philip lit a fire, and his father sat down and rested from the long journey. And the shepherd after milking his flocks returned and prepared dinner—bread and cheese and milk. And Dicaeopolis said, "Look, friend, a huntsman, whom we met on the way, gave us this hare. Do you want to roast it for dinner?" And he (replied), "Yes, certainly; for so we will dine most pleasantly; and after dinner, the boy will sing songs." And so they roasted the hare and dined well; then Philip sang songs, and the shepherd told stories, until all were so tired that they fell into a deep sleep.

[ὁ παῖς μέλη ᾄσεται (45): "the boy will sing songs": at Greek dinner parties, eating was followed by drinking and singing of songs; many of these were traditional, and everyone was expected to be able to perform. The telling of traditional stories was another regular form of entertainment, especially among the less literate.]

Principal Parts

We give here two more verbs in which τ is added to the stem (κόπτω and τύπτω). Τύπτω is irregular in that ε is added to the stem that produces the future, thus giving τυπτήσω instead of the expected τύψω, which appears in late Greek. Other tenses of τύπτω are supplied by other verbs, πατάσσω, παίω, etc. Τύπτω is included in the list here to provide a reminder that not all verbs follow regular patterns.

Word Building

1. up; above
2. into; within
3. out; outside
4. in; within
5. down; below
6. toward; forward

Grammar 2

Notes:

Grammar 3

Notes:

Grammar 4

Notes:

Exercise 19c

1. Those on the island were suffering many bad things.
2. The old man is not prudent; for he does not know the ways of fortune.
3. The men of today are no worse than their ancestors.
4. All wise men honored those who died in that battle.
5. The Greeks, understanding the ways of the sea, could defeat the barbarians although they had fewer ships.
6. As we do not have the resources of war, we can scarcely stand up to our enemies.
7. The ships of the barbarians were bigger and slower than those of the Greeks.
8. The sailors in that ship don't know how great a storm there will be.
9. Did you meet the shepherd who was driving his flocks up the road?
10. Virtue is hard; so say the wise, and they are right (not wrong).

Exercise 19d

1. καλὴ ἡ παρθένος. ἆρ' οὐ
θαυμάζεις τὸ καλόν;
2. οἱ ἀγαθοὶ τοὺς μὲν φίλους
ὠφελοῦσι, τοὺς δὲ ἐχθροὺς βλάπ-
τουσιν.
3. ἆρα τὸ ἀληθὲς/τὰ ἀληθῆ λέγεις, ὦ
παῖ; οἱ τὰ ψευδῆ λέγοντες κακῶς
πράττουσιν.
4. ὁ τοῦ βασιλέως οὐκ ἠπίστατο τὰ
τῆς τύχης.
5. τὸ ἄστυ ἔρημον ηὕρομεν καὶ
νεκροὺς ἐν ταῖς ὁδοῖς κειμένους.

The ideas expressed in no. 2 were
part of traditional Greek morality, and
in Plato *Republic* 1334b they are offered
as a definition of justice: τοῦτο ἔμοιγε
δοκεῖ, ὠφελεῖν μὲν τοὺς φίλους ἡ
δικαιοσύνη, βλάπτειν δὲ τοὺς ἐχθρούς.
Socrates then proves that it can never be
just to harm anyone else (335e5).

Additional Exercises:

*Identify the following forms and trans-
late each:*

1. εἶσιν
2. εἰσίν
3. δοῦναι
4. ἦμεν
5. τιθέντα
6. ἴασι
7. ἰδόντες
8. ἑλεῖν
9. ᾔει
10. ἰδεῖν
11. ἔδοσαν
12. θεῖναι
13. δός
14. ἔσται
15. ἴμεν

Answers:

1. 3rd person sing. of εἶμι: "he/she
will go"
2. 3rd person pl. present of εἰμί: "they
are"
3. aorist active infinitive of δίδωμι:
"to give"
4. 1st person pl. imperfect of εἰμί: "we

were going"
5. acc. masc. sing. present participle
active of τίθημι: "placing"
6. 3rd person pl. of εἶμι: "they will go"
7. nom. masc. pl. aorist active participle of ὁράω: "having seen"
8. aorist active infinitive of αἱρέω: "to
take"
9. 3rd person sing. imperfect of εἶμι:
"he/she was going"
10. aorist infinitive of ὁράω: "to see"
11. 3rd person pl. aorist of δίδωμι:
"they gave"
12. aorist infinitive active of τίθημι:
"to put"
13. 2nd person sing. aorist imperative
active of δίδωμι: "give!"
14. 3rd person sing. future of εἰμί:
"he/she will be"
15. 1st person pl. of εἶμι: "we will go"

*Give the imperfect, future, and aorist of
the following:*

1. βαίνω
2. δίδωμι
3. θαυμάζω
4. τρέχω
5. γίγνομαι
6. μένω
7. τίθημι
8. νῑκάω
9. δουλόω
10. ἔρχομαι
11. πλέω
12. νομίζω

Answers:

1. ἔβαινον, βήσομαι, ἔβην
2. ἐδίδουν, δώσω, ἔδωκα
3. ἐθαύμαζον, θαυμάσω, ἐθαύμασα
4. ἔτρεχον, δραμοῦμαι, ἔδραμον
5. ἐγιγνόμην, γενήσομαι, ἐγενόμην
6. ἔμενον, μενῶ, ἔμεινα
7. ἐτίθην, θήσω, ἔθηκα
8. ἐνίκων, νῑκήσω, ἐνίκησα
9. ἐδούλουν, δουλώσω, ἐδούλωσα
10. ᾔειν, εἶμι, ἦλθον
11. ἔπλεον, πλεύσομαι, ἔπλευσα
12. ἐνόμιζον, νομιῶ, ἐνόμισα

In the following phrases put the nouns and adjectives into the correct cases and genders to match the given articles:

1. τοῦ (μέγας βασιλεύς)
2. τῷ (σώφρων πατήρ)
3. τῆς (ταχύς ναῦς)
4. τοὺς (βραδύς βοῦς)
5. τοὺς (ὑγιής παῖς)
6. (οὗτος) τοῦ (τεῖχος)
7. (οὗτος) τοῖς (ποιμήν)
8. οἱ (εὐμενής ἱερεύς)
9. (οὗτος) ταῖς (μήτηρ)
10. τῷ (μείζων ἄστυ)

Answers:

1. τοῦ μεγάλου βασιλέως
2. τῷ σώφρονι πατρί
3. τῆς ταχείας νεώς
4. τοὺς βραδεῖς βοῦς
5. τοὺς ὑγιεῖς παῖδας
6. τούτου τοῦ τείχους
7. τούτοις τοῖς ποιμέσι(ν)
8. οἱ εὐμενεῖς ἱερεῖς
9. ταύταις ταῖς μητράσι(ν)
10. τῷ μείζονι ἄστει

ΟΙ ΕΛΛΗΝΕΣ
ΤΟΥΣ ΠΕΡΣΑΣ
ΚΑΤΑ ΘΑΛΑΣΣΑΝ
ΔΕΥΤΕΡΟΝ ΝΙΚΩΣΙΝ

Title: "The Greeks Vanquish the Persians at Sea a Second Time"

Students will remember the adverb δεύτερον from the title of the reading at the end of Chapter 17.

Translation

Lines 1–8

At the beginning of spring the fleet of the Greeks gathered at Aegina, one hundred and ten ships in number. From there they sailed to Delos, wanting to free the Ionians. And while the fleet was at Delos, messengers came from Samos, who asked them to sail to Samos and attack the barbarians. "The barbarians," they said, "have not many

ships, and the Ionians on seeing you will at once revolt from the Persians. So you can both free men of Greece and ward off the barbarians." And so the general of the Greeks accepted these proposals and led the ships toward Samos. [ἀποστήσονται (6; see also lines 15 and 20): students met this verb in Chapter 16 (passage α:21); see also Chapter 20, Grammar 1, page 49.]

Lines 9–16

When they arrived at Samos and prepared for (sea) battle, the Persians at once sailed away to the mainland; for they decided not to fight by sea (make a sea battle); for their ships were not battle-worthy. And so, sailing away to Mycale, they beached their ships and built a wall around them. And the Greeks, learning this, pursued them to Mycale. And when they were near the camp of the enemy and no one appeared putting out to sea but they saw the ships beached inside the wall, first they sailed past and called to the Ionians, telling them to revolt from the Persians; and then they disembarked onto land and attacked the wall.

Lines 17–20

At first the barbarians fought bravely, but when the Greeks charged in a concerted effort (with one onset) and took the wall, they turned and fled. And when the Ionians saw the Greeks winning, they deserted to them and fell on the barbarians. So the Ionians revolted from the Persians for the second time. [The first Ionian revolt had broken out in 499 B.C. (See essay, Book I, page 88.)]

Exercise 19e

1. τῶν Ἰώνων αἰτησάντων, τῷ στρατηγῷ ἔδοξε τῷ ναυτικῷ πρὸς τὴν Σάμον ἡγεῖσθαι.
2. οἱ ἄγγελοι, "οὐ προδώσομεν ὑμᾶς," ἔφασαν, "ἀλλ' ἀπὸ τῶν Περσῶν ἀποστησόμεθα."
3. οἱ βάρβαροι τὰς τῶν Ἑλλήνων ναῦς προσιούσας ἰδόντες, πρὸς τὴν ἤπειρον ἔφυγον.
4. οἱ Ἕλληνες ἐκ τῶν νεῶν ἐκβάντες

τῷ τείχει προσβαλόντες εἷλον.

5. οἱ Ἴωνες ἰδόντες τοὺς Ἕλληνας
  νῑκῶντας ἀπέστησαν ἀπὸ τῶν
  Περσῶν καὶ τοῖς Ἕλλησιν
  ἐβοήθουν/ἐβοήθησαν.

In the student's book we provide
hints in this exercise about use of genitive absolutes and participles. Such
hints will not always be given in the future. Students should be told to keep the
genitive absolute construction in mind
as a possiblity in future English to
Greek translations. They should also be
reminded that clauses such as "When
the barbarians saw the ships of the
Greeks approaching" (no. 3), in which
the subject of the subordinate clause is
the same as the subject of the main
clause, may best be translated into
Greek with a participle in the nominative case (circumstantial participle) =
"the barbarians having seen the ships of
the Greeks approaching, they. . . ." Finally, students should be reminded that
one or more coordinate main verbs in
English such as "disembarked . . . and
attacked . . . and took" in no. 4 may best
be translated with participles in Greek
(= "having disembarked . . . and having attacked, they took." Students
should be alert to using participles wherever possible in translating from
English to Greek.

20
Ο ΝΟΣΤΟΣ (γ)

Title: "The Return"

The purposes of this chapter are:

1. Reading: (γ) to continue the story of Dicaeopolis's and Philip's return to Attica, with a visit to the ruins of Mycenae; (δ) to describe an overnight stay with a farmer, a hostile encounter in Corinth on the eve of the outbreak of the Peloponnesian War, flight and an overnight stay in a ditch, bypassing of Megara, and arrival, exhausted, in Eleusis; to present an adapted excerpt from Thucydides, in which Athenian ambassadors, present at the meeting of the Peloponnesian League at which the League resolved to declare war on Athens, remind the Spartans of their debt to Athens (July, 432 B.C.)
2. Grammar: (γ) to present the forms, meanings, and uses of the verbs ἵστημι, ἀφίσταμαι, and καθίστημι; (δ) to present some verbs that take supplementary participles
3. Background: to sketch the events that led to the outbreak of the Peloponnesian War

Illustration

Ruins of the great court and megaron of the palace at Mycenae.

Caption under Illustration

"They were standing in the very palace of Agamemnon": we use the Homeric word δώματα (*plural*) "palace," which is not used in Attic prose, to supply a Homeric flavor here and in line 9 of the first reading passage in this chapter; students will have to be given the meaning of the word.

Encourage students to deduce the imperfect ἵσταντο from their knowledge of ἔστην and ἀφίσταμαι (See Book I,

pages 184 and 194). Call attention to the temporal augment and the secondary ending.

Vocabulary

In presenting the verbs ἵστημι and καθίστημι/καθίσταμαι, be sure students understand the terms *transitive* and *intransitive* and the force of the middle voice.

Verbs

Students have seen forms of ἵστημι since Chapter 15 (see especially Chapter 15, Grammar 1, for ἔστην). The following forms of ἵστημι and its compounds ἀνίστημι, ἀφίσταμαι, and καθίστημι have occurred in the reading passages in Chapters 15–19: ἀναστάς (15α:10), ἀνέστη (15β:36), ἀναστάς (16α:12), ἀνέστη (16β:25), καταστήσεσθε (19β:18), κατέστη (19β:29), ἀποστήσονται (19 tail reading:6), ἀποστῆναι (19 tail reading:15), and ἀπέστησαν (19 tail reading:20).

The verb ἵστημι is formally presented in the current chapter; the following forms occur in passage γ: ἑστηκότα (3), στήσας (4), ἑστηκότα (5), and ἵσταντο (22). The perfect participles (3 and 5) need not be discussed at this time, but the occurrences of the verb in the earlier chapters should be reviewed while the verb is being studied in the current chapter.

Translation

Lines 1–12
When day dawned, they bade farewell to the shepherd and went on their way and finally arrived at the top of the mountains, from which they looked down on the plain lying below and some walls standing on a hill. And Philip, stopping his father, said, "Papa, I see some great walls standing on that hill. But tell me what they are." And Dicaeopolis looking at the walls for a long time said, "Those, my boy, are, I

think (as it seems to me), the walls of
Mycenae." And Philip said, "Do you
really mean it (are you telling the
truth)? Did Agamemnon live there?
May we go down there and look at
Agamemnon's palace?" And Dicaeopolis (replied), "We may go down, if you
like (if it seems good to you). For the
walls are not far from the road, and—for
it is late—we will spend the night safe
inside the walls."

Lines 13–23

So saying he led the boy down the
mountain. And soon they were approaching the walls, and, going up the
hill, they arrived at the gates. Philip,
gazing at the walls, was amazed at their
size and said, "Father, surely giants
built these walls; for men could not have
raised such large stones." And Dicaeopolis said, "You are right, son. For
the Cyclopes, as they say, made these.
But look, look up." And Philip, looking
up, saw two stone lions guarding the
gates. And, having looked at these, they
went forward, and arriving at the top of
the hill they were standing in the very
palace of Agamemnon (the palace itself), looking down on the plain and the
sea shining in the sun.
[θεώμενος (15) and θεᾱσάμενοι (21): the
verb θεάομαι ("I look at") used here may
be contrasted with θεωρέω ("I see" in the
sense of viewing or sightseeing) used in
line 10.

ὥς φᾱσιν (18–19): note that the pro-
clitic preceding the enclitic takes an
acute accent and that the enclitic is not
accented.

Compound verb to be deduced: ἀνα-
βλέπων (20).]

Lines 24–29

But suddenly Philip shuddered and
fell into an icy fear. "Father," he said,
"I do not like this place (this place does
not please me). For it smells of blood."
And Dicaeopolis said, "Don't be afraid,
child. Perhaps the Furies of Agamemnon and his completely evil wife are
even now wandering about. But they

will not hurt you, son. Come, give me
your hand. I will lead you." And so
speaking, he led the boy down as quickly
as possible.

Principal Parts

Verbs with guttural stems (ending
in γ, κ, or χ) are given in this and the
next group of principal parts.
We list πρᾱ́ττω first because it shows
a complete set of regular forms.
Most verbs with -ττ- (-σσ-) have
guttural stems and follow the pattern of
πρᾱ́ττω.
Be sure students note the reduplication of the stem ἀγ- in the aorist ἤγαγον
and the deponent future and second
aorist of φεύγω.

Word Study

1. *photograph*: from τὸ φῶς, τοῦ
    φωτός (light) + γράφω. A photo-
    graph is a light-drawing, i.e., a
    picture made "by means of the
    chemical action of light on a sensi-
    tive film" (OED).

2. *seismograph*: ὁ σεισμός (shaking,
    shock, earthquake) + γράφω. A
    seismograph is an instrument for
    recording earthquakes; it does this
    by drawing a graph of the shocks.

3. *telegraph*: τῆλε (far, at a distance)
    + γράφω. A telegraph is an in-
    strument for transmitting mes-
    sages to a distance in written form
    (compare telephone, which is an
    instrument for transmitting the
    spoken word, φωνή.

4. *paleography*: παλαιός, -ᾱ́, -όν
    (old) + γράφω, γραφή = ancient
    writing, the study of ancient
    writing and inscriptions.

5. *cryptography*: κρύπτω (I hide) +
    γράφω = a secret method of writing,
    hidden from all except those who
    have the key.

telegram: τῆλε + τὸ γράμμα (something
    written, message, etc.) = writing
    from a distance, i.e., a message

sent by telegraph (see 3 above).

telephone: τῆλε + ἡ φωνή (voice).

telepathy: τῆλε + πάσχω (παθ-) = suffering/experiencing emotions from afar: "the communication of impressions from one mind to another, independently of the recognized channels of sense" (OED).

telescope: τῆλε + σκοπέω (I look at, examine), τηλέσκοπος, -ον = far-seeing = an instrument making it possible to examine/look at objects that are far-off.

television: τῆλε + Latin *video* (a hybrid coinage) = an instrument making it possible to see things that are far-off (coined 1909).

Grammar 1

It should be stressed that ἵστημι, στήσω, and ἔστησα are transitive and will normally take direct objects, while ἔστην is intransitive and will not. To say simply "I stand" (intransitive), Greek generally uses the perfect ἕστηκα, which will be presented in Chapter 28, Grammar 3, page 164, or less commonly the present middle ἵσταμαι.

Grammar 2

The dog put the stranger into a panic.

The stranger got into a panic.

The people appointed Pericles general.

Pericles was appointed general.

The Athenians established laws (for themselves).

Exercise 20a

1. Singular imperative, 2nd aorist active: "stand!"
2. Present infinitive active: "to set up"
3. 2nd aorist infinitive: "to stand"
4. 2nd person pl. present indicative middle: "you are setting up (for yourselves)"
5. Aorist infinitive middle: "to set up (for oneself)"

6. (a) 3rd pl. 1st aorist indicative: "they set up"
   (b) 3rd pl. 2nd aorist indicative: "they stood"
7. 3rd sing. imperfect indicative active: "he/she was setting up"
8. Singular imperative, 1st aorist: "set up!"
9. 2nd aorist participle: "having stood," "standing"
10. Aorist participle middle: "having set up (for himself)"
11. 3rd sing. present indicative middle: "he/she revolts from"
12. 3rd pl. imperfect indicative middle: "they were revolting from"
13. 3rd pl. future indicative middle: "they will revolt from"
14. 1st aorist participle: "having set up"
15. Singular imperative, present middle: "revolt!"

Exercise 20b

1. The shepherd stopped his dog.
2. The farmer suddenly stood still (stopped) in the agora.
3. The boy stood up.
4. The father made his son stand up.
5. The Athenians got into (a state of) war.
6. The enemy will put you to flight.
7. Who appointed you a judge of us?
8. Theseus was appointed king of the Athenians.
9. The Athenians established laws (for themselves).
10. The sailors, after leaving the harbor, set up the mast.
11. The Greeks appointed the Spartans leaders.
12. The generals got into a panic and wanted to flee.
13. After defeating the Persians, Pausanias set up a trophy (for himself).
14. Don't flee, friends, but stand and fight bravely.
15. After suffering so much, we will never get into a war again.

Exercise 20c

1. ὡς/ἐπεὶ τὸν ξένον εἴδομεν, στάντες
   ἠρόμεθα ποῖ πορεύεται.
2. ὁ νεανίας τὸν ἵππον ἔστησε καὶ τὴν
   ὁδὸν ἡμῖν ἐδήλωσεν/ἐσήμηνεν ἣ
   πρὸς τὸ ἄστυ ἔφερεν.
3. ὁ δῆμος τοῦτον στρατηγὸν αὖθις
   κατέστησεν.
4. οὗτος, ἐπεὶ στρατηγὸς κατέστη, τῷ
   δήμῳ παρήνεσεν μὴ μάχεσθαι.
5. ἐκέλευσεν ἡμᾶς τοῦ πολέμου
   παύσασθαι καὶ τὴν πόλιν εἰς
   εἰρήνην κατέστησεν.

War Clouds

For further reading, see *The World of Athens*, pp. 24–28.

Ο ΝΟΣΤΟΣ (δ)

Vocabulary

Explanation of the meaning and use of λανθάνω (+ *participle*) should wait until students have seen the examples in lines 27, 29, and 31–32 of passage δ; further examples of verbs that take supplementary participles are given in Grammar 3.

New usage of preposition: ἐπί (+ *gen.*) = toward, in the direction of: ἐπὶ τῆς Κορίνθου (12).

Lines 1–14

And so they decided not to spend the night near Mycenae, but, leaving the walls behind, they went on toward Corinth. Soon, when the sun had already set, they arrived at a certain village. And there a certain farmer, meeting them resting by the roadside, took pity on them and led them home. And so his wife offered them food, and the farmer told them to sit near the fire. And when they had dined, the farmer asked them where they were going, and, hearing that they were going to Corinth, "Corinth," he said, "is a long way off. And so you cannot arrive there today. But if you like (if it seems good to you), you may spend the night here." They

thanked him most heartily and lay down near the fire. The next day, as the sun was rising, they bade farewell to the farmer and hurried in the direction of Corinth. But the road was long, and they arrived at the city when evening was already falling and looked for an inn.

Lines 15–23

And so approaching a man who was going by on the road, they asked where there was an inn. But he, giving a terrible look and getting into a rage, said, "By the gods, You are clearly Athenians. What do you want? What are you doing in Corinth?" And shouting to passers-by (those present) he said, "Come here, friends. Some Athenians are here; they are surely spies, who have come to spy on the shipyards." But Dicaeopolis said, "What are you saying, man? We are not spies but farmers who are returning from Epidaurus to Athens." But already a crowd of Corinthians had gathered, who were shouting savagely; and some were even taking stones to pelt them.
[The Corinthian would have known that the strangers were Athenians by their accent and dialect; the Corinthians spoke a version of the Doric dialect, of which the most obvious feature was ᾱ instead of Attic η. Dicaeopolis did not know that by now war was about to be declared on Athens by the Peloponnesian League (see the next chapter).

κατασκεψόμενοι (20): future participle, here without ὡς, to express purpose.]

Lines 24–34

And so Dicaeopolis, terrified (having got into fear), said, "Flee, Philip, as fast as you can." And so they fled toward the gates, and the Corinthians in hot pursuit (pursuing) threw stones. But Philip and his father, running, escaped their pursuers and hid in a certain ditch unseen (escaped [their] notice hiding in a certain ditch), in which they remained the whole night. And when day came, they set out at once and hurried quickly, unseen by anyone

(they escaped the notice of all men, hurrying quickly). And when they approached Megara, they did not go into the city but passed by outside the walls. And so at last they entered Attica unseen (they escaped notice entering Attica), and as soon as they arrived at Eleusis they lay down and rested by the roadside; for after suffering many terrible (hardships) they were very tired, so that they could not go on.
[Megara was another Dorian city, at this time in the Peloponnesian League.]

Principal Parts

Note the aspiration of the final consonant of the stem in the perfect active of διώκω and φυλάττω and in the aorist passive of διώκω and δοκέω.

In the present and imperfect, δοκέω is conjugated like a regular -ε- contract verb, but in the other tenses it is a regular guttural stem verb.

Word Building

1. τῑμα-: honor; I honor
2. ἀναγκα-: necessity; I compel
3. ὀργα-: anger; I get angry
4. οἰκο/ε-: house, home; I dwell; dwelling; dweller; dwelling, room
5. δουλο-: slave; I enslave; enslavement
6. κηρυκ-: herald; I proclaim; proclamation

In each case a noun is formed from the root stem, and a denominative verb is formed from this noun. The list is arranged thus: 1, 2, and 3 give first declension nouns; 4 and 5 give second declension nouns; and 6 (consonant stem) gives a third declension noun. The suffixes -αζ- and -ιζ- were originally added to form verbs from stems in γ and δ, e.g., ἀρπαγ- > ἀρπάζω and ἐλπιδ- > ἐλπίζω, but they were then widely extended to other stems.

Grammar 3

With φαίνομαι we give the second future passive (φανήσομαι), the future

middle (φανοῦμαι), the second perfect active (πέφηνα), and the second aorist passive (ἐφάνην), which are used in the sense "I will appear," "I have appeared," and "I appeared." Students will not be taught the formation of these tenses until later; they will be able to recognize the forms from the Overview of the Greek Verb, and they have already seen the second aorist passive ἐφάνη in 18α:2. For the principal parts of φαίνω and φαίνομαι, see the list of principal parts after reading 22α, page 73.

Exercise 20d

1. The Corinthians seemed to be (to become) hostile.
2. The Corinthians are shown to be hostile/are clearly hostile.
3. Come on, Philip, escape the notice of our pursuers by hiding in this ditch.
4. Philip got down the hill before his father (anticipated his father getting down the hill).
5. When her husband approached, his wife happened to be sitting (was at that moment sitting) in the courtyard.
6. "You are clearly idle, wife," he said; "Why aren't you working?"
7. The Persians sailed away to the mainland before the Greeks. (*or*) The Persians anticipated the Greeks in sailing away to the mainland.
8. The Persians were clearly unwilling to fight by sea.
9. The master happens to be asleep.
10. They anticipated the storm, sailing into the harbor. (*or*) They sailed into the harbor before the storm.

ΟΙ ΑΘΗΝΑΙΟΙ ΤΟΥΣ ΛΑΚΕΔΑΙΜΟΝΙΟΥΣ ΑΝΑΜΙΜΝΗΙΣΚΟΥΣΙΝ

Title: "The Athenians Remind the Spartans"

You will have to give the meaning of the verb ἀναμιμνῄσκουσιν.

The Corinthians persuaded the Spartans to call a meeting of the Peloponnesian League in July, 432 B.C., after the Megarian Decree had been passed and the siege of Potidaea had begun (see Thucydides 1.66). The Corinthians addressed the conference last, accusing the Athenians of open aggression and the Spartans of being dilatory. They contrasted the national characters of Athens and Sparta and ended by demanding that they invade Attica immediately. Athenian ambassadors, who happened to be in Sparta on other business, asked permission to address the Spartans and made the speech from which the following extracts are taken. The Spartan king, Archidamus, then addressed the Spartan Assembly and tried to dissuade them from embarking on a war with Athens and advised them to make further diplomatic overtures. The issue was put to the vote, and the Spartan Assembly resolved by a large majority that the truce had been broken by the Athenians and that war should be declared. Nevertheless, diplomatic activity continued until spring 431 B.C. (see Chapter 21, readings α and β).

Translation

Lines 1–6
"We say that at Marathon we took the risk of fighting the barbarians alone, and when they came the second time, not being able to defend ourselves by land, we boarded our fleet, all together, and fought by sea at Salamis, so that the barbarians could not sail against the Peloponnesus and destroy it city by city. And the barbarians themselves gave the greatest proof of this; for when we defeated them with our ships, they retreated as fast as possible with the greater part of their army.

Lines 7–14
And in these actions we Athenians provided the three most useful things, the greatest number of ships, the man who was the most skillful general, and a most resolute spirit (eagerness). For we provided two-thirds of all the ships, and Themistocles as general, who persuaded the other generals to fight by sea in the straits, and we showed such spirit that when no one helped us by land, we left our city and destroyed our property, and having boarded our ships we faced the danger. For you came to help when you were afraid for yourselves and not for us (for when we were still safe, you did not come); but we by endangering ourselves (running a risk) saved both you and ourselves.

Lines 15–19
After showing such spirit then and such judgment, do we deserve (are we worthy of), Spartans, such great hostility from the Greeks because of the empire that we hold? For this very empire we took not by force, but because you refused to stand fast against the remnants of the barbarians, and the allies approached us and themselves asked us to become their leaders.

Exercise 20e

1. οἱ Λακεδαιμόνιοι, καὶ τὰ τῶν συμμάχων ἐγκλήματα ἀκούσαντες καὶ τοὺς τῶν Ἀθηναίων λόγους, ἐβουλεύοντο μόνοι περὶ τοῦ πράγματος.
2. πολλοὶ ἔλεγον ὅτι οἱ Ἀθηναῖοι ἀδικοῦσι καὶ δεῖ εὐθὺς στρατεύεσθαι.
3. ὁ δὲ Ἀρχίδᾱμος, βασιλεὺς ὤν, αὐτοῖς παρῄνεσε μὴ εἰς πόλεμον καταστῆναι.
4. "ἐκείνοις γάρ," ἔφη, "πλεῖστά τε χρήματά ἐστι καὶ πλεῖσται νῆες. οὐ δυνάμεθα αὐτοὺς κατὰ θάλατταν νῑκᾶν. ἡμεῖς οὖν αὐτοὶ κακὰ πεισόμεθα μᾶλλον ἢ ἐκείνους βλάψομεν."
5. τοὺς δὲ Λακεδαιμονίους οὐκ ἐδύνατο πεῖσαι, οἷς ἔδοξε στρατεύεσθαι.

21
Η ΕΚΚΛΗΣΙΑ (α)

Title: "The Assembly"

The purposes of this chapter are:

1. Reading: (α) to continue the story of Dicaeopolis's and Philip's return to Attica, to describe their meeting on the road with farmers hurrying to Athens to attend the Assembly, at which, as Dicaeopolis and Philip learn, the alternatives of war or peace with Sparta will be discussed, and to bring Dicaeopolis and Philip to Athens and the Assembly; (β) to present an adapted version of Pericles' speech to the Assembly as reported by Thucydides, sketching the diplomatic situation of Sparta and Athens, the respective military powers of the two states, Pericles' proposed reply to the Spartan ambassadors, and his belief in the inevitability of war; and in the final reading to give an adapted version of Thucydides' account of how the Athenians, in obedience to Pericles' policy moved their households into Athens in anticipation of a Spartan invasion of Attica
2. Grammar: (α) to introduce the forms of the subjunctive, and its use in exhortations, prohibitions, deliberative questions, and purpose clauses; (β) to present the verb ἵημι
3. Background: to sketch the development of Athenian democracy from Solon to Pericles

Illustration

The Pnyx, photographed from the north; the bema (speakers' platform) can be seen in the middle of the far side. The Pnyx is a huge semicircular terrace built on the slopes of a hill, about 500 yards due west of the Acropolis.

Caption under Illustration

"They hurry to the Pnyx in order to be present at the Assembly on time."

The Subjunctive

This chapter formally introduces the forms and uses of the subjunctive. The following information about the use of the subjunctive is presented in this and subsequent chapters:

Chapter 21
Grammar 3, pages 62–63:
hortatory, deliberative questions, prohibitions, purpose, conditional clauses
Chapter 22
Grammar 1, page 74:
clauses of fearing
Grammar 2, pages 75–77:
indefinite or general clauses (including temporal clauses)
Chapter 27
Grammar 2, page 156:
πρίν + ἄν + subjunctive
Chapter 30
Grammar 1, pages 192–194:
conditional clauses
Grammar 2, pages 200–202:
optional change of subjunctive to optative in subordinate clauses in indirect speech

Vocabulary

Note that the verb ἀγορεύω is used only in the present and imperfect in Attic Greek in uncompounded forms, and thus we give only the present form in the vocabulary list; the remaining principal parts as used in compound verbs are given in the Greek to English Vocabulary at the end of the student's book. We include ἵημι in order to show the principal parts of this verb that appears in the compound form ἀφίημι in passage α and is presented formally in Grammar 4.

Note that the stem vowel of θύω is long in the first three principal parts and short in the others, just as with λύω.

We give the singular πρέσβυς
(poetic for πρεσβύτης) because it is used
in the selections from the *Acharnians* in
Chapter 31 (line 67). The plural πρέσβεις
is declined like πόλις in the plural.

New usage of preposition: περί
(+ *gen.*) = about, concerning: περὶ τοῦ
πολέμου (16).

For ἐάν with the subjunctive in conditional clauses, see Grammar 3e in
this chapter and Grammar 2 in Chapter
22. For ἵνα (or ὅπως or ὡς) with the subjunctive in purpose clauses, see Grammar 3d.

Verbs

The following subjunctive forms
occur in passage α: σπεύδωμεν (3; *hortatory*), ἀκούωμεν (9; *purpose*),
ποιησώμεθα . . . σώσωμεν (12–13; *deliberative*), ἀφῆτε (20; *future more vivid
condition*), ἀφῶμεν . . . ποιησώμεθα (21–
22; *deliberative*), σπεύδωμεν (25; *hortatory*), and πάρωμεν (25; *purpose*).

Translations in the glosses will
help students with these new forms and
uses; they should be carefully reviewed
after students have studied Grammar 1–
3.

Translation

Lines 1–13
A little later (later by not much) Dicaeopolis stood up and said to Philip,
"Stand up, son; (for) it is time to go. And
so let us hurry straight to the city." And
so they set out and soon met many farmers journeying to Athens. And so Dicaeopolis approached an old man, who
was walking near him, and asked why
(because of what) so many people were
hurrying to Athens. And he said,
"What do you say, man? Don't you
know this, that today there will be an
Assembly? And so we are all hurrying
to the city for this reason, to hear the
speakers in the Assembly. For most important matters lie before the people about
which it is necessary to debate." And
Dicaeopolis (asked), "What (issues) lie

before the people, old man?" And he
(replied), "But who does not know this,
that we must debate whether we are to
make war against the Peloponnesians
or preserve the peace?"
[πολλῷ (1): provide help as necessary
with this dative of degree of difference,
"a little later."

ὦ ἄνθρωπε (6): this is a rather
disparaging form of address, e.g., "My
good man, . . . "

ἆρα τοῦτο ἀγνοεῖς, ὅτι. . . . (7) and
τούτου ἕνεκα, ἵνα. . . . (8): Greek frequently uses demonstratives that antici-
pate a following clause; we use them
much more sparingly in English, and
they can sometimes be omitted in translation.]

Lines 14–25
But Dicaeopolis (said), "But what is
new? For the Peloponnesians have long
been hostile, but we did not get into a war
but the truce still stands. Then why
must we decide about war now?" And
the old man replied, "Are you ignorant
of this also, that the Spartans lately sent
ambassadors who said this, 'The Spartans want there to be peace; and there
will be peace, if you let the Greeks go free
(independent).' And so they are telling
us to give up our empire. And so this is
what we must debate, whether we are to
give up our empire or make war against
the Peloponnesians." And Dicaeopolis
said, "Zeus, that's it (this is that). (For)
now I understand why the Corinthians
got into a rage and attacked us, when
they learned that we were Athenians.
But let's hurry, son, so that we may be
present in time."
[αἱ σπονδαί (16): this refers to the
Thirty Years' Peace, made between
Athens and Sparta in 446 B.C.; it termi-
nated the First Peloponnesian War and
was the basis of all negotiation until the
great Peloponnesian War broke out. In
demanding that the Athenians give up
their empire, the Spartans were in fact
contravening the terms of this peace,
since both sides undertook not to inter-

fere in the other's sphere of influence
and to submit disagreements to the arbitration of a third party.

Λακεδαιμόνιοι βούλονται. . . . (18–
20): this was the final Spartan ultima-
tum to Athens, following a flurry of
diplomatic activity (see Thucydides
1.139).

ἀφῆτε (20): note the accent of the
aorist subjunctive forms of ἵημι in compounds.]

Lines 26–39

And so they hurried on at once and
arriving at the gates ran to the Pnyx.
There the people were already gathering
and thousands were present, waiting for
the presidents. Soon the presidents and
the chairman and the other councilors
came in and sat down. Then those present became silent (*ingressive aorist*),
and the priest approached the altar and
sacrificed the victim and prayed to the
gods, that they might be kindly to the
people. Then the chairman told the herald to read out the motion for debate.
And the herald read out the motion and
asked the people whether they wanted (it
seemed good) to vote straightway or to
debate the matter first. And the people
voted, showing that all wanted to debate
the matter, since it was so important.
Then the herald said, "Who wishes to
speak?" And many of the speakers
came to the platform and spoke, some
saying that they should make war,
others that nothing should stand in the
way of peace.

[For the Pnyx and the procedure at the
Assembly, see essay, Chapter 22, page
78; we have a presentation of the
Assembly in action in the opening scene
of Aristophanes' *Acharnians* at the end of
this book (see Chapter 31α and β).

"τίς ἀγορεύειν βούλεται;" (37): this
question, put by the herald, was the customary way of opening a debate.

ῥητόρων (37): this is the word used to
described those who regularly addressed
the Assembly.

The last sentence of this section is

adapted from Thucydides 1.139 and
leads into the speech of Pericles
(Thucydides 1.140–144), which forms
the second part of this chapter.]

Principal Parts

Verbs with dental stems (ending in
δ, ζ, θ, or τ) are given in this and the
next group of principal parts.

We give the -δ- stem verb σπεύδω
first, but φράζω shows the most complete
set of forms. Students should note that
θαυμάζω is deponent in the future.

Word Study

1. *anthropology*: ὁ ἄνθρωπος + ὁ
    λόγος, -λογίᾱ: the study of
    mankind (coined 1593, but
    ἀνθρωπολογέω occurs in Philo
    1.282, 3rd century B.C.).
2. *philanthropy*: φιλέω + ὁ ἄνθρωπος;
    ἡ φιλανθρωπίᾱ: love of mankind,
    benevolence.
3. *anthropomorphous*: ὁ ἄνθρωπος +
    ἡ μορφή (= shape); ἀνθρωπόμορφος,
    -ον: of human shape.
4. *anthropophagous*: ὁ ἄνθρωπος +
    φαγ- (cf. ἔφαγον = I ate);
    ἀνθρωπόφαγος, -ον: man-eating.
5. *misanthrope*: τὸ μῖσος (μῖσέω = I
    hate) + ὁ ἄνθρωπος; μῖσάνθρωπος,
    -ον: a hater of mankind.
6. *pithecanthropus*: ὁ πίθηκος + ὁ
    ἄνθρωπος: an ape-man (coined by
    Haeckel in 1876 to describe the
    missing link between ape and
    man).

Grammar 1

Notes:

Grammar 2

Occurrences and uses of the subjunctive in passage α are listed under
"Verbs" at the beginning of the teacher's
notes to this chapter. These should be re-

viewed with students after studying
Grammar 3.

Grammar 3

Notes:

Exercise 21a

1. λύωμεν
2. λύσῃ
3. τιμᾷ
4. δηλῶμεν
5. λύωνται
6. λάβω/λάβωσι
7. ὦσι
8. ἴωμεν
9. γένηται
10. φιλήσῃς
11. μαχώμεθα
12. ᾖ
13. ἴδητε
14. βουλεύσηται
15. αὔξηται

Exercise 21b

1. Stop, friends; let us consider what
   we should do.
2. Are we to return home or go on?
3. Since evening is falling, let us not
   stay in the mountains, but let us
   hurry home.
4. How are we to reach home? For we
   do not know the way.
5. Look, we can ask that shepherd
   which road we should take.
6. Don't run away, old man, but tell
   us which road leads to the city.
7. Don't set out to that place now; for
   you won't arrive before night.
8. What are we to do, friends? For the
   shepherd says that we cannot arrive before night.
9. Going down into the plain, let us
   look for a house so that we may rest.
10. And when day comes, let us set out
    at once.

In nos. 1 and 5 be sure that students

who have had Latin do not confuse the
use of the subjunctive here with the use of
the subjunctive in indirect questions in
Latin.

Exercise 21c

1. οἱ Ἀθηναῖοι βουλεύονται πότερον
   πόλεμον ποιήσωνται πρὸς τοὺς
   Πελοποννησίους.
2. πρὸς τὸ ἄστυ σπεύδωμεν καὶ τῶν
   ῥητόρων ἀκούωμεν.
3. πότερον τοῖς πολεμίοις εἴξωμεν ἢ
   τὴν πόλιν σώσωμεν;
4. μὴ ἀκούσητε τῶν πρέσβεων· οὐ γὰρ
   λέγουσι τὰ ἀληθῆ.
5. εὐθὺς αὐτοὺς ἀποπέμψωμεν.

The Athenian Democracy

For further reading, see *Civilization
of the Ancient Mediterranean*, Vol. I, pp.
451–455 and 463–478; *The World of
Athens*, pp. 5–10; and *The Oxford History
of the Classical World*, pp. 31–35 and
136–141.

Η ΕΚΚΛΗΣΙΑ (β)

Vocabulary

New usage of preposition: κατά
(+ *acc.*) = at (of time): κατ' ἐκεῖνον τὸν
χρόνον (1–2).

Spelling

Note that in this reading, in Exercise 21e, in the passage at the end of the
chapter, and in the translations of the
sentences in Exercise 21g we use the
Thucydidean spellings that are described on page 66 of the student's book.

Translation

Lines 1–12
And finally Pericles, son of Xan-
thippus, the leading man at Athens (of
the Athenians) at that time and the most
capable in words and action (to speak
and act), came forward and gave this
advice (advised things of this sort): "I

always hold to the same opinion, Athenians, not to yield to the Peloponnesians. For it is clear that the Spartans have plotted against us before and are doing so now (are plotting against us both formerly and now). For in the treaty it was (had been) stated that we must give and accept arbitration of (our) differences, and that each side should keep what we hold. But now they have not asked for arbitration themselves nor do they accept (arbitration) when we offer it but want to settle their complaints by war rather than discussion. For they impose many other conditions (things) on us and this last lot (of envoys) tells us to let the Greeks go free. And so I advise you not to yield at all but to preserve the empire and prepare for war.

[ἐν . . . ταῖς ξυνθήκαις (5): the Thirty Years' Peace (446 B.C.).

εἴρητο (6): this is a classic example of the difference between Greek and English tense usage; Greek uses the pluperfect to stress that the provisions of the treaty were fixed and unchangeable, while the English idiom is to use a simple past.

Word glossed earlier in chapter: αὐτονόμους independent, free.

μηδὲν εἴκειν (11–12): μηδέν is an adverbial accusative.]

Lines 13–21

"And if we get into war, we shall have military resources no weaker (than theirs); listen and learn. The Peloponnesians are farmers, and they have no money either privately or in their treasury. And people of this sort can neither man ships nor send out infantry armies often; for they are unwilling to be away from their farms for a long time, and they have to contribute money from their own resources. And so in one battle the Peloponnesians and their allies are capable of holding out against all the Greeks, but they are incapable of conducting a long war against us.

[τὰ τοῦ πολέμου (13): for this use of the

article with the genitive, see Chapter 19, Grammar 4, page 43.]

Lines 22–26

"For we rule the sea. And if they march against our land on foot, we will sail against theirs. For sea power is a great thing. For we live in a city like an island, which no enemy can take. And so we must give up our land and houses and guard the sea and the city.

Lines 27–30

"And now let us send away (these ambassadors), answering them that we will let the cities (of our empire) go free, if they too give up the cities they hold subject, and that we are willing to submit to arbitration in accordance with the treaty, and that we will not start a war, but if they start one, we will defend ourselves.

[τούτοις (27): dative of indirect object with ἀποκρῑνάμενοι.

Word glossed earlier in chapter: αὐτονόμους independent, free.]

Lines 31–36

"You must understand this, that war is inevitable (it is necessary to go to war), and that from the greatest dangers come (result) the greatest honors both for the city and for the individual (the private person). Your fathers drove away the barbarians and advanced the city to its present power, and you must not become worse men than they but must defend yourselves against your enemies by every means and pass on the city to your descendants no less powerful (lesser)."

Lines 37–40

And so Pericles said this (such things), and the Athenians, thinking that he had given the best advice, voted for what he had ordered and answered the ambassadors point by point as he explained. And the ambassadors departed for home and did not come again after this (later) as ambassadors.

[Compound verb to be deduced: ἀπεχώρησαν (39).]

Principal Parts

Verbs in -ίζω form a subset of dental stem verbs and most have principal parts like those of κομίζω.

Note the two perfects of πείθω and their different meanings.

To this list of verbs with dental stems may be added the following verb used in Book I with stem in τ found mainly in Homer:

ἐρέσσω (ἐρετ-), ἤρεσα I row.

For "I row" Attic usually uses ἐλαύνω.

Word Building

1. ἡ δίκη; root word = custom, right, judgment, lawsuit, penalty.
   δίκαιος; δικα- + -ιος = just.
   ἡ δικαιοσύνη; δικαιο- + -σύνη = justice.
   ἄδικος; ά-privative + δικ- + -ος = unjust.
   ἀδικέω; ἀδικέ-ω = I commit injustice, do wrong.
   ἀδίκημα; ἀδίκη-μα = injustice, wicked deed.
2. βουλή; primitive noun from root βουλ- (βούλ-ομαι); = will; counsel, plan; the Council.
   βουλεύω; βουλ- + -εύω; = I take counsel, deliberate; I am a member of the Council.
   βουλευτής; βουλευ- + -τής = councilor.
   βούλευμα; βουλευ- + -μα = resolution, decision.
   προβουλεύω; προ- + βουλεύω = I deliberate beforehand, frame a προβούλευμα.
   προβούλευμα; προ- + βούλευμα = preliminary decree of the Council.

Grammar 4

Have students locate and identify the four occurrences of ἀφίημι in passage β. They are:

ἀφιέναι (11): present infinitive
ἀφεῖναι (26): aorist infinitive

ἀφήσομεν (28): future indicative, first person pl.

ἀφῶσι (28): aorist subjunctive, third person pl.; future more vivid condition

Exercise 21d

1. Present infinitive middle; ἵημι
2. 3rd pl. present indicative active; ἵημι
3. Present participle middle; ἵημι
4. 3rd sing. aorist indicative active; ἀφίημι
5. Aorist active participle; ἀφίημι
6. 3rd pl. aorist indicative active; ἀφίημι
7. Singular aorist imperative active; ἀφίημι
8. 2nd pl. aorist indicative middle; ἀφίημι
9. 3rd pl. imperfect indicative middle; ἵημι
10. 1st pl. aorist subjunctive active; ἀφίημι
11. Singular aorist imperative middle; ἀφίημι
12. Infinitive; εἶμι
13. Present infinitive active; ἵημι
14. Infinitive; εἰμί
15. Aorist infinitive active; ἵημι

Exercise 21e

1. The merchants hastening to the harbor looked for a ship that was going to sail to Athens.
2. The ambassadors said: "Let your empire go free, Athenians, if you want there to be peace."
3. But Pericles advised the Athenians not to let the empire go.
4. When the Peloponnesians approached Attica, the farmers had to give up their houses and come together to the city.
5. This slave came hurrying here to save us from danger.
6. And so hurrying home let us ask our father to let him go free.
7. The woman/wife said, "Don't let the slave go, husband."

8. But the husband let the slave go and hurried to Athens to buy another slave.

Exercise 21f

1. ὁ Περικλῆς τοῖς 'Αθηναίοις παρή-νεσεν τὴν ἀρχὴν μὴ ἀφῑέναι/ ἀφεῖναι.
2. οἱ 'Αθηναῖοι τὴν ἀρχὴν οὐκ ἀφεῖσαν ἀλλὰ παρεσκευάζοντο ὡς πολεμήσοντες.
3. ὁ αὐτουργὸς ἱέμενος οἴκαδε ἐπαν-ῆλθεν ἵνα τῇ γυναικὶ εἴπῃ/λέγῃ τί ἐγένετο.
4. τοὺς δούλους ἐλευθέρους ἀφήσομεν, ἐὰν ἐκεῖνοι λέγωσιν ὅτι ἐθέλουσιν ἡμῖν βοηθεῖν.

In no. 2, advise students to use ὡς + future participle.

ΟΙ ΑΥΤΟΥΡΓΟΙ ΑΝΙΣΤΑΝΤΑΙ

Title: "The Farmers Move (Are Forced to Move)"

Help students deduce the meaning of ἀνίστανται, here used in a very specific sense of being compelled to get up and move from one's usual place of residence: "are forced to move."

Translation

Lines 1–10
The Athenians obeyed Pericles and brought in (to the city) from the country their children and wives and besides them the equipment (literally, the other equipment; see below) that they used at home; the flocks and beasts of burden they sent to Euboea and the nearby islands. The removal was difficult for them, because the majority were always accustomed to living in the country. And they were distressed at leaving their houses and temples, and being about to change their way of life. And when they arrived at the city, only a few had houses ready for them (for some few there were houses ready); but the majority lived in the deserted parts of the city and the temples. And many set up house even in the towers on (of) the walls and wherever (as) each could. For the city was not large enough for them when they all gathered, but later they set up house in the Long Walls and most of the Piraeus.

[τὴν ἄλλην κατασκευήν (2): not "the other equipment" but "besides them the equipment that. . . ."

ἐρῆμα (7): so accented in Thucydides, instead of the usual Attic ἔρημα.]

Exercise 21g

1. τῶν πολεμίων ἐς τὴν 'Αττικὴν προχωρούντων, τῷ Περικλεῖ πειθόμενοι πάντες πρὸς τὸ ἄστυ ἤλθομεν.
2. μάλα ἐβαρῡνόμεθα τοὺς οἴκους καταλιπόντες.
3. ἐπεὶ ἐς τὸ ἄστυ ἀφῑκόμεθα, οὐδεὶς οἶκος/οὐδεμία οἴκησις ἡμῖν ὑπῆρχεν.
4. πρῶτον μὲν οὖν ἐν πύργῳ τινὶ ᾠκοῦμεν/ᾠκήσαμεν, ὕστερον δὲ κατεσκευασάμεθα ἐγγὺς τῶν μακρῶν τειχῶν.
5. ἐπεὶ δὲ οἱ πολέμιοι ἀνεχώρησαν, ἡμεῖς ἐς τοὺς οἴκους ἐπανήλθομεν.

22
Η ΑΝΑΣΤΑΣΙΣ (α)

Title: "The Removal"

The noun and the related verb ἀνίσταμαι are given in the vocabulary list.

The purposes of this chapter are:

1. Reading: (α) to bring Dicaeopolis and Philip home (at long last!) with Philip's sight restored but with the bad news of the momentous decisions made in the Assembly and the necessity to move into the city before the Peloponnesians invade in the spring; (β) to describe the family's preparations for the removal and their journey to the city and the final diplomatic moves prior to the invasion of Attica; and in the final reading to describe the plague that struck Athens when the Peloponnesians invaded Attica the second time in 430 B.C.
2. Grammar: (α) to present further uses of the subjunctive (in clauses of fearing and in indefinite or general clauses); (β) to present the verb δείκνῡμι and to describe the structures used in indirect statements with ὅτι and ὡς and in indirect questions
3. Background: to present a sketch of Athenian political institutions at the time of the outbreak of the Peloponnesian War

Illustration

This red figure stamnos in the British Museum (ca. 500 B.C.) shows a farewell scene, which was a common subject for vase painting of this period. Often the departing warrior is shown taking the omens.

Caption under Illustration

"I am afraid that we will soon get into war; for the young man is saying goodbye to his father and wife": encourage students to find a satisfactory translation of the clause of fearing after φοβοῦμαι. Ask "What is the speaker afraid of?" Then explain briefly that Greek introduces a fear that something *will* happen with the word μή and that something *will not* happen with the words μή and οὐ. Be sure students recognize that the verb is in the subjunctive. The first part of the caption recurs in lines 11–12 of passage α.

Vocabulary

Conjugation of λούω: λούω, λούεις, λούει, λοῦμεν, λοῦτε, λοῦσι(ν). The rule here is that the υ of the stem drops before a short vowel of the ending, and the ο contracts with that short vowel. The same happens in the imperfect, giving ἔλουν, etc.

New usage of preposition: ὑπό (+ *gen.*) = by: ὑπὸ τῶν πολεμίων (23). Students have seen this usage of ὑπό in tail reading 17:17, ἀδικούμενοι ὑφ' ὑμῶν, where it was glossed.

Since it cannot be determined with certainty whether the α of ἐπειδάν is long or short, we do not mark it with a macron.

Spelling

In the α and β readings and the grammatical exercises we return to the regular Attic spellings (e.g., εἰς, Μέλιττα), associated from the beginning of the course with the language of Dicaeopolis and his family. In the reading from Thucydides at the end of the chapter we retain his spellings (e.g., ἐς instead of εἰς).

Translation

Lines 1–9
When the Assembly had ended and the citizens were going away, Dicaeopolis said, "Come on, son; let's hurry home to tell mother all that has hap-

pened." And so they traveled very quickly, and when night had already fallen they reached home. When Dicaeopolis had knocked on the door, out came Myrrhine and seeing Philip sound (being healthy) and no longer blind (seeing) she embraced him and burst into tears (*ingressive aorist*) of joy (rejoicing began to weep). And when they had come in and washed and supped, Philip related everything that had happened on the journey and at the sanctuary of Asclepius; and she enjoyed listening.

Lines 10–19

And Dicaeopolis related all that they had heard the speakers saying in the Assembly. "And so," he said, "I am afraid that soon we shall be at war (get into a state of war). And we must obey Pericles and prepare everything to remove to the city; for when the Peloponnesians invade Attica, it will be necessary to leave home and remove to Athens." But Myrrhine said, "Oh dear, what are you saying, husband? For how shall we be able to leave home and the flocks and the oxen? And if we remove (having removed) to Athens, where will we live? For there is no house ready for us in the city. But it is not possible to do these things."

[φοβοῦμαι μὴ δι᾽ ὀλίγου εἰς πόλεμον καταστῶμεν (11–12): see discussion under "Caption under Illustration" above.

ἀναστάντες (18): the circumstantial participle may be translated with conditional force here: "if we remove."]

Lines 20–26

And Dicaeopolis (replied), "But it will be necessary to do these things for the following reasons (because of these things); (for) when the Peloponnesians invade the land, we will not be able to stand up against them in battle since they are so many (being so many); and so whoever stays outside the walls will be killed by the enemy; but if we gather in(to) the city, we will all be safe, and there will be no danger that the enemy

will hurt us, if/provided we give up (giving up) our land and homes and keep guard (keeping guard) over the sea and the city.

[Notice the translation of the circumstantial participles in this paragraph: τοσούτοις οἶσιν (22) "since they are so many" (causal); ξυνελθόντες . . . εἰς τὴν πόλιν (24) "if we gather in(to) the city" (conditional); τὴν μὲν γῆν ἀφέντας . . . δὲ . . . ἔχοντας (25–26) "if/provided we give up . . . and keep" (conditional).]

Principal Parts

Verbs with liquid stems (ending in λ, μ, ν, or ρ) are given in this and the next two groups of principal parts.

Note the metathesis of vowel and consonant of the stem of βάλλω in the perfects and aorist passive.

The following meanings of the various forms of φαίνω may be noted. The second future passive φανήσομαι means "I will appear/seem"; the future middle φανοῦμαι may mean either "I will show" or "I will appear/seem." The second perfect active πέφηνα means "I have appeared." A first perfect active form πέφαγκα "I have shown" is rare in Attic. A first aorist passive ἐφάνθην "I was shown" is rare in prose.

For the use of φαίνομαι, etc., with infinitives and participles, see Chapter 20, Grammar 3, page 55.

Word Study

1. *mathematics*: τὰ μαθηματικά = the things suitable for learning, mathematics (since the Greek thinkers considered that mathematics was the pattern of rational learning).

2. *arithmetic*: ἡ ἀριθμητική (τέχνη) = the skill, science, concerned with numbers (ὁ ἀριθμός).

3. *geometry*: ἡ γεωμετρίᾱ = land measurement, surveying; then geometry (see Teacher's Handbook I, page 23).

4. *physics*: τὰ φυσικά = things concerned with nature, physics (ἡ φύσις

= nature).

5. *biology*: ὁ βίος + ὁ λόγος, -λογίᾱ = the study of life (coined, 1813; Longinus, 3rd century A.D., has τὰ βιολογούμενα = incidents sketched from life, but the Greeks did not have a name for a branch of science corresponding to biology).

6. *zoology*: τὸ ζῷον (living creature, animal, cf. ζάω) + -λογίᾱ = the study of living creatures; coined 1669.

Grammar 1

Note that if the introductory verb or clause expressing fear is in a primary tense, we translate the subjunctive with "will" or "may," but if the introductory verb or expression of fear is in a secondary tense, we translate the subjunvtive with "would" or "might." These translations will be used in the exercises.

Exercise 22a

1. Aren't you afraid that we will (may) suffer some disaster (something bad)?
2. There is danger that a storm will (may) arise quickly.
3. Although fearing that the removal will (may) be difficult, the wife obeys her husband.
4. The old man lamented, fearing he would (might) never return.
5. I am afraid the guards will (may) refuse to open the gates.
6. The slaves were afraid their master would (might) be angry with them.
7. We are not afraid to stay outside the walls.
8. The children were afraid to tell the truth.
9. Fearing to return by night, the peasants stayed in the city.
10. The captain was afraid the storm would (might) destroy the ship.

Exercise 22b

1. φοβοῦμαι μὴ οὐκ ἐν καιρῷ

ἀφικώμεθα εἰς τὴν πόλιν.
2. κίνδῡνός ἐστι μὴ οἱ πολέμιοι δι' ὀλίγου εἰς τὴν γῆν εἰσίωσιν.
3. πρὸς τὸ ἄστυ εὐθὺς ὡρμήσαμεν, φοβούμενοι ἐν τοῖς ἀγροῖς μένειν.
4. οἱ αὐτουργοὶ ἐφοβοῦντο μὴ οἱ πολέμιοι τοὺς οἴκους διαφθείρωσιν.
5. ἆρ' οὐ μᾶλλον φοβῇ οἴκαδε πλεῖν ἢ κατὰ γῆν ἰέναι;

Grammar 2

In this section we discuss relative, temporal, and conditional clauses, and it is important to make sure that students are familiar with these terms and can recognize and produce clauses of these three types. Begin by having students make up sentences in English with first relative, then temporal, and then conditional clauses. The temporal conjunctions discussed here are "when(ever)" and "until."

Then have students study the examples of *definite* and *indefinite* clauses on page 75 and carefully compare the corresponding sentences. Note that we have provided two sentences introduced by ὅστις ἄν to point up the contrast between use of the present and the aorist subjunctive.

Conditional sentences will be treated more fully in Chapter 30, Grammar 1, pages 192–194.

Be sure students learn the forms of ὅστις, as they will be expected to recognize them in future readings and use them in exercises.

Exercise 22c

1. Whoever stays outside the walls, will be in danger.
   ὅστις ἂν πρῶτος ἀφίκηται, δέξεται τὸ ἀργύριον.
2. Whenever the Assembly meets (takes place), the citizens hurry to the Pnyx.
   ἐπειδὰν οἱ πολέμιοι εἰς τὴν γῆν εἰσβάλωσι, πάντες εἰς τὸ ἄστυ συνερχόμεθα.
3. We will stay in the agora until the

messenger returns.

οὐκ ἐπάνιμεν οἴκαδε ἕως ἂν
γένηται ἡ ἡμέρᾱ.

4. Don't board the ship until the captain orders.

μὴ ἀνάβητε ἐπὶ τὸ ὄρος ἕως ἂν
γένηται τὸ ἔαρ.

5. If the Peloponnesians come
against our land on foot, we will
sail against theirs with our ships.

ἐὰν σπεύδωσιν οἱ αὐτουργοὶ εἰς τὸ
ἄστυ, ἀσφαλεῖς ἔσονται.

6. Whatever the boys have, they are
willing to give us all (of it) (the
boys are willing to give us whatever they have).

δεῖ ἡμᾶς ποιεῖν ὅσ' ἂν κελεύῃ ὁ
βασιλεύς.

7. When the farmer drove (had
driven) the oxen into the field, he
soon began to plow.

ἐπεὶ/ἐπειδὴ/ὡς ὁ παῖς εἰσῆλθεν εἰς
τὸν ἀγρόν, εὐθὺς τὸν πατέρα
ἐκάλεσεν.

8. The shepherds will pasture their
flocks on the mountains until
winter comes.

οἴκαδε οὐκ ὁρμησόμεθα ἕως ἂν ὁ
ποιμὴν τὴν ὁδὸν ἡμῖν δηλοῖ.

9. Whenever the master is away, the
slaves stop working.

ὅταν προσχωρῇ/προσέλθῃ ὁ
δεσπότης, οἱ δοῦλοι ἀνίστανται
καὶ (ἀνιστάντες) ἐργάζονται.

10. You will get into danger, boys, if
you do not do all that we advise.

εἰ μή μου ἀκούσεσθε, δεινὰ
πείσεσθε.

11. These boys, who were helping
their fathers, worked until night
fell.

ἐκεῖναι αἱ γυναῖκες, αἳ ἐν τῷ ἀργῷ
ἐκαθίζοντο, ἔμενον ἕως οἱ ἄνδρες
ἐπαύσαντο ἐργαζόμενοι.

12. If (ever) anyone drinks (of) this,
he dies.

ἐάν τις τοιοῦτο ποιήσῃ,
ὀργιζόμεθα αὐτῷ.

Note the use of the future indicative
in the sentences in No. 10, which express
warnings.

Athenian Democracy in Action

For further reading, see *Civilization
of the Ancient Mediterranean*, Vol. I, pp.
470–473; *The World of Athens*, pp. 199–
230; and *The Oxford History of the Classical World*, pp. 136–141.

Η ΑΝΑΣΤΑΣΙΣ (β)

Vocabulary

Notes:

Translation

Lines 1–13

After hearing this Myrrhine fell silent and obeyed her husband, although
fearing that the removal would be difficult. And so all winter they prepared to
move to Athens when the Peloponnesians invaded. At the beginning of
spring a messenger arrived from
Athens saying that the Spartans and
their allies were already gathering at
the Isthmus. And so Dicaeopolis sent
Philip and Xanthias to take the flocks to
Euboea. Then he himself and Myrrhine
brought out the wagon and put into it all
that they could carry. And when all was
ready, Dicaeopolis yoked the oxen and
put the grandfather, who was grieving a
lot, onto the wagon. Finally Myrrhine
and Melissa themselves got up (onto the
wagon). So they went on their way,
weeping and lamenting, afraid that they
would never return.

[ἐξαγαγόντες (8): compound verb to be
deduced.

εἰσέθεσαν (9): compound verb to be
deduced.

πολλὰ ὀδῡρόμενον (10): πολλά is
adverbial accusative.]

Lines 14–24

The road was long and difficult.
For they had to go along the wagon road,

and they met many farmers who were hurrying to the city and were getting in one another's way. Finally, as evening was falling, they arrived at the gates, and entering with difficulty they stayed for the night in a shrine of a hero. The next day Dicaeopolis went to his brother to ask him if he could help in any way. But the brother could not receive them into his house as they were so many, but he showed him a tower, which would hold them all. And so Dicaeopolis returned to his family and led them to the tower, in which they were going to live the whole time (throughout all) until the Peloponnesians went away and they themselves returned to the country.

[τὴν ἁμάξιτον (ὁδόν) (14): the road for wagons, as opposed to the footpaths and mule tracks, which would be more direct.

ἐν ἡρῴῳ τινί (17–18): heroes were humans who were worshiped after death for the services they had done for men in their lifetime, such as founding cities. Their cults were very common, and there must have been many shrines to them in the city.

πύργον τινά (21): the city walls had towers at intervals, the ground floors of which provided shelter for the refugees.

ἕως ἄν . . . ἀπίωσιν . . . ἐπανίωσιν (23–24): although the sequence is secondary, ἕως ἄν + subjunctive is used here, since the clause is virtually an indirect statement ("we will stay until. . . . ").]

Lines 25–35

Meanwhile a herald arrived at Athens, Archidamus, king of the Spartans, having sent (him); but the Athenians did not admit him into the city or to the Council; for it was Pericles' decision (judgment) not to admit a herald or (and) embassy when the Spartans were already on the march; and so they send him away before hearing him and told him to be outside the boundaries that very day, and they send with him escorts, so that he would not contact any-

one. And when he was at the boundaries and was about to part (from his escort) he went on his way after saying just this: "This day will be the beginning of great troubles for the Greeks." And when he reached the (Peloponnesian) camp and Archidamus knew that the Athenians would make no concessions at all, then he set out with his army and advanced into their land.

[κῆρυξ (25): heralds were sacrosanct and could therefore travel through enemy territory unmolested.

πρὶν ἀκοῦσαι (29–30): help students as necessary with this use of πρίν + infinitive.

πω (34): this particle is common with a negative, e.g., οὔπω "not yet," but is rare in positive sentences; here it seems to mean "at all."

This paragraph is taken from Thucydides 2.12 with little change.]

Principal Parts

Students should be told that ἀποθνῄσκω is used in Attic as the passive of ἀποκτείνω. Forms of these verbs without the prefix ἀπο- are frequent in poetry, but rare in prose.

The uncompounded verb κρίνω is given in Chapter 25α.

Word Building

1. I do; action; act, affair, business; fit for action, active```
2. I marshal, draw up in battle array; arrangement, position, order; division of soldiers; ordered; disordered, undisciplined
3. I confuse; confusion; freedom from confusion, calmness; without confusion, calm
4. I guard; guard; guarding, guard post

Grammar 3

Notes:

Grammar 4

After studying Grammar 4, have students look back through passage β and locate examples of indirect statements and questions. They are as follows:

λέγων ὅτι . . . συλλέγονται οἵ τε Λακεδαιμόνιοι καὶ οἱ σύμμαχοι. . . . (5–6)

αἰτῇ αὐτὸν εἴ πως βοηθεῖν δύναται. (19)

εἰπὼν . . . ὅτι, "ἥδε ἡ ἡμέρᾱ τοῖς Ἕλλησι μεγάλων κακῶν ἄρξει." (32–33; this is a combination of indirect and direct statement)

ἔγνω ὁ Ἀρχίδᾱμος ὅτι οἱ Ἀθηναῖοι οὐδέν πω ἐνδώσουσιν. . . . (34–35)

Exercise 22d

1. 3rd pl. present indicative active: "they show"
2. Present infinitive middle: "to show for oneself," "to display"
3. 3rd sing. imperfect indicative active: "he was showing"
4. Nom. fem. sing. present active participle: "showing"
5. 2nd sing. imperfect indicative middle: "you were showing (for yourself)"
6. Aorist infinitive active: "to show" *or* 2nd sing. aorist imperative middle: "show (for yourself)!"
7. 2nd pl. indicative or imperative active present: "open!"
8. 3rd pl. aorist indicative active: "they broke"
9. Nom. masc. sing. aorist participle active: "having yoked"
10. 3rd sing. aorist indicative active: "he opened"
11. 3rd pl. future indicative active: "they will break"
12. 2nd sing. present imperative middle: "show (for yourself)!"
13. Nom. pl. masc. aorist participle active: "having opened"
14. Present infinitive active: "to break"
15. 1st pl. present subjunctive active: "let us yoke"

Exercise 22e

1. The father asked the girl from where she had come.
2. She replied saying (answering said) that she had come from the house and would soon return there.
3. The messenger said that the ambassadors were already approaching and would soon be present.
4. The general told the messenger to open the gates and receive the ambassadors.
5. The messenger asked the guards why they were not opening the gates.
6. The farmer yoked the oxen and started to plow.
7. Calling the slave, he showed him a huge stone and told him to carry it out of the field.
8. But the slave said that it was not possible to lift so large a stone.
9. But the master answered that so big a stone would break the plow; and so it was necessary to lift it.
10. The slave said that unless the master helped, he would not be able to lift the stone.

In no. 5 students are to deduce the meaning of τοὺς φύλακας or to recall it from the Word Building exercise in this chapter.

Η ΝΟΣΟΣ

Title: "The Plague"

Encourage students to deduce the meaning of the title from the verb νοσέω, which they have had. Here, of course, the "sickness" is the plague.

Translation

Lines 1–4

As soon as the summer began (the summer beginning straightway) the

Peloponnesians and their allies invaded Attica; and when they had been in Attica for a few (not many) days, the plague first began to fall on (happen to) the Athenians. They say that before this it had fallen upon many places, but it had not been so terrible (so great) a plague nor had so many people died. [ὄντων . . . πολλὰς ἡμέρας (2): help students with this idiomatic use of the present participle with an accusative of duration of time = "when they had been. . . . "]

Lines 5–9

For neither could doctors help at first, as they were not familiar with the disease, but they themselves especially died because they most consorted with the sick, nor could any other human skill help. The plague began first (originated), as they say, from Ethiopia, south of Egypt, and then it spread to (came down on) Egypt and the greater part of the (Persian) king's land.

Lines 10–13

It fell on the city of the Athenians suddenly and at first attacked men in the Piraeus; and later it reached the upper city (i.e., Athens itself), and far more men died now. I will say what it was like, having had the plague myself and having myself seen others suffering (from it).

[Thucydides' description of the plague that follows this passage is highly scientific (2.49–53). He uses contemporary medical terminology and describes the symptoms in such detail that doctors since his time have often tried to identify it (but have failed to agree). The most likely diagnosis is typhus fever; "Two doctors who read Thucydides' account, with great experience of typhus, but innocent of all knowledge of the Athenian epidemic, said, 'Typhus, of course.'" (See Gomme, *Historical Commentary on Thucydides,* Volume II, page 153.) Thucydides not only describes the physical symptoms of the plague but goes on to discuss the psychological effects it had on the survivors and in particular the breakdown of traditional morality.]

Exercise 22f

1. οἱ ἰᾱτροὶ τοῖς νοσοῦσιν προσιέναι φοβοῦνται.
2. ὅστις γὰρ ἂν νοσοῦντος ἅπτηται, αὐτὸς ἐς τὴν νόσον ἐμπεσὼν ἀποθνῄσκει.
3. οἱ ἰᾱτροὶ εἶπον ὅτι οὐ δύνανται ὠφελεῖν, τὴν νόσον ἀγνοοῦντες.
4. καίπερ φοβούμενοι μὴ ἐς τὴν νόσον ἐμπέσωμεν, ἐν τῷ ἄστει δεῖ μένειν ἕως ἂν ἀπίωσιν οἱ πολέμιοι.
5. ἐὰν δι' ὀλίγου ἀπίωσιν, ἐς τοὺς ἀγροὺς σπεύσομεν ἵνα τὴν νόσον φύγωμεν.

23
Η ΕΣΒΟΛΗ (α)

Title: "The Invasion"

The word is given in the vocabulary list.

The purposes of this chapter are:

1. Reading: (α) to give an adapted version of Thucydides' account of the Peloponnesian invasion of Attica in 431 B.C. and of Archidamus' strategy for drawing the Athenians out into battle; (β) to continue Thucydides' account of the invasion with his description of the consternation of the Acharnians over the ravaging of their territory, their eagerness to go out to attack the invaders, Pericles' methods of maintaining his policy of not going on the attack, and the eventual withdrawal of the Peloponnesian army; and in the final reading to present Thucydides' summary of the achievements of Pericles

2. Grammar: (α) to present the passive voice of the present and imperfect tenses and to present a note on prepositional prefixes and euphony; (β) to continue the presentation of the forms of indirect statement from the previous chapter, giving here the structures using infinitives and participles, and to direct students to learn the forms of the verb φημί

3. Background: to sketch the course of the first phase of the Peloponnesian War (431–421 B.C.), picking up the story from where the essay in Chapter 20 left off

Caption under Map

"The Attic land is ravaged by the enemy": the verb is given in the vocabulary list; help students deduce the sense of the passive voice (the prepositional phrase will help).

The arrows show the route of Archidamus' invasion (see passage α) and withdrawal (see passage β).

The site of Oenoe is uncertain; it may have been on the Boeotian side of the border. Nor is it clear why Archidamus went out of his way to try to take this fort. Perhaps he was delaying the invasion proper in the hope that the Athenians would still negotiate. His route from Eleusis is clearly defined by Thucydides (2.21–23); from the Thriasian Plain he turned north ("keeping Mount Aegaleus on his right") and advanced to Acharnae. After leaving Acharnae, he moved east and ravaged some demes between Mount Parnes and Mount Brilessus (= Pentelicon), west of Marathon. He left Attica via Oropus and returned through Boeotia.

Vocabulary

Notes:

Spelling

Since all three of the reading passages in this chapter are based on Thucydides, we use his spellings (e.g., ἐς and τάσσω) throughout the readings and exercises in this chapter. In the vocabulary lists the regular Attic spellings are given first with the Thucydidean spellings in parentheses.

Verbs

This chapter formally introduces the passive voice (see caption under map), and after reading and translating passage α and studying Grammar 1 students should come back to the reading passage and locate the passive verb forms. The meanings of these forms should be carefully distinguished from those of the middle/deponent forms in the passage. The passive forms are:

ἐτετείχιστο (5; pluperfect, see Overview of the Greek Verb, pages 4–5, in the student's book), λέγεται (18), τεμνομένην (21), and διαφθειρόμενα (27). The meaning of the passive voice should be discussed while translating the sentences in which these forms occur, and it should be pointed out that the forms are the same as for the middle voice and that it is the context that shows that the forms are passive here.

Translation

Lines 1–9

The Peloponnesian army (the army of the Peloponnesians) advanced and arrived first in Attica at Oenoe, where they were about to (intended to) invade. And when they were encamped (literally "were sitting down," "were settled"), they prepared to make attacks on the wall with siege engines and other methods; for Oenoe, being on the borders of Attica and Boeotia, had been fortified, and the Athenians used it (as) a fortress whenever war occurred. And so they prepared assaults and wasted time around it in vain. And Archidamus received considerable (not little) blame from this; for the Athenians brought in (to Athens) all (their goods) during this time.

[τῆς Ἀττικῆς (1): partitive genitive with πρῶτον, "first in Attica."

παρεσκευάζοντο . . . ποιησόμενοι (3): the verb παρασκευάζομαι has frequently been used with ὡς + a future participle expressing purpose (see 22β:3 and Chapter 17, Grammar 3, page 17). Here ὡς is omitted. Translate "they prepared to make attacks on the wall" (note the dative τῷ τείχει with the verbal phrase προσβολὰς . . . ποιησόμενοι = προσβαλοῦντες).

μηχαναῖς (3): siege engines. The Greeks were notoriously incompetent at siege warfare in this period; the whole Peloponnesian army failed to reduce the fortified village of Oenoe on this occasion, and they did not even attempt to

storm the walls of Athens on any of their invasions of Attica. Archidamus was a "guest friend" of Pericles, i.e., if, in peacetime, Archidamus came to Athens he would have stayed with Pericles, and vice versa. Hence the Spartans suspected that he would not prosecute the war vigorously. Pericles fell under similar suspicions from the Athenians and announced publicly that if the invading army did not sack his country estates, he would give them to the state.

ἐτετείχιστο (5): pluperfect passive (to be introduced formally in Chapter 27, Grammar 1, pages 146–150). Students can easily locate the form on the chart at the beginning of the book.

ὁπότε πόλεμος γένοιτο (5–6): the optative will be easily recognized from the information provided in the Overview of the Greek Verb. The use of the optative in indefinite clauses in secondary sequence will be discussed in Chapter 25, Grammar 2b, page 117, and may be touched on here if students are curious.

ἐσεκομίζοντο (8): compound verb to be deduced. Note the force of the middle voice: they brought everything in "for themselves" or "in their own interests."]

Lines 10–13

But when they had attacked Oenoe and tried every method but failed to take it, and the Athenians made no more peace proposals (sent no heralds at all), then they set out from Oenoe and invaded Attica; and Archidamus, king of Sparta, led them.

[οὕτω δή (12): this phrase is often used after a long protasis to mark the beginning of the main clause.]

Lines 14–21

And encamping they first ravaged Eleusis and the Thriasian plain. Then they advanced until they arrived at Acharnae, the largest district in Attica of the so-called demes, and settling down in it they pitched camp and stayed there a long time ravaging (the country). It is said that Archidamus stayed around Acharnae with his troops drawn up as for battle (having drawn himself up as for battle) and did not go down into the plain (of Athens) on that invasion with the following intention; he hoped that the Athenians would go out against him and would not disregard the destruction of their land (their land being ravaged).

[τὸ Θριάσιον πεδίον (14–15): the Thriasian plain was one of the grain-producing districts of Attica, as was the plain of Athens; in Greek warfare, when an invading army destroyed standing crops (the Peloponnesians invaded just as harvest was due to take place), their opponents normally had three options: (1) to come out and fight, (2) to make terms, and (3) to take no action and starve. Since the Athenians ruled the seas and could import all they needed, Archidamus' calculations proved wrong. Pericles had already warned the Athenians of the sacrifice they must make.

ἤλπιζε . . . (20–21): help students as necessary with the indirect statement with accusative and infinitive, which will be formally introduced in Grammar 3 of this chapter (pages 94–95).]

Lines 22–27

And so when they did not go to meet him at Eleusis and the Thriasian plain, he (Archidamus) settled down around Acharnae and tested (made trial) whether they would come out against (him); for at the same time the district seemed to him suitable for camping in, and (at the same time) he thought that the Acharnians, being a great part of the (whole) city (for they were three thousand hoplites) would not disregard the destruction of their own property (their own things being destroyed) but would rouse all the people to battle.

[πεῖραν ἐποιεῖτο . . . εἰ ἐπεξίᾶσιν (23): help students see the relationship between πεῖραν ἐποιεῖτο and εἰ ἐπεξίᾶσιν "made trial (as to) whether. . . . "

ἐνόμιζε . . . (25–27): as with lines 20–21 above, help students as necessary

with the indirect statement.

τρισχίλιοι . . . ἐγένοντο (26): the total of Athenian front line hoplites was 13,000, apart from 16,000 reserves. If Thucydides refers to the first figure, the Acharnians provided nearly a quarter of the total force.

καὶ τοὺς πάντας (27): literally, "also the all," i.e., the whole population as well (as themselves). The article with πᾶς indicates "the whole lot."]

Principal Parts

This group of principal parts completes the presentation of liquid stem verbs.

The long α of the stem ἀρ- appears in the unaugmented forms of the aorist, e.g., ἄρω, ἄραιμι, ἄρον, ἄραι, ἄρᾱς.

Many Greek verbs show three grades of stem vowel, similar to the pattern *sing, sang, sung* in English (see Reference Grammar, paragraph 59). One such gradation of vowels in Greek consists of the following:

Strong grade 1: ε
Strong grade 2: ο
Weak grade: either no vowel or α

The three grades of stem vowel for φθείρω are: φθερ-, φθορ-, and φθαρ-.

The three grades of stem vowel for ἐγείρω are: ἐγερ-, ἐγορ-, and ἐγρ-.

Some linguists refer to the three grades of stem vowel as *e-grade, o-grade* and *zero-grade*. The term zero grade covers both possibilities for weak grade given above, namely no vowel or α (i.e., neither ε nor ο).

More verbs with three grades of stem vowel will be found after reading 26b, page 136.

The compound verb διαφθείρω is found more frequently than the uncompounded verb.

Word Study

1. *politics*: τὰ πολῑτικά = the affairs of the city, politics.

2. *demagogue*: ὁ δημαγωγός (ὁ δῆμος + ἀγωγός, -όν) = leader of the people; but by the time of Xenophon it had already acquired the sense of mob leader.

3. *rhetoric*: ἡ ῥητορική (τέχνη) = the art of oratory.

4. *democracy*: ἡ δημοκρατίᾱ (ὁ δῆμος + τὸ κράτος) = rule of the people.

5. *monarchy*: ἡ μοναρχίᾱ (μόνος, -η, -ον + ἀρχ- + -ίᾱ) = the rule of one man only.

6. *tyranny*: ἡ τυραννίς, τῆς τυραννίδος (ὁ τύραννος) = government by a single ruler with absolute power.

7. *ochlocracy*: ἡ ὀχλοκρατίᾱ (ὁ ὄχλος = mob + τὸ κράτος) = mob rule (Polybius 6.4).

8. *autonomy*: ἡ αὐτονομίᾱ (αὐτόνομος, -ον) = freedom to have one's own laws, independence.

It is worth noting that Plato, *Republic*, Book 8, lists five types of constitutions in descending order of merit:

ἡ ἀριστοκρατίᾱ: the rule of the best, i.e., of the philosopher kings

ἡ τῑμοκρατίᾱ: the rule of those for whom honor is the mainspring of action, e.g., as in Sparta

ἡ ὀλιγαρχίᾱ: the rule of the few; in this constitution money is the qualification for power, e.g., as in Corinth

ἡ δημοκρατίᾱ: the rule of the people, of which the distinguishing characteristic is liberty, or, as Plato saw it, chaotic license

ἡ τύραννις: tyranny, where the state is subject to a single evil individual (Hitler's Germany and Stalin's Russia provide good examples)

Grammar 1

Notes:

Exercise 23a

1. The hoplites were being drawn up (as) for battle by the general. (ὡς = "as" may be omitted in translation.)

2. The child being chased by the bull gave (used) a very loud shout.

3. The farmers were afraid that their fields might be ravaged by the enemy.

4. The women riding on (being carried on) the wagon were being conveyed to the temple quickly.

5. Those who fought in that battle were always honored by the people.

6. There is no danger that we may be conquered by the enemy, although they are so many.

7. It is said that the citizens are becoming angry seeing their property destroyed.

8. Let us hurry to the city so that we may not be harmed by the invaders.

9. At the beginning of spring the flocks were always driven to the mountains.

10. Whoever is caught outside the walls will be in the greatest danger.

In no. 7, τὰ σφέτερα is to be recalled from passage α:26, where it is glossed.

Exercise 23b

1. ἐπειδὰν γένηται ἡ ἑσπέρᾱ, οἱ βόες οἴκαδε ἐλαύνονται ὑπὸ τοῦ αὐτουργοῦ.

2. οἱ ὑπὸ ἐκείνου τοῦ κυνὸς διωκόμενοι μόλις ἐς τὴν οἰκίᾱν ἔφυγον.

3. τὰ μῆλα ὑπὸ τούτων τῶν παίδων διωκόμενα ἐς φόβον κατέστη.

4. φοβοῦμαι μὴ ὑπὸ τῶν πολεμίων νῑκώμεθα.

5. ὅσοι ἂν ὑπὲρ τῆς πατρίδος ἀνδρείως μάχωνται ὑπὸ τοῦ δήμου τῑμῶνται.

Grammar 2

Remind students if necessary that γ

is pronounced as *ng* before γ, κ, μ, ξ, and χ·

The Peloponnesian War–First Phase (431–421 B.C.)

For further reading, see *The World of Athens*, pp. 28–34.

Η ΕΣΒΟΛΗ (β)

Vocabulary

Notes:

Translation

Lines 1–10

As long as the army was around Eleusis and the Thriasian plain, the Athenians had some hope that they would not advance nearer (to the city); but when they saw the army around Acharnae twelve miles (60 stades) distant from the city, they no longer considered it tolerable, but as their land was being ravaged before their eyes (visibly), it seemed to them a terrible thing, and all, especially the youth, resolved (it seemed good to both the others and especially the young men) to go out against them and not neglect (the situation). And they assembled into groups and argued furiously (were in great strife), some telling them to go out, others forbidding (not allowing) it. And the Acharnians thinking that they formed the greatest part of the Athenians, since their land was being ravaged, were urging the attack most.

Lines 11–19

The city was excited in every way, and they (the citizens) were angry with Pericles (held Pericles in anger), and they remembered nothing of his earlier advice (of those things that he had formerly advised them), but they were abusing him, because he was general and he was not leading (them) out

against (the enemy), and they thought him responsible for everything they were suffering. But Pericles, seeing that they were angry regarding the present state of affairs and not in a good frame of mind (not thinking the best things), and confident that he was right about not going out to attack, did not hold an Assembly or any other meeting, lest if they gathered together in anger rather than good judgment they might make some mistake, but he guarded the city and kept them quiet (in quietness) as far as he could.

[ἐν ὀργῇ εἶχον (11–12): help with the idiom as necessary–"they held X in anger" = "they were angry with X."

ὧν (12, 14): explain to students that relative pronouns that would be accusative direct objects of the verbs in their clauses are often attracted into the case of a genitive or dative antecedent (see Grammar 6, page 97). This provides a good opportunity to review agreement and case usage of relative pronouns.

περὶ τοῦ μὴ ἐπεξιέναι (16): we gloss the articular infinitive here; it will be formally presented in Chapter 27, Grammar 3, page 157.

μάλιστα (18) belongs with ὅσον ἐδύνατο and is untranslatable.]

Lines 20–24

And the Peloponnesians, when the Athenians did not come out to battle with them, setting out from Acharnae, ravaged some of the other demes (some other of the demes) and after staying in Attica for a considerable time retired through Boeotia (the Boeotians), not the way they had invaded. And arriving at the Peloponnesus they disbanded their army and they returned each to his own city.

[ἄραντες (21): note the intransitive use of the verb αἴρω here, "setting out"; cf. 22β:35 and the gloss there.

διέλυσαν τὸν στρατόν (24): the Peloponnesian army consisted of farmers who were called up for particular campaigns; the only standing army in the

alliance was that of the Spartans themselves. The others had to return to their
farms to get the harvest in. Pericles in
his speech to the Assembly (see Chapter
21β) had remarked on this.]

Principal Parts

Verbs with nasal infixes (consisting of ν or ν in combination with
some vowel) are given in this and the
next group of principal parts.

In λαμβάνω and μανθάνω another
nasal (μ, ν) is inserted within the stem
(λαβ-, μαθ-), and the nasal infix -αν-
is then added.

The perfect of λαμβάνω is formed by
placing the prefix εἰ- before the stem instead of by regular reduplication.

Note that many verbs with the -αν-
infix extend the stem with an ε in
forming the other tenses (but not the second aorist), e.g., αὐξάνω (αὐξε-) and
μανθάνω (μαθε-).

Word Building

1. I say, word, etc.
   I turn; turn, way, manner
   I draw, write; drawing, writing
   I fight; battle
2. I make, compose; maker, poet
   I judge; judge
   I write; writer
   I become, am born; parent
   I save; savior
   I give; giver
   I heal; healer, doctor
3. I loose; loosing
   I make, compose; making, compo-
   sition
   I judge; judgment
   I say; saying, report
   I get to know, learn, judge, think;
   opinion, judgment, intention
4. I make, compose; anything made,
   composition
   I do; act, affair, business
   I write; writing, letter, (plural) let-
   ters, literature

Grammar 3 and 4

After studying Grammar 3 and 4,
have students look back through passages α and β and locate examples of
indirect statement. They are as follows:

Passage α:

λέγεται . . . ὅτι . . . ὁ Ἀρχίδᾱμος . . . ἔμεινε καὶ . . . οὐ κατ-
έβη. . . . (18–20).
ἤλπιζε . . . τοὺς Ἀθηναίους ἐπεξιέναι καὶ . . . οὐ περιόψεσθαι . . .
(20–21)
ἐνόμιζεν τοὺς Ἀχαρνέᾱς . . . οὐ
περιόψεσθαι . . . ἀλλὰ ὁρμή-
σειν. . . . (25–27)
περιόψεσθαι τὰ σφέτερα διαφθειρόμενα. . . . (26–27)

Passage β:

ἐλπίδα τινὰ εἶχον αὐτοὺς . . . μὴ
προϊέναι. . . . (2)
εἶδον τὸν στρατὸν . . . ἀπέχον-
τα. . . . (3–4)
οἱ . . . Ἀχαρνῆς οἰόμενοι αὐτοὶ
μέγιστον μέρος εἶναι τῶν Ἀθηναίων. . . . (8–9)
αἴτιόν τε ἐνόμιζον αὐτὸν εἶναι. . . .
(13–14)
Περικλῆς . . . ὁρῶν . . . αὐτοὺς . . .
ὀργιζομένους καὶ οὐ . . . φρο-
νοῦντας. . . . (14–15)
πιστεύων . . . ὀρθῶς γιγνώσκειν. . . .
(15–16)

Grammar 5

Notes:

Exercise 23c

1. The messenger said that the ambassadors had already arrived at
   the gates.
   ὁ γέρων ἔφη τὸν παῖδα ἤδη οἴκαδε
   ἐπανελθεῖν.
2. The young men think that they will
   easily defeat the enemy.
   οἰόμεθα τὴν πόλιν ῥᾳδίως

αἱρήσειν.

3. The boys said that they had not
   (denied that they had) seen their
   father in the agora.
   οἱ ξένοι οὐκ ἔφασαν τὸ ἀργύριον
   εὑρεῖν.

4. I see that you are suffering many
   troubles.
   ὁρῶμεν αὐτοὺς ἁμαρτάνοντας.

5. As a storm was rising, the sailors
   realized that they would arrive at
   the harbor with difficulty.
   αἱ γυναῖκες ἔγνωσαν ἐς μέγαν
   κίνδυνον καταστησόμεναι.

6. The girl thought that she would see
   her mother by the spring.
   ὁ ποιμὴν ᾤετο τὸν κύνα εὑρήσειν
   πρὸς τῷ ποταμῷ.

7. The slaves hoped that their master
   would not be angry with them.
   ἐλπίζομεν τὸν κύνα μὴ βλάψειν τὰ
   μῆλα.

8. The women knew that there was no
   food for them in the house.
   οἱ αὐτουργοὶ ἠπίσταντο οὐδεμίαν
   οἴκησιν σφίσιν ὑπάρχουσαν ἐν τῷ
   ἄστει.

9. The Athenians thought that their
   enemies were plotting against
   them.
   ᾠόμεθα τὸν ξένον ἡμῖν ἡγεῖσθαι/
   ἡμᾶς ἄγειν πρὸς τὸ ἱερόν.

10. The woman was confident that she
    was right and her husband wrong.
    ἕκαστος ᾤετο αὐτὸς μὲν ἀσφαλὴς
    εἶναι, τοὺς δὲ ἄλλους ἐν κινδύνῳ.

Grammar 6

Notes:

Exercise 23d

1. Let us not trust the ambassadors
   that the Spartans sent. οὕς

2. Be worthy, men, of the freedom that
   you have won. ἥν

3. You must judge the matters from
   what you know yourselves. ἐκείνων
   ἅ

4. The general arrived, leading an
   army from the cities that he persuaded. ἅς

5. You are the most ignorant of the
   Greeks that I know. Ἑλλήνων οὕς

Ο ΠΕΡΙΚΛΗΣ

Translation

Lines 1–6
   Saying this Pericles tried to rid the
Athenians of their anger against him.
And publicly they obeyed his words, and
they sent no more ambassadors to the
Spartans and were more enthusiastic
(in a greater state of eagerness) for the
war, but privately they were depressed by
their sufferings. But they did not stop
being angry with him (having him in
anger) until they had fined him (penal-
ized him with money). But not much
later they chose him as general again
and entrusted (to him) all their affairs.
[οὔτε ... τέ (2–3): a common combination where a negative clause is followed
by a positive.

   πρότερον (4): "before," looking forward to πρίν (5) "until"; there is no need
to translate πρότερον. Students have
seen πρίν + infinitive = "before" in
22β:29–30. It can also be used with a fi-
nite verb, usually after a negative
clause, and mean "until," as here.

   ἐζημίωσαν χρήμασιν (5): the Assembly was sovereign and kept strict control
over all its officers. Each month at a
meeting of the Assembly, the people were
asked whether they wished to keep all officials in office; it may have been at
such a meeting that Pericles was accused of embezzlement and deposed
from office and fined. Such fines were a
common way of punishing officials,
and embezzlement of public funds was
one of the most common accusations in
prosecutions that might be purely political in purpose. Our sources differ both
on the charge brought against Pericles
and the amount of the fine.]

Lines 7–11

For as long as he was at the head of the city in time of peace, he led it with moderation and guarded it safely, and in his time it became its greatest; and when war broke out, Pericles was proved to have foreseen the power of the city in war, too. He lived on for two years and six months; and when he died, his foresight with regard to the war was recognized even more.

[φαίνεται . . . προγνούς (9): "was proved" (for the supplementary participle, see Chapter 20, Grammar 3, page 55).]

Lines 12–17

For he said that if they (the Athenians) kept quiet and guarded the fleet and did not try to increase the empire in time of war and avoided putting the city at risk, they would win; but they (i.e., his successors) did everything opposite to this (to the opposite) and pursued bad policies for private ambition and private gain. And the reason was that he was capable and was not led by the people so much as he led them himself. There was (under Pericles) in theory a democracy, but in fact rule by the leading man.

[This is a hard paragraph, not made easier by the omissions that were necessary; students may need help.

μὴ ἐπικτωμένους (12–13): the negative is μή because this and the other participles are conditional and conditional clauses have εἰ μή. Remind students that participles can be translated with conditional force. Thucydides, in attributing this advice to Pericles, is perhaps writing with hindsight, thinking of the Sicilian expedition, which was largely responsible for the downfall of Athens. He was strongly biased against Pericles' successors, especially Cleon.

λόγῳ μὲν . . . ἔργῳ δέ (16): "in word . . . but in deed," very commonly used to mean "in theory . . . but in practice."

Word to be deduced: δημοκρατίᾱ (16).]

Exercise 23e

1. τοῦ Περικλέος ἀποθανόντος/ ἐπειδὴ/ὡς ἀπέθανεν ὁ Περικλῆς, οἱ ὕστερον οὐκ ἦγον τοὺς πολίτᾱς ἀλλ' ἤγοντο ὑπ' αὐτῶν.

2. ἕκαστος γὰρ βουλόμενος πρῶτος εἶναι, "τοῖς πολίταις," ἔφη, "πάντα δώσω ὅσ' ἂν βούλωνται."

3. πολλὰ δὲ ἥμαρτον καὶ τὸν στόλον ἀπέπεμψαν πρὸς τὴν Σικελίᾱν, ἐλπίζοντες οὕτω τῷ δήμῳ χαριεῖσθαι.

4. ἐπειδὴ/ὡς δὲ ἤκουσαν τοὺς στρατηγοὺς ὑπὸ τῶν πολεμίων νῑκωμένους/ὅτι οἱ στρατηγοὶ ὑπὸ τῶν πολεμίων νῑκῶνται, βοήθειαν οὐκ ἔπεμψαν.

5. ἀγωνιζόμενοι γὰρ πρὸς ἀλλήλους περὶ τῆς τοῦ δήμου προστασίᾱς, τοῦ πολέμου ἀμελεῖν ἐπείθοντο.

24
EN ΔΙΔΑΣΚΑΛΩΝ (α)

Title: "At School"

Try to get students to deduce the meaning of the title, beginning with ὁ διδάσκαλος in the vocabulary list. With ἐν διδασκάλων, supply οἴκῳ, "in the house of the teachers."

The purposes of this chapter are:

1. Reading: (α and β) to describe the education that Philip received while in Athens, and to present the description of Greek education contained in Plato's *Protagoras*; to move by means of a clever transition at the end of reading β to the writer Herodotus, from whom the readings in Chapters 25–28 are drawn; and in the reading at the end of the chapter to present an adapted version of the prologue to Herodotus' history.
2. Grammar: (α) to continue the presentation of the passive voice from the previous chapter, by giving the forms of the aorist and future passive and discussing the aorist of deponent verbs (sometimes middle and sometimes passive in form), and to present clauses with ὅπως and the future indicative; (β) to present further information about the comparison of adjectives (building on what was given in Chapter 14)
3. Background: to give an overview of Greek education in the fifth and fourth centuries B.C.

Illustration

This and the illustration on page 107 show two sides of a red figure cup by Douris, ca. 480 B.C. (Berlin, Staatliche Museen). The boy in the middle is reciting his lesson. On the walls behind hang cups (φιάλαι), lyres (κιθάραι), and an object that is perhaps a charcoal brazier.

Caption under Illustration

"At school: on the left the boy is being taught to play the lyre by the music teacher; on the right sits his παιδαγωγός; in the middle the writing master teaches letters": students will find many of the words (or related words) in the vocabulary list. The word παιδαγωγός (the slave who accompanied a boy to and from school, a tutor) will be familiar to students who have studied Latin, and its derivation from παῖς and ἄγω may be discussed.

Vocabulary

ζάω: in Attic ἐβίων is used instead of ἔζησα, and βεβίωκα is used instead of ἔζηκα. The future is often deponent, ζήσομαι or βιώσομαι.

Spelling

With this reading passage and the exercises accompanying the grammatical presentations in this chapter, we resume use of the Attic spellings εἰς and -ττ-, e.g., πράττω, as the story returns to the family and Philip's education. These spellings are also used in the passage adapted from Plato's *Protagoras* in the second reading passage, since Plato used them. At the end of the chapter in the reading from Herodotus we use the Ionic spelling ἐς.

Verbs

The chapter formally introduces the aorist and future passive. The first paragraph of passage α contains two examples of the aorist passive (ἠγγέλθη, 5, and καταλειφθείς, 11). The paragraph provides a good opportunity to sort out and discuss middle, deponent, and passive verb forms:

> ἐπολιορκοῦντο (2): imperfect passive
> ἤγετο (2): imperfect passive
> ἐδιδάσκετο (3): imperfect passive
> (note that verbs such as διδάσκω

that take two accusatives when used actively–e.g., "the teacher taught the boy letters"–retain one of the accusatives in the passive, thus "he was taught letters" (τὰ γράμματα, accusative)

ἠγγέλθη (5): aorist passive

λελυμένοι (7): perfect passive participle (see Overview of the Greek Verb, pages 4–5)

ἤρετο (8): aorist middle deponent

παύηται (9): present middle

παιδευόμενος (10): present passive participle

δεξάμενος (10): aorist middle deponent participle

ἐπορεύετο (11): imperfect deponent

καταλειφθείς (11): aorist passive participle

ἐπαιδεύετο (12): imperfect passive (again with accusative object, πλέονα)

Translation

Lines 1–12

As long as the Peloponnesians stayed in Attica and the Athenians were being besieged, Philip was taken every day by his cousins to school. And so he was taught letters by the grammar teacher and music by the lyre teacher; and he also went to the trainer's to practice gymnastics. But when it was announced that the Peloponnesians had gone away, all the farmers, freed from their fear, returned to the country. And so Dicaeopolis was going to take his wife and children home, but his brother asked him if he wanted to leave Philip at his house so that he would not stop his education (stop being educated). And so Dicaeopolis gladly accepted this and entrusting his son to his brother went off, and Philip, left behind, continued his education (was educated even more things).

[εἰς διδασκάλων (3): students will deduce the meaning of this phrase from their knowledge of the title of the chapter.]

Lines 13–17

What this education was like, one can learn by studying a dialogue of Plato, in which a sophist called Protagoras tries to prove that virtue is teachable. For Protagoras says that all parents consider this most important, that their children should be (become) good.

[Protagoras has said to a prospective pupil whom Socrates has brought to see him, "Young man, if you come to me, you will go home that very day a better man, and the same the next day; and every day you will become better." Socrates replies that he had not thought that virtue (goodness, excellence) was teachable, and that even the wisest and best fathers fail to pass on their virtue to their children (he quotes the example of Pericles' children). Protagoras replies at length, and one of his arguments is taken from the education of children both at home and at school; he tries to show that the primary purpose of all education is moral. The extract begins at *Protagoras* 325c.]

Lines 18–25

"Starting from (when they are) little children," he says, "as long as they live, they (the parents) teach and warn them. And when he (a child) first understands speech, both nurse and mother and tutor and the father himself strive hard for this, that the child may be as good as possible, in (respect of) each deed and word teaching (him) and showing that this is right but that is wrong, and (that) this is good but that is shameful, and (that) this is holy but that is unholy, and do this but don't do that; and if he obeys (well and good!)—, but if not, they straighten him out with threats and blows."

[παιδαγωγός (20): students will be familiar with this word from the caption under the illustration.]

Principal Parts

We here show verbs with the nasal infixes -ν-, -νε-, -ιν-, and -νῡ-/-νυ- in that order. We include δείκνῦμι in this list, even though it was just given in Chapter 22, Grammar 3, pages 82–83, in order to show students how it fits into the sets of verbs with nasal infixes.

Note the accent of ἀφῖγμαι. The accent cannot precede augment or reduplication.

Grammar 1

It should be noted that the υ is short in the aorist passive and future passive of λύω.

The aorist passive subjunctive forms are contractions of λυθή-ω, λυθή-ῃς, λυθή-ῃ, λυθή-ωμεν, λυθή-ητε, λυθή-ωσιν, thus producing the circumflex accents.

Grammar 2

Notes:

Grammar 3

The verb ἥδομαι is given in the vocabulary for the second half of this chapter.

Grammar 4

Notes:

Exercise 24a

1. When it was announced that the Peloponnesians were invading Attica, the majority of the farmers immediately journeyed to the city.
2. Some, who refused to leave their homes, were caught by the enemy.
3. When the Peloponnesians went away, all, freed from fear, prepared to return home.
4. Weren't you delighted to return (returning) to the country?
5. Let us do everything, friends, to

avoid being caught (so as not to be caught) by the enemy.
6. The father did everything (to see to it) that his son would be well educated.
7. If you fight bravely, men, our country will be freed, and you will be praised by all.
8. The man seeing his wife talking to a stranger grew extremely angry.
9. Don't talk to this young man, wife; for he is a stranger.
10. The wife, told by her husband to go in, hastened into the house.

Note the partitive genitive τῶν αὐτουργῶν with οἱ πολλοί in no. 1.

Exercise 24b

1. οἱ ὁπλῖται ὑπὸ τῶν πολεμίων νῑκηθέντες εἰς τὸ ἄστυ ἠλάθησαν.
2. ἄγγελοι ὑπὸ τοῦ δήμου ἐπέμφθησαν ὡς σπονδὰς αἰτήσοντες.
3. ὁ δοῦλος φοβούμενος μὴ ὁ δεσπότης ὀργισθείη/ὀργίζοιτο ἀπέφυγεν.
4. τὸ ἄστυ νυκτὸς λιπεῖν ἐπειρᾶσατο ἀλλ' ὀφθεὶς κατελήφθη.
5. ἑκατὸν νῆες πεμφθήσονται ὡς τοῖς συμμάχοις βοηθήσουσαι.

Students may need to be reminded that in no. 4 "by night" is to be rendered by a simple genitive of time without a preposition (see Book I, page 165).

Greek Education

Illustration (page 105)

A black figure cup, ca. 550 B.C. (London, British Museum).

Illustration (page 107)

The pipe is a double pipe (the only sort the ancients used). On the wall behind the music lesson are hung a papyrus scroll and a writing tablet.

For further reading, see *Civilization of the Ancient Mediterranean*, Vol. II, pp. 1077–1086; *The World of Athens*, pp. 172–177 and 287–288; and *The Oxford*

History of the Classical World, pp. 227–232 and 236–237.

ΕΝ ΔΙΔΑΣΚΑΛΩΝ (β)

Vocabulary

New usage of preposition: ἐπί (+ *gen.*) = on: ἐπὶ τῶν βάθρων (6).

New usage of preposition: πρός (+ *dat.*) = in addition to: πρὸς . . . τούτοις (11).

Translation

Lines 1–9

"After this they send (their children) to school and tell the teachers to pay much more attention to the good behavior of the children than to letters and music (lyre-playing); and the teachers do pay attention to this, and when they (the children) are learning letters and are about to understand writing, as earlier (then) (they were about to understand) the spoken word (the voice), they set in front of them (as they are sitting) on the benches the poems of good poets to read, and they make them learn (these) thoroughly, (poems) in which there are many warnings and many eulogies (praises) of good men of old, so that the child may imitate (them) and want to become like them.

[ἀναγιγνώσκειν (6): explanatory infinitive.]

Lines 10–16

"And again the music teachers are concerned with self-discipline and to see that the young do no wrong. And besides this, when they learn to play the lyre, they teach them the poems of other good poets, songwriters, setting them to the lyre, and they make (compel) the rhythms and harmonies (of the songs) to be made (to become) familiar to the souls of the children, so that they may be gentler, and (so that) becoming more graceful (well-rhythmed) and more co-ordinated (harmonious) they may be useful in/for both speech and action.

[σωφροσύνης (10): ἡ σωφροσύνη (σῴ-ζω + ἡ φρήν, φρεν-ός/φρον- + -σύνη) = (1) soundness of mind, prudence; (2) temperance, self-control. Together with ἡ σοφίᾱ (wisdom), ἡ ἀνδρείᾱ (courage), and ἡ δικαιοσύνη (justice), it is one of Plato's four cardinal virtues, which together make up ἡ ἀρετή = (human) excellence. Plato (430d5) describes it as "a sort of discipline (κόσμος τις) and control of certain pleasures and desires, as when people describe someone as being in some indefinable way 'master of himself.'" Plato in Book III of the *Republic* attaches great importance to music in education and is much concerned with the moral effects of music— its influences on the soul, e.g. 401d4: "For these reasons is not education in music of the greatest importance, because rhythm and harmony sink down into the innermost part of the soul and grasp it most firmly, bringing with them grace, and if a man is rightly educated, they make him graceful, and, if not, the opposite?"

ποιήματα . . . εἰς τὰ κιθαρίσματα ἐντείνοντες (12–13): literally, "stretching poems to lyre music," i.e., writing music to fit the poems; ἐντείνω is used both of tuning a lyre (by stretching the strings) and of putting words into verse. Its meaning of setting words to music, although natural enough, seems to occur here only.

ἡμερώτεροι (15): the word ἥμερος means "tame," "cultivated," "civilized," "gentle." This term and the following terms (εὐρυθμότεροι and εὐαρμοστότεροι) deserve special attention and discussion, as does the phrase χρήσιμοι . . . εἰς τὸ λέγειν τε καὶ πρᾱ́ττειν (16).

εἰς τὸ λέγειν τε καὶ πρᾱ́ττειν (16): note the use of εἰς + accusative to express purpose and the use of the articular infinitive.]

Lines 17–20

"And also besides this they send them to the trainer's, so that having their bodies in better condition they may serve their intellect that will be (being) good and not be compelled to play the coward through physical weakness (faultiness of their bodies) whether in war or in other transactions (both in war . . . and . . .)."

[The commonly accepted view of education was that "music" (i.e., everything concerned with the Muses, including literature and music proper) was for training the soul, and gymnastics (physical training) for training the body. Plato in Book III of the *Republic* argues that both music and gymnastics aim at educating the soul; he here attributes a similar view to Protagoras.

παιδοτρίβου (17): παῖς + τρίβω I rub, pound, spend or waste (time), wear out (a person). The παιδοτρίβης is the one who makes the boys exercise and practice so that they become experts (τετρῐμμένοι).]

Lines 21–32

Such was the education Philip received, and delighting in this education he proved so good a pupil that the teacher gave him some books to read to himself. Of these books (there was) one he particularly enjoyed, the history of Herodotus, in which Herodotus relates the Persian Wars; for Herodotus not only writes of the war with the Medes (Persians) and all the battles but also shows the causes of the war, showing how (in what way) the Medes increased their power and what peoples they conquered one after the other. In this account (in which things) many stories are told including the story of Croesus (both many other things and the story of Croesus). For Croesus was king of the Lydians; he became exceedingly wealthy and powerful and subdued the Greeks in Asia but finally was conquered by Cyrus, king (being king, who was king) of the Medes (Persians). [ἀναγιγνώσκῃ (23): the verb means to read aloud; this was the normal practice; hence αὐτὸς πρὸς ἑαυτὸν ἀναγιγνώσκειν = to read to himself.

Ἡρόδοτος (25): the latest events recorded in his history belong to 431/430, and he may have died before he had finished it completely; Philip, in spring 431, is therefore reading an unfinished version (but Herodotus was said to have made public readings of parts of his work at the Olympic games some years before).

τὰ Μηδικά (25): Cyrus, a Persian prince, had at the beginning of his career conquered his neighbors, the Medes, and so was king of the Medes and of the Persians. Herodotus usually uses οἱ Μῆδοι and τὰ Μηδικά, while we usually say "Persians" and "the Persian Wars"; Herodotus generally keeps the name Πέρσαι for the Persians proper, who formed the aristocracy of Cyrus' court and army.

δυνατώτατος (30): "exceedingly powerful," a new meaning for this word, which has occurred previously with the meanings "possible, "capable."]

Principal Parts

The suffix -(ί)σκω is usually referred to as *ingressive, inceptive,* or *inchoative,* but only a few of the verbs that use it have any sense of "beginning," e.g., γηρά-σκω. In the first principal part, the suffix -ίσκω is added to the stem if it ends with a consonant and -σκω, if with a vowel (note the iota subscript in ἀποθνή-σκω). The suffix appears only in the first principal part and thus shows up in the present and imperfect tenses only. Students should be informed that only certain verbs in Greek use this suffix; it is not one that can be added to any verb stem.

Note that the perfect tense of ἀπο-θνῄσκω does not use the prefix ἀπο-.

The verb γιγνώσκω shows reduplication in the present stem, consisting of the first consonant of the stem + ι (see the group of verbs after reading 26α, page 130, for more examples of present reduplication). This verb does have an ingressive force = I get to know, learn.

The aorist imperative of εὑρίσκω is εὑρέ/εὑρέτε (note the irregular accent).

Word Study

1. *music*: ἡ μουσική (τέχνη) (αἱ Μοῦσαι) = art, skill concerned with the Muses, then music in our sense.
2. *harmony*: ἡ ἁρμονίᾱ = means of fastening, stringing an instrument, music, harmony.
3. *rhythm*: ὁ ῥυθμός.
4. *orchestra*: ἡ ὀρχήστρᾱ (ὀρχέομαι = I dance) = the circular space in the theater in which the chorus danced. In English = (1) the part of the theater assigned to the band and chorus of singers (1724) and (2) the band of musicians itself (1720).
5. *chorus*: ὁ χορός = dance, band of dancers and singers.
6. *symphony*: ἡ συμφωνίᾱ (συν + ἡ φωνή, -φωνίᾱ) = concord of sounds, then orchestra; symphony had the same meaning in English, e.g., "And with preamble sweet of charming symphonie . . . " (Milton, *Paradise Lost* III, 367–368) until the time of Handel (in the Messiah, 1760, "The Pastoral Symphony" is an orchestral interlude).
7. *melody*: ἡ μελῳδίᾱ (τὸ μέλος = song + ἡ ᾠδή = song, ode)
8. *chord*: ἡ χορδή = (1) the gut of an animal, (2) the string of a lyre, and (3) a musical note. The modern meaning of chord in music is properly speaking a "concord," i.e., the notes added to a bass to make up a "chord."
9. *diapason*: διὰ πᾱσῶν = ἡ διὰ πᾱσῶν χορδῶν συμφωνίᾱ (the concord through all the notes of the scale). The meaning is now generally limited to two stops on the organ, which extend through the whole compass of the instrument.

Your students may be able to think of other musical terms derived from Greek, e.g., organ (τὸ ὄργανον) and harmonica (cf. harmony).

Word Building

1. honor; I honor
2. house, home; I dwell
3. slave; I enslave
4. king; I am king, I rule
5. necessity; I compel
6. anger; I grow angry

Grammar 5

Notes:

Exercise 24c

1. Take care, friend, (to see to it) that you play the lyre better than your brother.
2. The good are not always more prosperous than the wicked and do not live more easily.
3. I am afraid that the ships of the enemy are swifter than ours.
4. If you do this, you will become most hateful to me.
5. Whoever reads the poems of good poets will become a better man.

Word glossed earlier in chapter: ποιήματα (in β:6, here in no. 5).

Ο ΗΡΟΔΟΤΟΣ ΤΗΝ ΙΣΤΟΡΙΑΝ ΑΠΟΔΕΙΚΝΥΣΙΝ

Title: "Herodotus Displays His Inquiry"

Students will try to translate τὴν ἱστορίᾱν as "his history," but the word is used here in its original sense of "inquiry." Students had δείκνῡμι "I show" in Chapter 22β; from this they should be encouraged to deduce the meaning of ἀποδείκνῡσιν here ("makes known," "displays").

Translation

Lines 1–4

This is the display of the inquiry of Herodotus of Halicarnassus, so that the

past (what happened) may not become
faded from men's memory (from men)
through (lapse of) time, and the great
and wonderful deeds performed some by
the Greeks and others by the barbarians
may not lose their fame (become without
fame), including the reason why (both
other things and for what reason) they
made war on each other.
[ἡ ἀπόδειξις (1): "exhibition," "display"; Herodotus would have "dis-
played" his work by reciting it before an
audience. Thucydides, on the other
hand, wrote his history for a reading
public and says (1.22.4): "(My history)
is composed to be a possession forever,
not a performance to please an immedi-
ate public."

It is characteristic of Herodotus to
tell the old mythical stories without crit-
ical comment; the next paragraph
makes it clear that he does not necessar-
ily believe them himself.]

Lines 5–9

That is what the Persians say, and
they find the origin of their hatred toward the Greeks in the sack of Troy
(find the origin of . . . is because of). On
this subject I am not going to say that it
happened like this or in some other way,
but after telling of the man whom I myself know began wrong action against
the Greeks, I will go forward further into
my account.
['Ιλίου (5): the initial iota is long, but we
do not place macrons over capital letters.]

Lines 10–14

Croesus was Lydian by race and the
son of Alyattes, and ruler (tyrant) of the
peoples this side of (within) the river
Halys. This Croesus was the first man

(Croesus first) of whom we know who
subdued some of the Greeks and made
others friends. He subdued the Ionians
in Asia, and he made friends of the
Spartans. But before the reign of
Croesus all Greeks were free.
[Croesus became king of Lydia ca. 565
B.C.; the eastern border of his empire
was the river Halys; he in fact completed the conquest of the Ionian Greeks,
which had been begun by Alyattes. He
made an alliance with Sparta, on learning that the Spartans were the most powerful state in Greece.]

Exercise 24d

1. τοῦ πατρὸς ἀποθανόντος, ὁ Κροῖσος
    βασιλεὺς ἐγένετο, ὃς ἐπὶ τοὺς ἐν
    Ασίᾳ Ἕλληνας στρατευόμενος
    κατεστρέψατο.

2. πάντων τῶν ἐν Ἀσίᾳ Ἑλλήνων
    νῑκηθέντων, πλείστᾱς ναῦς ποιησά-
    μενος παρεσκευάζετο ὡς ἐπὶ τοὺς
    νησιώτᾱς στρατευσόμενος.

3. Ἕλλην δέ τις ἐς τὰς Σάρδῑς
    ἀφικόμενος καὶ ἀκούσᾱς τί ἐν νῷ
    εἶχεν ὁ Κροῖσος, "ὦ βασιλεῦ," ἔφη,
    "οἱ νησιῶται πλείστους ἱππέᾱς συλ-
    λέγουσιν ὡς ἐπί σε στρατευσό-
    μενοι/ἵνα ἐπί σε στρατεύσωνται.

4. ὁ δὲ Κροῖσος, οἰόμενος τὸν Ἕλληνα
    τὰ ἀληθῆ λέγειν, "ἐγὼ μέν," ἔφη,
    "ἐλπίζω τοὺς νησιώτᾱς στρατεύ-
    σεσθαι ἐπί με· σαφῶς γὰρ νῑκηθή-
    σονται."

5. ὁ δὲ Ἕλλην τάδε ἀπεκρίνατο· "ἆρ'
    οὐκ οἴῃ καὶ τοὺς νησιώτᾱς ἐλπίζειν
    σὲ κατὰ θάλασσαν ἐπὶ σφᾶς
    στρατεύσεσθαι, πιστεύοντας σὲ
    νῑκήσειν;"

6. οὕτως οὖν ἐπείσθη ὁ Κροῖσος μὴ
    ἐπιστρατεύεσθαι ἐπὶ τοὺς νησιώτᾱς
    ἀλλὰ φίλους ποιήσασθαι.

25

Ο ΚΡΟΙΣΟΣ
ΤΟΝ ΣΟΛΩΝΑ
ΞΕΝΙΖΕΙ (α)

Title: "Croesus Entertains Solon"

The new verb is in the vocabulary list.

The purposes of this chapter are:

1. Reading: (α, β, and the end reading) to give an adapted version of Herodotus' story of how Croesus entertained Solon and their discussion of true happiness
2. Grammar: (α) to introduce the optative mood and its use in main clauses expressing wishes and its use as an alternative to the subjunctive in subordinate clauses in secondary sequence; (β) to present the use of the optative as an alternative to the indicative in indirect statements and indirect questions in secondary sequence
3. Background: to present information about Herodotus and his history

Illustration

This red figure cup by Douris, ca. 480 B.C. (London, British Museum) illustrates a symposium (dinner party). This is a very common subject on cups of this period. Although the scene of this chapter is set in Sardis, it may not be wildly wrong to illustrate it with an Athenian symposium, since relations between Greece and Lydia were close in this period.

Caption under Illustration

"Solon, having arrived at Sardis to look at everything, was entertained by Croesus": introduce θεωροίη as an optative and briefly explain its use as a substitute for the subjunctive in subordinate clauses in secondary sequence.

The Optative

This chapter formally introduces the forms and uses of the optative. The following information about the use of the optative is presented in this and subsequent chapters:

Chapter 25
  Grammar 1, page 116:
    wishes
  Grammar 2, pages 116–117:
    the optative as an alternative to the subjunctive in subordinate clauses in secondary sequence
  Grammar 4, pages 124–125:
    the optative as an alternative to the indicative in indirect statements and questions in secondary sequence
Chapter 29
  Grammar 4, pages 187–188:
    potential optative
Chapter 30
  Grammar 1, pages 192–194:
    conditional sentences
  Grammar 2, pages 200–202:
    optional change of indicative and subjunctive to optative in complex sentences in indirect speech

Vocabulary

Students have already seen some of the principal parts of κρίνω in ἀποκρίνομαι, given in the list of principal parts after passage 22β.

New usage of preposition: κατά (+ *acc.*) = through: κατὰ τοὺς θησαυρούς (13).

Note that we keep Herodotus' genitive 'Αλυάττεω.

Spelling

With the readings from Herodotus in Chapers 25 and 26 we continue to use his spellings ἐς and -σσ-; with Chapter 27 more of Herodotus' Ionic dialect will be preserved in the readings, and students will be given a note on the Ionic dialect at the beginning of that chapter.

Verbs

This chapter formally introduces the optative. The caption under the illustration at the opening of the chapter provides an example of the optative in a purpose clause in secondary sequence, and attention should be called to the use of the optative here. There are no examples in passage α. The following examples occur in passage β:

ἴδοι (2): indirect question in secondary sequence.

παραγένοιτο (8): purpose clause in secondary sequence.

εἴη (13): indirect statement in secondary sequence.

εἴη (19): indefinite relative clause in secondary sequence.

There are two examples in the tail reading:

παραμεῖναι (10): optative in a future less vivid protasis of a mixed conditional sentence.

κελεύοι (16): optative in a subordinate clause in indirect statement in secondary sequence.

Translation

Lines 1–14

When Alyattes died, Croesus the son of Alyattes inherited (received) the kingdom, being thirty-five years old, who attacked and subdued the Greeks in Asia in turn. When he had subdued the Greeks in Asia, there arrived at Sardis (other) wise men from Greece including Solon, an Athenian, who after making laws for the Athenians went abroad for ten years, sailing off ostensibly for sightseeing but in fact so that he might not be forced to repeal (loose, untie) any of the laws that he had enacted. The Athenians themselves could not do this; for they were constrained by great oaths to use for ten years whatever laws Solon enacted for them. And so leaving the country he arrived in Egypt and also at

Sardis to (visit) Croesus. On arrival he was entertained in the palace by Croesus. And afterwards, on the third or fourth day, on Croesus' order (Croesus having ordered) servants led Solon through the treasures and showed (him) that they were all great and prosperous (all being great and prosperous).

[For Solon, see essay, Chapter 21, pages 64–65. His archonship, when he was appointed arbitrator and carried through his reforms, is traditionally dated to 594/593 B.C., though some modern scholars argue for a later date. Croesus did not become king of Lydia until 565 B.C., and so the whole of the famous story that follows may belong to the realm of myth rather than history.

ἄλλοι . . . σοφισταί (4–5): for Herodotus the word does not mean "sophist" but simply "wise man." Solon was one of "the seven wise men" of this time. Herodotus says that they all came to visit Croesus when Sardis was at the height of its prosperity.

Compound verb to be deduced: ἐκπλεύσας (7).

κατείχοντο . . . οὓς ἄν . . . θῆται (9–10): this is a past indefinite or general relative clause following a main verb in the imperfect tense. Normally Greek would use the optative without ἄν in the subordinate clause, but Herodotus here used the subjunctive with ἄν, because it is virtually indirect speech, part of what they swore; in indirect speech the tenses and moods of the original words may be retained.

οὕς (9): note that the pronoun is not assimilated to the case of its antecedent here.

θῆται (10): help students as necessary with this aorist subjunctive form. Compare ἔθετο (8).]

Lines 15–28

After he had seen and examined it all, Croesus asked him this, "Athenian guest, many reports (much account) have come to us about you because of your wisdom and your travels (wandering), (telling) that you have passed through much of the world (much land) to see things (for the sake of seeing). And so now I want to ask you who is the happiest of all the men whom you have seen." He asked this expecting that he himself was the happiest, but Solon without any flattery (flattering nothing) spoke the truth (using the truth) and said, "O king, Tellus the Athenian." Croesus was surprised at what was said and asked, "How do you judge Tellus to be happiest?" And Solon said, "Tellus had handsome and good sons, and he also saw children born to his sons and all surviving, and the end of his life was most brilliant; for when the Athenians had a battle with their neighbors at Eleusis, he came to help and routed (made a rout of) the enemy and died most gloriously, and the Athenians buried him publicly where he fell and honored him greatly."

[ξένε (16): ὁ ξένος means (1) guest-friend, i.e., one who receives or gives hospitality to another, whether a guest or a host, (2) stranger, and (3) foreigner.
ὧν (19): genitive by attraction.]

Principal Parts

These three verbs belong to the -μι class of verbs, which in the present and imperfect are athematic, that is, they add endings to the stem without thematic vowels. The forms are similar to those of ἵσταμαι.

It should be noted that the second person singular imperfect of δύναμαι is ἐδύνασο or more commonly ἐδύνω and of ἐπίσταμαι it is ἠπίστασο or more commonly ἠπίστω.

The verb κεῖμαι is used in the present and imperfect instead of the perfect and pluperfect passive of τίθημι, "I place."

Word Study

1.   *history*: ἡ ἱστορίᾱ = inquiry, history.

2.   *chronicle*: χρονικός, -ή, -όν = concerned with time; τὰ χρονικά = annals, records of events year by year (via Middle English *cronicle*).

3.   *chronology*: ὁ χρόνος + ὁ λόγος, -λογίᾱ = study of times and dates (coined, 1593).

4.   *genealogy*: ἡ γενεαλογίᾱ (τὸ γέν-ος + -λογίᾱ) = study of family, tracing descent.

5.   *paleography*: παλαιός, -ά, -όν (old) + ἡ γραφή, -γραφίᾱ = ancient writing, the study of ancient writing (coined, 1818).

6.   *archaeology*: ἡ ἀρχαιολογίᾱ (ἀρχαῖος, -ᾱ, -ον + -λογίᾱ) = study of things ancient.

Grammar 1

While it is worth emphasizing to students that the optative may be easily recognized from the diphthongs οι, αι, or ει, the actual signals of the optative mood are -ι- and -ιη-, which combine with other vowels in the verb forms to make the easily identifiable diphthongs.

Grammar 2

The first two examples in section b have the same pattern as past general conditions, namely, subordinating conjunction without ἄν + optative in the subordinate clause and the imperfect indicative in the main clause (see Chapter 30, Grammar 1a, page 193).

Grammar 3

Students should be alerted to the fact that the diphthongs οι and αι are counted as long in the optative endings, producing accents as follows: λύσοι, λύσαι, φιλήσαι.

On the top of page 118 we give only the first and second person singular forms. Students may be asked to write out the remaining forms for practice.

Students may also consult the charts of forms in the Reference Grammar, paragraph 43.

There are alternative forms of the

plural optative of contract verbs, which correspond to those of the plural of εἰμί as given on page 118: φιλοίημεν, φιλοίητε, φιλοίησαν; τῑμῷημεν, τῑμῷητε, τῑμῷησαν; and δηλοίημεν, δηλοίητε, δηλοίησαν.

Exercise 25a

1. λύωσιν, λύοιεν
2. λύηται, λύοιτο
3. λύσωμεν, λύσαιμεν
4. λυθῇ, λυθείη
5. βούλωμαι, βουλοίμην
6. νῑκῶμεν, νῑκῷμεν
7. φιλῇ, φιλοίη
8. στῇ, σταίη
9. ἦ, εἴη
10. τῑμᾷ, τῑμῷη
11. θῶμαι, θοίμην
12. λάβω/λάβωσι, λάβοιμι/λάβοιεν
13. γένηται, γένοιτο
14. φιλήσωμεν, φιλήσαιμεν
15. ἴωσιν, ἴοιεν

Exercise 25b

1. May our mother arrive quickly!
2. May we never get (involved) in war again.
3. May I not see the wicked faring well!
4. May you be sensible, children, and always love your parents!
5. May all who do such things die horribly!

Exercise 25c

1. οἱ νέοι ἐπαιδεύοντο ἵνα ἀγαθοὶ γένοιντο.
   The young were being educated so that they might become good.
   (It may be useful to point out to students that in English we use *may* in primary sequence, e.g., "The young men are being educated so that they *may* become good," and *might* in secondary sequence, as in the sentence above. This corresponds to the use of the subjunctive and the optative in Greek.)
2. ὁ Σόλων ἀπεδήμησεν ἵνα μὴ

ἀναγκασθείη τοὺς νόμους λῦσαι.
Solon went abroad so that he might not be forced to repeal his laws.

3. ὁ πατὴρ τοῖς τέκνοις ἐδίδου ὅσα βούλοιντο ἔχειν.
   The father used to give his children whatever they wanted to have.

4. οἱ ὁπλῖται ἐφοβοῦντο μὴ οὐκ ἀμύνοιεν τοὺς πολεμίους.
   The hoplites were afraid they might not ward off the enemy.

5. οἱ Ἀθηναῖοι μεγάλοις ὅρκοις κατείχοντο νόμοις χρήσεσθαι οὓς θεῖτο ὁ Σόλων.
   The Athenians were bound by great oaths to use whatever laws Solon proposed.

6. φοβούμενος τὸν κίνδῡνον, τοὺς φίλους ἐκάλεσα ὅπως ὑμῖν βοηθοῖεν.
   Fearing the danger, I called our friends to help you.

Exercise 25d

1. οἱ Ἕλληνες τοὺς παῖδας εἰς διδασκάλων ἔπεμπον ἵνα/ὅπως τὰ γράμματα μάθωσιν/μάθοιεν.
2. ὁ παῖς ἐφοβεῖτο μὴ οὐδέποτε οἴκαδε ἐπανίῃ/ἐπανίοι.
3. ὁπότε γένοιτο ὁ χειμών, οἱ ποιμένες τὰ μῆλα ἤλαυνον εἰς τὸ πεδίον.
4. οἱ δοῦλοι αἰεὶ ἐποίουν (πάντα) ὅσα κελεύοι ὁ δεσπότης.

N.B. In nos. 1 and 2 either the subjunctive or the optative is correct, but in 3 and 4, which are indefinite clauses, only the optative without ἄν is correct.

For the use of μὴ οὐδέποτε in no. 2, see Chapter 22, Grammar 1, page 74.

Illustration (page 119)

Marble portrait herm of Herodotus, Roman copy of a late fifth-century original (New York, Metropolitan Museum).

Herodotus

For further reading, see *Ancient Writers*, Vol. I, pp. 209–232; *Cambridge History of Classical Literature*, Vol. I, pp.

426–441; and *The Oxford History of the Classical World*, pp. 186–191.

Ο ΚΡΟΙΣΟΣ
ΤΟΝ ΣΟΛΩΝΑ
ΞΕΝΙΖΕΙ (β)

Vocabulary

Notes:

Translation

Lines 1–11

When Solon had said this about Tellus, Croesus asked him who was the second happiest man he had seen after him, thinking that he would certainly carry (off) the second prize. And Solon said, "Cleobis and Biton. For they were Argives by birth (being Argives) and had sufficient wealth and besides that physical strength (strength of body) like this: both were prize winners (in athletic contests) and, further, this story is told (about them). The Argives had a festival for Hera, and their mother absolutely had to be carried by a team of oxen (by a yoke) to the temple, and the oxen did not arrive from the field in time. And the young men, so that their mother might arrive in time, themselves dragged the wagon, and on the wagon rode (was carried) their mother, and they carried her eight and a half miles (forty-five stades) and arrived at the temple.

Lines 12–23

After they had done this (for them having done this) and had been seen by the assembly (those present), the end of their life was excellent, and god showed in this that it is better for a man to be dead rather than to live. For the Argives standing around praised the strength of the young men, and the Argive women praised their mother, because she had such children. And the mother, standing in front of the statue of the goddess (Hera), prayed that the goddess should give to Cleobis and Biton, her own children, who had honored her greatly, whatever it was best for a man to get. And after this prayer, when they had sacrificed and feasted, the young men having gone to sleep in the actual temple never got up again but died like this. And the Argives made statues of them as (being) very good men and set them up at Delphi.

[ὀφθεῖσι (12): help students as necessary with this aorist passive participle of ὁράω.

τεθνάναι (14): besides having the first perfect forms τέθνηκα, etc., θνῄσκω has second perfect forms, found most commonly in the participle τεθνεώς, τεθνεῶσα, τεθνεός and the infinitive τεθνάναι. Similarly, ἵστημι, besides having the first perfect forms ἕστηκα, etc., has second perfect forms, the participle ἑστώς, ἑστῶσα, ἑστός and the infinitive ἑστάναι (see Chapter 27, tail reading, lines 10 and 13).]

Illustration (page 123)

These archaic statues of brothers, dated about 590 B.C., were found in excavations at Delphi, complete with an inscription naming them and saying that they were dedicated by the people of Argos.

Lines 24–26

And so Solon gave the second prize for happiness to these men, and Croesus got angry and said, "Athenian guest, do you despise our happiness so much that you don't (didn't) even consider us worth comparing to (worthy of) private individuals?"

Principal Parts

These verbs that begin with vowels augment to εἰ- instead of following the usual rules for temporal augment. This irregularity is accounted for by the disappearance of an initial ϝ or σ or both. Note that ἐργάζομαι augments to εἰ- in the aorist and perfect as well as the imperfect, as do all other regular verbs with this augment, such as ἐάω, ἐάσω, εἴᾱσα, εἴᾱκα, εἴᾱμαι, εἰάθην I allow, let be.

The εἰ- augment does not appear in the aorist and perfect of ἕπομαι and ἔχω.

The unaugmented aorist forms of ἕπομαι are σπῶμαι, σποίμην, σποῦ, σπέσθαι, σπόμενος.

The unaugmented aorist forms of ἔχω are σχῶ, σχοίην or σχοῖμι, σχές, σχεῖν, σχών.

Word Building

1. citizen (city); sailor (ship)
   horseman (horse); priest (holy)
2. (a) dear, friendly; friendship, love
       true; truth
   (b) just; justice
       prudent, self-disciplined; prudence, self-control
   (c) equal; equality
       young; youth
3. son of Alcmeon, descended from Alcmeon
4. (a) little child
   (b) little house
   (c) young boy
   (d) youth

Grammar 4

For further information and examples, see Chapter 30, Grammar 2, pages 200–202.

Exercise 25e

1. ἡ γυνὴ ἡμᾶς ἤρετο εἰ τῷ παιδὶ αὐτῆς ἐν τῇ ὁδῷ ἐντύχοιμεν.
   The woman asked us if we had met her boy on the road.
2. ἀπεκρῑνάμεθα ὅτι οὐδένα ἀνθρώπων ἴδοιμεν ἀλλ᾽ εὐθὺς ἐπανίοιμεν ὡς αὐτὸν ζητήσοντες.
   We answered that we had seen no one (of men) but we would return at once to look for him.
3. τῷ παιδὶ ἐντυχόντες εἴπομεν ὅτι ἡ μήτηρ ζητοίη αὐτόν.
   Meeting the boy, we said that his

mother was looking for him.

4. ὁ ἄγγελος εἶπεν ὅτι τῶν πολεμίων ἀπελθόντων τοῖς αὐτουργοῖς ἐξείη οἴκαδε ἐπανιέναι.
   The messenger said that as the enemy had gone away the farmers could return home.
5. ὁ Πρωταγόρᾱς εἶπεν ὅτι τοῦτο περὶ πλείστου ποιοῖντο οἱ πατέρες, ὅπως ἀγαθοὶ γενήσοιντο οἱ παῖδες.
   Protagoras said that fathers considered this the most important thing, that their sons should become good.
6. ὁ Ἡρόδοτος ἐξηγήσατο ὅπως εἰς πόλεμον καταάσταιεν οἵ τε βάρβαροι καὶ οἱ Ἕλληνες.
   Herodotus related how the barbarians and Greeks got involved in (got into) war.
7. ὁ Σόλων ἠπίστατο ὅτι οἱ Ἀθηναῖοι οὐ λύσοιεν τοὺς νόμους.
   Solon knew that the Athenians would not repeal the laws.
8. ὁ Κροῖσος τὸν Σόλωνα ἤρετο τίνα ὀλβιώτατον ἴδοι.
   Croesus asked Solon who was the happiest man he had seen.
9. ὁ Σόλων εἶπεν ὅτι οἱ νεᾱνίαι, τὴν μητέρα εἰς τὸ ἱερὸν κομίσαντες, ἀποθάνοιεν.
   Solon said that the young men, after carrying their mother to the temple, died.
10. οὕτως ἔδειξεν ὁ θεὸς ὅτι ἄμεινον εἴη ἀνθρώπῳ τεθνάναι ἢ ζῆν.
    So god showed that it was better for a man to die than to live.

Students will recall the second perfect infinitive τεθνάναι in no. 10 from passage β:14, where it is glossed.

Notice the future optatives in nos. 5 and 7, representing future indicatives of direct speech; students should be reminded that this is the only use of the future optative.

Ο ΣΟΛΩΝ
ΤΟΝ ΚΡΟΙΣΟΝ ΟΡΓΙΖΕΙ

Title: "Solon Angers Croesus"

Students will deduce the meaning of the verb from their knowledge of the middle verb ὀργίζομαι.

Translation

Lines 1–6

But Solon said, "Croesus, you ask me about the human predicament (human affairs), and I know that all divinity is jealous and troublemaking. For in (the course) of a long time it is possible to see many things that one does not want to see and to suffer many things (that one does not want to suffer). I set the bounds of a man's life (of life for a man) at seventy years. These years, seventy in number (being seventy) provide 26,200 days; and each of these days brings something different from the others (and the one of them brings nothing like to the other).

[πᾶν τὸ θεῖον φθονερὸν ὂν καὶ ταραχῶδες (2): the notion that God was hostile to mankind was not unfamiliar to some writers in the Old Testament, e.g., Exodus 20:5, "I the Lord thy God am a jealous God," i.e., He will not tolerate the neglect of honors due to Him or the paying of honors to other gods. The Greeks consistently believed that God (the gods) would humble those who enjoyed too much prosperity; for too much prosperity or power results in ὕβρις (pride) and this will inevitably be followed by νέμεσις (divine retribution). No man therefore could feel secure, and the prosperous might well consider that the gods were "troublemaking."]

Lines 7–13

"You seem to me to be very rich and to be king over many men; but as for what (that which) you ask me, I do not yet say this of you, until I learn that you have ended your life well. For the very (greatly) rich man is not happier than the one having livelihood for a day, unless luck should stay with him, so that he finishes his life well. For many rich people among mankind (of men) are unhappy, and many having a moderate

livelihood are lucky. One must examine the end of every event, (to see) how it will turn out. For god gives a glimpse of happiness to many men and then overturns them root and branch."

[ἐκεῖνο . . . οὔπω σε λέγω (8): "I don't yet say that of you. . . . " When λέγω means "I say something of someone," it takes two accusatives, e.g., κακά σε λέγω "I speak ill of you."

The profound pessimism of this passage illustrates one strand of Greek thought; it was based on the conviction that life was a lottery in which no man could rely on the protection of the gods, however well he lived. It led Theognis to say (425–429): "The best of all things for men is never to be born, nor to see the rays of the burning sun, and being born to pass as soon as possible the gates of Hades and lie clothed in deep earth"—a sentiment echoed, for instance, in Sophocles' *Oedipus at Colonus*, 1224–1227.]

Lines 14–16

Solon in saying this no longer found favor with Croesus but Croesus sent (sends) him away, thinking that he was a stupid man who ignored present goods and told him to look at the end of everything.

Exercise 25f

1. ὁ μὲν Κροῖσος ᾤετο ὀλβιώτατος εἶναι ἀνθρώπων, ὁ δὲ Σόλων εἶπεν ὅτι πολλοὺς εἶδεν/ἴδοι ὀλβιωτέρους.

2. ὁ οὖν Κροῖσος τὸν Σόλωνα ἤρετο διὰ τί κρίνει/κρίνοι ἄλλους ὀλβιωτέρους εἶναι.

3. ὁ δὲ Σόλων ἀπεκρίνατο ὅτι οὐδένα ὄλβιον καλεῖ/καλοίη πρὶν ἂν μάθῃ/πρὶν μάθοι αὐτὸν τὸν βίον εὖ τελευτήσαντα.

4. ὁ οὖν Κροῖσος τῷ Σόλωνι ὀργισθεὶς ἀπέπεμψεν, οἰόμενος/δόξας ὅτι ἀμαθής ἐστιν/ἀμαθὴς εἴη or αὐτὸν ἀμαθῆ εἶναι.

5. μετὰ δὲ ταῦτα ὁ Κροῖσος δεινὰ παθὼν ἔγνω τὸν Σόλωνα ὀρθῶς γιγνώσκοντα.

26
Ο ΚΡΟΙΣΟΣ
ΤΟΝ ΠΑΙΔΑ
ΑΠΟΛΛΥΣΙΝ (α)

Title: "Croesus Loses His Son"

The verb is given in the vocabulary list.

The purposes of this chapter are:

1. Reading: (α, β, and tail reading) to give an adapted version of Herodotus' story of Croesus, Adrastus, and Croesus' son Atys
2. Grammar: (α) to review and consolidate the correlatives; (β) to review and consolidate uses of the genitive, dative, and accusative cases (including the new accusative absolute)
3. Background: to offer information on shame and guilt in Greek culture as background for the story of Adrastus

Illustration

The painting on this black figure vase by the Amasis Painter (New York, Metropolitan Museum, ca. 540 B.C.) shows a wedding procession. The bride and groom are in a cart drawn by mules, preceded by the bride's mother carrying torches; at the right, the bridegroom's mother, holding a torch, welcomes the procession.

Caption under Illustration

"Croesus gets his son a wife; look! Atys is bringing his bride home in a carriage": students may need help with the idiom ἄγεται τῷ παιδὶ γυναῖκα. The meaning of the word νύμφην "bride" will have to be given to students, to avoid confusion with "nymph." The alpha of Ἄτῡς is long, but we do not place macrons over capital letters.

Vocabulary

New usage of preposition: ἐπί (+ acc.) = to or for (of direction or purpose): ἐπὶ πόλεμον (9).

New usage of preposition: κατά (+ acc.) = with regard to: κατὰ τὸν παῖδα (4).

Translation

Lines 1–12

When Solon had gone away, a terrible retribution from god fell on (took) Croesus, because he thought that he was the happiest of all men. For while he was asleep (to him sleeping), a dream appeared to (stood over) him, which showed him the truth of the things that were going (were destined) to happen with regard to his son. Croesus had two sons, of whom one was mute, but the other far the first of those the same age; and his name was Atys. Well, the dream shows to Croesus that this Atys will die from the blow of a spear (struck by an iron spear point). When he woke up, in fear of (fearing) the dream, he gets his son a wife, and no more did he send him out to/for war, and the javelins and spears and all (the weapons) that men use for war he took out of the men's chambers and piled up in the storerooms, lest one fall on his son. [μελλόντων γενέσθαι (4): the aorist infinitive with μέλλω is rare.

βληθέντα (8): help as necessary with this aorist passive participle; the aorist passive was given on page 103, and the principal parts were given after passage 22α, page 73, with the meaning "I strike," as needed here.

ἐξηγέρθη (8): again, help as necessary with this aorist passive form; the principal parts of ἐγείρω were given after passage 23α, page 88.

ἐκκομίσας (11): compound verb to be deduced.

τι (11): "some one" (of the weapons).]

Lines 13–23

But while the boy has his marriage

on his hands (is busy with his mar-
riage), there arrives at Sardis a man
whose hands are unclean (being unclean as to his hands). This man came
to Croesus' palace and asked to obtain
purification. And Croesus purified
him. And when Croesus had performed
the customary rituals, he inquired
where he had come from and who he
was, saying this, "Man, who are you
and where have you come from to my
palace (being who and coming from
where have you arrived at my palace)?"
And he answered, "King, I am the son of
Gordias, and I am called Adrastus, and
I am here after involuntarily slaying
my own brother, having been driven out
by my father." And Croesus replied,
"You are the offspring of friends and
you have come to friends, where you will
lack nothing as long as you stay in my
palace. And I advise you to bear this
misfortune as lightly as possible.
[On the concepts of pollution and purification underlying the content of this
paragraph, see essay, pp. 132–133.

τὰς χεῖρας (14): for the accusative of
respect, see Grammar 4c, page 139, in
this chapter.

The nominative of Γορδίου (19) is
Γορδίης (Ionic) or Γορδίᾱς (Attic).

The English spelling of Ἄδρηστος
(19) is Adrastus.]

Principal Parts

Present reduplication consists of the
first letter of the stem + ι.

We repeat γιγνώσκω here from the
list of principal parts after passage 24β to
show how it fits into the group of verbs
with present reduplication and to set it
alongside γίγνομαι, with which it is often
confused by students.

The verb διδάσκω was given in the
vocabulary for Chapter 24α with full
principal parts, but it is repeated here to
show how it fits into the group of verbs
with present reduplication; it is irregular in retaining the prefix δι- in all
tenses.

The verb γίγνομαι shows three
grades of stem vowel (see explanation in
the notes in the teacher's handbook to the
set of principal parts after reading 23α;
also see the set of principal parts after
reading 26β, page 136). The o-grade of
the stem vowel is common in the perfect
active, especially with stems that end in
a liquid, e.g., γέγονα and διέφθορα.

The perfect active and middle of
γίγνομαι have the same meaning.

For πίπτω, see Appendix.

Word Study

1. *epic*: ἡ ἐπική (ποίησις) = epic poetry
    (τὰ ἔπη is used to mean the same);
    the root επ- is found in εἶπον = I
    said (epic poetry was declaimed
    rather than sung).

2. *lyric*: λυρικός, -ή, -όν = of the lyre
    (ἡ λύρᾱ); Greek lyric poetry was
    composed to be sung to the accom-
    paniment of the lyre.

3. *drama*: τὸ δρᾶμα (δράω = I do, act)
    = action on the stage, drama.

4. *tragedy*: ἡ τραγῳδίᾱ (ὁ τράγος =
    goat + ἡ ᾠδή = song) = goat-song
    (?). Greek writers say that origi-
    nally the prize for the winner of the
    tragic competition was a goat.

5. *comedy*: ἡ κωμῳδίᾱ (ὁ κῶμος =
    revel + ἡ ᾠδή = song) = revel song,
    so-called, according to Greek writ-
    ers because comedy first arose at
    revels in honor of Dionysus.

6. *biography*: ἡ βιογραφίᾱ (ὁ βίος +
    γράφω, ἡ γραφή); the word does not
    occur until late Greek, but a few bi-
    ographies were written in classical
    times.

The novel is missing from this list
of literary genres, since it was not a recognized form of literature, although ro-
mantic novels were written from the
first century B.C.

Grammar 1

Notes:

Exercise 26a

1. "How did you do this?" "I did it like this, as my father advised."
2. "Where have you come from?" "I don't know where from; for I missed the road."
3. "Where does the old man live?" "The old man lives there, near the river, where I saw him recently."
4. "In what sort of ship did you sail here?" "I sailed in the sort of ship which (such as) brings grain from Egypt."
5. We waited in the agora as long as (as much time as) you ordered.
6. The girl asked her father where he was going; but he did not wish (refused) to answer.
7. "When will mother come home?" "Mother will come home when she finds father."
8. "How many ships do the enemy have?" "I don't know how many ships they have."
9. The hoplite carried a spear in one hand and a sword in the other.
10. The general sent two messengers, who do not say the same things; which are we to believe?

Shame and Guilt

For further reading, see *Civilization of the Ancient Mediterranean*, Vol. II, pp. 959–979; *The World of Athens*, pp. 103–115; and E. R. Dodds, *The Greeks and the Irrational* (University of California Press, 1968), especially Chapter 2.

Ο ΚΡΟΙΣΟΣ
ΤΟΝ ΠΑΙΔΑ
ΑΠΟΛΛΥΣΙΝ (β)

Vocabulary

New usage of preposition: πρός (+ *gen.*) = from, at the hand of: πρὸς αὐτοῦ (5).

Translation

Lines 1–9
And so Adrastus lived in Croesus' palace. And at the same time on Mount Olympus a great boar is born. And this boar rushing (down) from this mountain destroyed the tilled fields of the Mysians, and the Mysians often went out against it and did it no harm but suffered harm from it. Finally messengers of the Mysians came to Croesus and said this, "King, a huge wild boar appeared in our land (in the land for us), which is destroying our farms. We've made every effort to take it but can't (being very eager to take it, we can't). And so now we ask you to send us your son and picked young men and dogs, so that we may remove it from our land." [τὰ ... ἔργα (3): students may need to be reminded of the meaning "tilled fields," seen previously in passage 19α:6, 11, and 19β:1.

ἑλεῖν (7): help as necessary with this aorist infinitive of αἱρέω (see Book I, Chapter 11, Grammar 5, page 135).

ἐξέλωμεν (9): compound verb to be deduced; help as necessary with the aorist subjunctive form.]

Lines 10–13
But Croesus remembering the words of the dream said this, "I refuse to send my son; for he is just married, and that is what concerns him now. But I will send picked young men and dogs and will tell those who go to remove the beast from your land."

Illustration (page 135)

The scene actually shows the Calydonian boar hunt (Meleager is about to kill the boar). Detail from the François vase (black figure volute krater signed by Kleitias and Ergotimus, ca. 575 B.C., Florence, National Museum).

Lines 14–26
But his son, hearing what Croesus had said to the Mysians, went to him and

said, "Father, why do you refuse to send
me to the hunt? Have you seen some
cowardice in me or lack of spirit?" And
Croesus answered with these (words):
"Son, I'm not doing this because I have
seen cowardice or anything else objec-
tionable, but a vision in a dream (of a
dream) appeared to (stood over) me in
my sleep and said that you would be
short-lived; for you would perish by an
iron spear point." And the young man
answers with these words: "You may be
pardoned for guarding me (there is par-
don for you to keep a guard around me)
since you saw such a vision. But you say
that the dream said that I would die by an
iron spear point. But what hands (what
sort of hands) has a wild boar (are there
of a wild boar), and what iron spear
point? And so since our battle (the battle
for us) is not against men, let me go."
Croesus replied, "Son, you convince
(conquer) me (by) revealing your opinion concerning the dream. And so I
change my mind and let you go to the
hunt."
[ἃ εἶπεν (14): note omission of the antecedent.

ἔσεσθαι (19): students may have
forgotten this future infinitive of the
verb εἰμί (Chapter 17, Grammar 1, page
10).

ἰδόντι (21): causal, "since."

μέθες (24): help students as necessary with this aorist imperative of
μεθίημι (Chapter 21, Grammar 4, page
69).]

Lines 27–33

After saying this Croesus sends for
Adrastus and says this to him:
"Adrastus, I purified you and received
you in my palace. And so now I want
you to become the guardian of my son as
he sets out to hunt." And Adrastus answered, "Since you are (so) earnest and
I must oblige you, I am ready to do this,
and you can expect (expect–*imperative*)
that your son whom you tell me to guard
will return home safe as far as his
guardian is concerned."

Lines 34–41

After this they went, equipped with
picked young men and dogs. And arriving at Mount Olympus they searched
for the wild beast, and after finding it
they stood around it in a circle and threw
their javelins at (it). Then the foreigner, the man who had been purified of
(as to) the murder, throwing his javelin
at the boar, missed it and hit Croesus'
son. And he, struck by the spear point,
fulfilled the warning (voice) of the
dream, and someone ran to tell Croesus
what had happened. And when he arrived at Sardis he told him of both the
battle and the fate (death) of his son.
[περιστάντες (36): compound verb to be
deduced.

ὁ καθαρθεὶς τὸν φόνον (36–37): "the
one who had been purified as to the murder"; the article is used to stress the
identity of the slayer of Croesus' son at
this dramatic moment.

τὸν φόνον (37): adverbial accusative of respect—a difficult example;
the genitive would have been expected.

ἀκοντίζων (37): here with an accusative object, though the verb usually
is followed by a genitive.

βληθείς (38): see passage α, line 8
and the note in this handbook on
βληθέντα.]

Principal Parts

These verbs show three grades of
stem vowel. For an explanation of this
pattern, see the notes in this handbook on
the set of principal parts in Chapter 23α
and Reference Grammar, paragraph 59,
in the student's book.

The verbs γίγνομαι and λείπω are
repeated here from earlier lists (26α and
19α) since they are particularly good examples of vowel gradation.

The form πάσχω is from the stem
παθ- + the suffix -σκω: *πά(θ)-σκω >
πάσχω. The future πείσομαι is from
*πένθ-σομαι.

Word Building

1. I leave; left, remaining
2. I enjoy, am glad, delighted; sweet, pleasant
3. I lie; false
4. war; of war, of an enemy, hostile
5. justice; just
6. I dwell; of the house, of the family, kin
7. war; warlike, hostile
8. I do; concerned with action, practical
9. stone; of stone
10. battle; fit for battle, warlike
11. I use; useful
12. I shine; shining, bright
13. I fear; fearful, frightened, frightening
14. I make, do; made, done
15. I write; written
16. I use; useful, good

Grammar 2

The grammar sections here mostly summarize uses of the cases with which students are already familiar. The accusative absolute (pages 139–140) is new.

Grammar 3

The dative in ταῖς ναυσὶ πλευσόμεθα (example e) may be thought of as either instrumental or of accompaniment.

Grammar 4

Notes:

Exercise 26b

1. Croesus, fearing that his son might be struck by a spear, told him to keep away from battle.
   δόρατι: dative of instrument.
   μάχης: genitive of separation.
2. A certain man, Phrygian by race, arrived at Sardis and asked Croesus for purification.

τὸ γένος: accusative of respect.
κάθαρσιν: αἰτέω takes two accusatives.

3. Croesus, when he had decided to purify him, asked where he had come from and from what father he was born.
   δόξαν: accusative absolute.
   τίνος πατρός: genitive of separation or origin.

4. As he had to tell the truth, the stranger answered, "I am the son of Gordias and my name is Adrastus and I am here after slaying my own brother involuntarily.
   δέον: accusative absolute.
   Γορδίου: genitive of separation or origin.
   μοι: dative of person concerned or of possession.

5. Croesus, receiving him, said, "You have come to friends; and so stay in our palace for as much time as you like."
   ὅσον . . . χρόνον: accusative of duration of time.

6. Some messengers, Mysian by race, arriving at Sardis, said, "Send us, king, your son so that we may remove a great wild beast from our country."
   γένος: accusative of respect.
   ἡμῖν: dative of indirect object or of the person concerned.
   τῆς χώρᾱς: genitive of separation.

7. Croesus replied, "I have two sons, of whom this one is much dearer to me than the other.
   μοι: dative of possession.
   πολλῷ: dative of degree of difference.
   τοῦ ἑτέρου: genitive of comparison.

8. "No by Zeus, I will not send him to you, but I will send Adrastus with young men and dogs."
   Δία: accusative of exclamation used in oaths.

ὑμῖν: dative of indirect object or
of the person concerned.

νεανίαις τε καὶ κυσίν: dative of
accompaniment.

9. The boy, not at all afraid of the
hunt, persuaded his father to send
him; "For," he said, "our battle is
not against men."

οὐδέν: adverbial accusative.

ἡμῖν: dative of the person concerned.

10. Being allowed to go to the hunt, Atys
set out at once.

ἔξον: accusative absolute.

11. After journeying a long way and
finding the beast, some of the young
men chased it and others stood
around in a circle and threw their
javelins.

μακρὰν . . . ὁδόν: accusative of
extent of space.

τῶν νεανιῶν: partitive genitive.

12. But Adrastus, aiming at the boar,
missed it and hit Croesus' son.

τοῦ ὑός and τοῦ and τοῦ . . .
παιδός: genitives with verbs of
aiming at, missing, and hit-
ting.

In no. 2, the meaning of Φρύγιος
and κάθαρσιν are to be deduced; τὸ γένος
appeared in Grammar 4c.

In nos. 11 and 12, the verb ἀκοντίζω
and the noun ὗς are to be recalled from
passage β:2 and 37.

Ο ΑΔΡΗΣΤΟΣ
ΕΑΥΤΟΝ ΣΦΑΖΕΙ

Title: "Adrastus Slays Himself "

Students will need to be given the
meaning of the verb.

Translation

Lines 1–6

Croesus was confounded by the
death of his son, and he was all the more
upset because his son had been killed by
the man whom he himself had purified
of murder (the man . . . had killed his

son). And grieving terribly at the disaster, he called on Zeus of purification,
calling (him) to witness what he had
suffered at the hands of his guest, and he
called on Zeus of hospitality, because he
had received the stranger in his palace
and had been sheltering unawares the
murderer of his child, and he called on
Zeus of companionship, because he had
sent Adrastus as a guard and found him
most hostile.

[φόνου (2): genitive of separation with
ἐκάθηρεν.

καθάρσιον . . . ἐφέστιον . . .
ἑταιρεῖον (3–5): the titles by which Croesus calls on Zeus are all regular cult titles, signifying different aspects of his
worship.

ἃ ὑπὸ τοῦ ξένου ἔπαθεν (3): we say
"suffered from . . . " or "suffered at the
hands of . . . " rather than "suffered
by . . . " Note omission of the antecedent.

ἐλάνθανε βόσκων (4): one may supply ἑαυτὸν with ἐλάνθανε, i.e., "he
escaped his own notice sheltering," "he
sheltered X unawares." See Chapter 20,
Grammar 3, page 55.

Compound verb to be deduced:
συμπέμψας (5).]

Lines 7–9

After this the Lydians arrived (were
present) carrying the corpse, and behind
(it) followed the murderer. And he,
standing before the corpse, tried to surrender himself to Croesus, stretching
forth his hands, telling him to slaughter
himself (Adrastus) over the corpse, saying that he ought to live no longer.

[παρεδίδου (8): conative imperfect,
"tried to surrender," but Croesus would
not accept his surrender.]

Lines 10–16

Hearing this, Croesus pities Adrastus, although in such deep trouble of his
own, and says to him, "I have all satis-
faction (justice) from you, since you
condemn yourself to death. You are not
responsible for this trouble of mine, but
one of the gods, who long ago fore-

warned me of what was (destined) to
be." And so Croesus buried his own son,
and Adrastus, this man (who was) the
murderer of his own brother and (was
the) murderer of (the son of) the man
who purified him, when there was no
man around the tomb, slaughters himself over the tomb.

Exercise 26c

1. ξένος τις, Φρύγιος τὸ γένος, ἐς
   Σάρδῑς ἀφικόμενος οὐ καθαρὸς ὢν
   τὰς χεῖρας, τὸν Κροῖσον ᾔτησεν
   ἑαυτὸν καθῆραι.
2. ὡς οἱ Μῡσοὶ τὸν Κροῖσον βοήθειαν
   ᾔτησαν, πρῶτον μὲν ὁ Κροῖσος οὐκ
   ἤθελεν/ἠθέλησε τὸν υἱὸν πέμψαι.
3. ὁ δὲ υἱός, "οὐ πρὸς ἄνδρας," ἔφη,

"ἡμῖν γίγνεται ἡ μάχη· μηδὲν οὖν
φοβοῦ ἀλλὰ πέμψον με."

4. ὁ οὖν Κροῖσος ἐπείσθη μὲν τοῖσδε
   τοῖς λόγοις, τὸν δὲ ξένον μεταπεμ-
   ψάμενος ἐκέλευσεν αὐτὸν φυλάσσειν
   τὸν παῖδα.
5. ἔξον ἰέναι, ὁ Ἄτῡς εὐθὺς ὁρμηθεὶς
   τῇ τρίτῃ ἡμέρᾳ ἐς τὸ ὄρος ἀφίκετο.
6. ὡς δὲ ηὗρον τὸν ὗν, ὁ ξένος
   ἀκοντίζων ἥμαρτεν μὲν τοῦ ὑός,
   ἔτυχε δὲ τοῦ παιδὸς τοῦ Κροίσου.

No. 1: it may be useful to review the
declension of χείρ (see teacher's handbook, Chapter 17, note after lines 43–50 of
passage β).

No. 3: remind students to use μηδέν
and not οὐδέν with the imperative.

27
Ο ΚΡΟΙΣΟΣ ΕΠΙ ΤΟΝ ΚΥΡΟΝ ΣΤΡΑΤΕΥΕΤΑΙ
(α)

Title: "Croesus Wages War against Cyrus"

The purposes of this chapter are:

1. Reading: (α and β) to give an adapted version of Herodotus' story of Croesus' campaign against Cyrus and of Cyrus' defeat of Croesus; in the final reading to give an adapted version of Herodotus' story of Labda, whose son, Cypselus, became tyrant of Corinth
2. Grammar: (α) to present the perfect and pluperfect, middle and passive; (β) to present the uses of πρίν and of the articular infinitive
3. Background: to present information on signs, dreams, and oracles as background for the story of Croesus and the Delphic oracle

Illustration

The photograph is taken from above the Treasury of the Athenians on the Sacred Way at Delphi, looking down on the theater and the temple of Apollo.

Caption under Illustration

"The messengers of Croesus, having arrived at Delphi, consulted the god": attention may be called to the perfect middle participle ἀφῑγμένοι, formally treated in this chapter. Students have seen the verb χράομαι (+ dat.) in the sense "I use, enjoy" since Chapter 14; they will have to deduce the new meaning here "consult" (a god or oracle). The new meaning is glossed at line 5 of passage α.

Vocabulary

New usage of preposition: ἐπί (+ acc.) = for (of time): ἐπὶ δύο ἔτεα (1).

New usage of preposition: πρός (+ acc.) = with (i.e., in relation to—not of accompaniment): πρὸς ᾽Αμασιν (45).

Dialect

The Ionic dialect. We introduce more Ionic forms in the readings in this and the following chapters, but we still allow a fair number of Attic spellings. Herodotus does not use movable ν. The only Ionic forms used in the exercises are the familiar ἐς (ἐσ-) and -σσ-.

Verbs

The following perfect and pluperfect passive forms appear in the readings: ἐστερημένος (α:2), τὰ γεγραμμένα (α:23), ἐπεποίητο (α:47), ἀφῑγμένος (β:6), τεταγμένοι ἦσαν (β:15), ἐσεσόφιστο (β:20), and διέφθαρτο (β:22).

Translation

Lines 1–13

Croesus sat in deep sorrow for two years after he was bereft of his son. After that, when Cyrus became king of the Persians and conquered the Medes and increased the power (the affairs) of Persia (the Persians), Croesus wanted, if he could, to stop their power before they became great. And so he decided to consult the best oracle, in order to learn whether he should wage war against the Persians; but first he had to find out (get to know) which oracle was the best. And so he made trial of all the oracles, sending messengers, some to Dodona, others to Delphi, and others to other places. And he told the messengers on the hundredth day from when(ever) they set out from Sardis to consult the oracles, asking what the king of the Lydians, Croesus, happened to be doing (at that moment), and to write down whatever the oracles said and bring it back to him.

[ποιῶν τυγχάνει (11): see Chapter 20, Grammar 3, page 55, for τυγχάνω with supplementary participle.

Δωδώνην (9): in the mountains of Epirus (in the northwest of Greece), was the seat of an ancient oracle of Zeus, the most prestigious oracle apart from that of Apollo at Delphi; the will of Zeus was revealed by the rustling of the leaves of a sacred oak.]

Lines 14–20

What the other oracles prophesied is told by no one, but at Delphi, as soon as the Lydians entered to consult the god, the Pythia says this:

I know the number of the sand(s) and the measures of the sea,
and I understand the dumb, and I hear him who does not speak.
A smell has come to my mind of a hard-shelled tortoise
being boiled in a bronze (kettle) along with the flesh of a lamb.

[The Pythia was the priestess of Apollo, who, after an elaborate ritual, sat upon a bronze tripod and, inspired by Apollo, delivered his response to the question put by the suppliant. On this occasion the Pythia gave the response without going through the ritual and before any question was put, but Apollo hears even "him who does not speak." On the hundredth day after his messengers had left Sardis, Croesus "cut up a tortoise and a lamb and boiled them together in a bronze pot" (Herodotus 1.48).]

Lines 21–26

When the Pythia had made this prophecy, the Lydians wrote it down and left for Sardis. And when the others also who had been sent around were present carrying their oracular responses, Croesus read all the writings. And of the others none pleased him, but when he heard the answer from Delphi, he at once prayed and accepted it, thinking that the only (true) oracle was that at Delphi, because it had found out what he himself had done.

[περιπεμφθέντες (22): compound verb to be deduced; help students as necessary with the aorist passive participle. The principal parts were given in the list

after passage 19α, page 35.
Compound verb to be deduced: ἐξηῦρεν (26).]

Lines 27–37

After this Croesus honored the god at Delphi and ordered all the Lydians each to sacrifice whatever each had/could. And he sent very many very beautiful gifts to Delphi and told those who were about to take them to ask the oracle whether Croesus should wage war against the Persians. And when the Lydians had arrived and dedicated (set up) their offerings, they consulted the oracle. And the Pythia answered as follows (these things), that if Croesus waged war against the Persians, he would destroy (break up) a great empire. And when Croesus learned the oracle, he was delighted, quite convinced (hoping altogether) that he would destroy the empire of Cyrus. And so with this hope he advanced into the Persian Empire. And when he arrived at the river Halys, he crossed with his army and took the city of the Pterians.

[ὅ τι ἔχοι ἕκαστος (28): the neuter of the pronoun ὅστις is usually written thus to distinguish it from ὅτι "that," "because." The optative is used here because the clause is indefinite in secondary sequence—"whatever each had." Note that ἔχω + an infinitive can mean "I can"; possibly we should supply θύειν here and translate "whatever each could sacrifice."

The river Halys (36) formed the eastern border of Croesus' empire, and the city of Pteria lay about 80 miles east of it, in the empire of Cyrus.]

Lines 38–49

And Cyrus gathered his own army and marched against (opposed) Croesus. And a great battle took place and many men fell on both sides; but finally they parted with neither side victorious (having conquered) as night came on. That is how the two armies fared in the contest (contended). But Croesus found fault with his army with regard to its size (for his army was much smaller than that of Cyrus), having found fault with this, when on the next day Cyrus did not attempt an attack (did not test/try him attacking), he marched off to Sardis, intending to summon the Egyptians according to their oath (for he had made an alliance with Amasis king of Egypt) and to send for the Babylonians (for an alliance had been made by him with them, too), and after calling these (allies) and gathering together his own army he intended to wage war against the Persians at the beginning of spring. [τὸ ἑαυτοῦ στράτευμα (42): be sure students take this as the object of μεμφθείς (41).

Compound verb to be deduced: ἀπήλαυνε (44).

στρατεύειν (49): Herodotus uses the active here, but usually he uses the verb in the middle voice.

According to Herodotus 1.77, Croesus also asked the Spartans, with whom he had an alliance, to send help.]

Principal Parts

In the Overview of the Greek Verb (page 3), we warned students that some verbs as they are presented by grammarians derive their parts from linguistically unrelated stems. The three verbs offered here exemplify that situation.

Note the irregular ε instead of the expected η in ἡρέθην.

Help students sort out the stems given with ἔρχομαι, and be sure they understand what principal parts come from what stems. In Attic prose ἔρχομαι is used only in the present indicative. Other forms in the present are supplied by forms of εἶμι (stems ἰ-/εἰ-): ἴω, ἴοιμι, ἴθι, ἰέναι, and ἰών. The imperfect is supplied by the imperfect of εἶμι: ᾖα. The future is supplied by εἶμι "I will go."

Note the Attic reduplication (see principal parts after reading 29β, page 187) in the second perfect ἐλ-ήλυθ-α.

Word Study

1. *philosophy*: ἡ φιλοσοφία (φίλος, -η, -ον + ἡ σοφία).
2. *logic*: ὁ λόγος = reason, λογικός, -ή, -όν, ἡ λογική (τέχνη).
3. *ethics*: τὸ ἦθος = custom, τὰ ἤθη = morals; τὰ ἠθικά = concerned with morals, a treatise on morals (Aristotle).
4. *epistemology*: ἡ ἐπιστήμη = knowledge (cf. ἐπίσταμαι = I know) + ὁ λόγος, -λογία = theory of knowledge (coined, 1856).
5. *metaphysics*: τὰ μετὰ τὰ φυσικά = the things after/beyond the natural; τὰ μεταφυσικά (Aristotle) = the branch of philosophy that deals with the first principles of things.
6. *political theory*: πολῑτικός, -ή, -όν + ἡ θεωρία = speculation, theory.

Grammar 1

Be sure that students understand why both the perfect passive participle (γεγραμμένα) and the pluperfect passive indicative (ἐπεποίητο) in the examples are translated with "had" in English. The "time" of the action described by a participle is always relative to the "time" of the action of the main verb.

Exercise 27a

1. ἐστερημένος (2): nominative masculine sing. of perfect participle passive of στερέω. Croesus sat for two years in deep grief after he was bereft of his son. Croesus was in a state of bereavement.
2. γεγραμμένα (23): accusative neuter pl. of perfect participle passive of γράφω. Croesus read all the writings, "the having been written things"; the act of writing had been done in the past, which resulted in a state (the written words) at the time when Croesus read them.
3. ἐπεποίητο (47): 3rd sing. pluperfect indicative passive of ποιέω. An alliance had been made by him

with them also. The alliance had been made and was in a state of completion at the time when Croesus summoned the Babylonians.

Exercise 27b

1. λέλυνται
2. λελυμένος
3. πεποίηται
4. νενΐκῆσθαι
5. γέγραπται
6. λέλειφθε
7. πεπρᾶγμένοι/αι/α εἰσίν
8. ἤγγελται
9. ᾠκῆσθαι
10. ἔψευσθε
11. πέπεισμαι
12. πεπεμμένοι/αι/α εἰσί.

1. ἐλέλυτο,
2. δεδεγμένοι ἦσαν
3. ἐπέπεισο
4. ἤγμην
5. ἀφῖκτο
6. ἐπεποίητο

Note that the accent of verbs, as in the case of ἀφῖκτο, does not precede the augment or reduplication.

Exercise 27c

1. An alliance had been made by Croesus with the Babylonians.
2. The hoplites, drawn up on the plain, were awaiting the enemy.
3. Everything had already been planned by the general.
4. Croesus had been persuaded by the oracle to invade Cyrus' empire.
5. The Lydians had been led out to battle to ward off the enemy.
6. The gates are open (have been opened); let us go in quickly.
7. Have you been persuaded by the doctor to take the boy to Epidaurus?
8. Do you understand the writing (the having been written things); for I can understand them.
9. The merchant denied that he (said that he had not) received the money.
10. The children left in the city by their fathers went to school every day.

Give special attention to the periphrastic pluperfect passive and perfect passive forms in nos. 5 and 6.

Exercise 27d

1. οἱ δοῦλοι τῷ δεσπότῃ λελυμένοι πάντες ἥδοντο/ἥσθησαν.
2. οἱ πρέσβεις ἤδη ἀφῑγμένοι ἦσαν ἐς τὰς πύλᾱς.
3. ὁ ἄγγελος ἔφη τὸν βασιλέᾱ πέπεισθαι τοῦ γέροντος φείσασθαι.
4. πεπέμμεθα ὡς λέξοντές σοι ὅτι ἡ ναῦς ἤδη ἐς τὸν λιμένα ἀφῖκται.
5. ἆρα τὸ ἀργύριον δέδεξαι ὃ ἔπεμψά σοι;

Signs, Dreams, and Oracles

For further reading, see *Civilization of the Ancient Mediterranean*, Vol. II, pp. 941–950; *The World of Athens*, pp. 97–100; and H. W. Parke, *Greek Oracles* (London, Hutchinson, 1967), chapter 7.

Ο ΚΡΟΙΣΟΣ ΕΠΙ ΤΟΝ ΚΥΡΟΝ ΣΤΡΑΤΕΥΕΤΑΙ (β)

Vocabulary

Note the double augment on the imperfect and aorist of ἀνέχομαι.

Translation

Lines 1–9

The moment Croesus marched off after the battle that had taken place at Pteria (Cyrus immediately, Croesus marching off), Cyrus, knowing that Croesus after marching away was going to disperse his army, resolved (deliberated with himself) to march as quickly as he could against Sardis. And after making this decision (when these things seemed good to him), he (also) did (it) quickly. For, marching his army into Lydia, he arrived himself as messenger to Croesus (i.e., he arrived before any messenger could report to

Croesus). Then Croesus, although he had reached desperation (having arrived at great difficulty), nevertheless led out the Lydians to battle. There was at that time no people in Asia braver or more stalwart than the Lydian; and they fought from (their fighting was from) horseback, and they themselves were good at riding.

[ἱππεύεσθαι (9): note the use of the infinitive to complete the meaning of the adjective ἀγαθός.]

Lines 10–23

When they (the two armies) came together on the plain before the city, when Cyrus saw the Lydians being drawn up for battle, fearing their cavalry, he did as follows; he ordered all his camels, which were carrying the food and baggage, to go in front of the rest of his army against Croesus' cavalry, and he told the infantry to follow the camels. And behind the infantry he posted all his cavalry. When they had all been drawn up, he exhorted (advised) them to kill all of the other Lydians without quarter (not sparing), but not to kill Croesus himself. And he posted the camels opposite the (i.e., Croesus') cavalry for the following reason; a horse is frightened of a camel and cannot endure either seeing the sight of it or smelling its smell. And so he had devised this (plan) so that Croesus' cavalry would be useless. And when they met in battle (came together to the battle), then, as soon as the horses smelled the camels and saw them, they turned back, and Croesus' hope was ruined.

[τῆς ἄλλης στρατιῆς (13): emphasize the idiom here, meaning "the rest of his army," not "the other army."

τῷ Κροίσῳ (20): dative of the person concerned, "the cavalry would be useless for Croesus" = "Croesus' cavalry would be useless." So also in the last line "the hope for Croesus" = "Croesus' hope."]

Lines 24–27

However, the Lydians were not cow-

ards. But when they learned what was happening, having leaped off their horses, they joined battle with the Persians on foot. But in time when many had fallen on both sides, the Lydians turned tail and were cooped up within (into) the walls and besieged by the Persians.

Principal Parts

The perfect active of λέγω is εἴρηκα and is formed from the verb εἴρω (ἐρ-/ ῥη-), which is found in Homer but is not used in Attic Greek and which also gives a future ἐρῶ, a perfect passive εἴρημαι, an aorist passive ἐρρήθην, and the noun ῥήτωρ, ῥήτορος. All of the alternative forms given in the set of principal parts (except εἴρω, which is enclosed in brackets) are used in Attic Greek with no difference in meaning between those derived from the three different stems.

The augment in εἶπον is retained in all moods.

Students should be reminded that λέγω introduces indirect statements with accusative and infinitive or with ὅτι/ὡς and that εἶπον introduces indirect statements with ὅτι/ὡς (see Chapter 23, Grammar 4, page 96).

The principal parts of the compound verb διαλέγομαι (+ *dat.*) "I talk to, converse with" are διαλέξομαι or διαλεχθήσομαι, διείλεγμαι, διελέχθην.

Word Building

Compound words are used freely by all Greek writers, especially by the poets, who seem to coin them freely. For example, Liddell and Scott list seventeen compounds formed from ναῦς, not counting adjectives, nouns, and verbs formed from these basic compounds.

N.B. All compound adjectives, including those compounded with ἀ-privative, are of two terminations, i.e., they have no separate feminine forms.

(a)
1. well-born
2. ill-born
3. lucky (with good luck)
4. unlucky (without luck)
5. unlearned, ignorant, stupid
6. ever remembered
(b)
1. loving mankind, benevolent
2. loving wisdom, philosophic
3. loving honor, ambitious
4. of short duration, short-lived
5. high-souled, generous
6. false prophet
(c)
1. ship battle, sea battle
2. shipowner, ship's captain
    (ὁ κλῆρος = lot, allotted portion,
    farm)
3. seafarer, sailor, passenger (ναῦς +
    βα-, βαίνω = one who goes on a
    ship)
4. people power, democracy
5. I rule the sea
6. child leader, tutor

Exercise 27e

1. ἀφῑγμένος (6): nominative mascu-
    line sing. of perfect participle of
    ἀφικνέομαι
2. τεταγμένοι ἦσαν (15): 3rd pl. of plu-
    perfect passive of τάσσω (τάττω)
3. ἐσεσόφιστο (20): 3rd sing. of pluper-
    fect of σοφίζομαι
4. διέφθαρτο (22): 3rd sing. of pluper-
    fect passive of διαφθείρω

Grammar 2

Notes:

Exercise 27f

1. The young man reached the city
    before day broke.
    οἱ αὐτουργοὶ ἐς τοὺς ἀγροὺς
    ἐπανῆλθον πρὶν γενέσθαι τὴν
    ἑσπέραν.
2. Before going away father told the

children to obey their mother in all
things.
πρὶν ἐπὶ τὸ ὄρος ἀναβῆναι, ὁ γέρων
πρὸς τῇ ὁδῷ ἀνεπαύετο.
3. Don't stop working until the sun
    sets.
    μὴ πειρώμεθα ἐς τὴν ναῦν ἐσβῆναι
    πρὶν ἂν κελεύσῃ ὁ ναύκληρος.
4. The messengers did not go away
    from Delphi until the Pythia had
    prophesied.
    ὁ Κροῖσος οὐκ ἐστρατεύσατο ἐπὶ
    τοὺς Πέρσας πρὶν τῷ μαντείῳ/τῷ
    χρηστηρίῳ ἐχρήσατο.
5. Before beginning battle Cyrus told
    his soldiers to spare Croesus.
    ὁ Κῦρος ἐς Σάρδῑς ἀφίκετο πρὶν τὸν
    Κροῖσον ἐπίστασθαι τί γίγνεται.

Grammar 3

Notes:

Exercise 27g

1. Themistocles especially was re-
    sponsible for the battle in the
    straits.
2. Croesus arrived at/reached a state
    of desperation (being at a loss).
3. What is justice? Justice is helping
    one's friends and harming one's
    enemies.
4. Are you skilled at playing the lyre?
5. By quickly pursuing the wild beast
    we will soon catch it.
6. Attacking the city, they came
    within hope of taking it.
7. Is there anything opposite to living,
    just as sleeping (is opposite) to be-
    ing awake?
8. Pericles, being general on this oc-
    casion, also had the same opinion
    about the Athenians not going out
    against (the enemy), as in the pre-
    vious invasion.

In no. 7, help as necessary with
ἐγρηγορέναι, the perfect active infinitive
of ἐγείρω; for principal parts, see the list
after passage 23α, page 88.

Η ΛΑΒΔΑ
ΣΩΙΖΕΙ ΤΟ ΠΑΙΔΙΟΝ

Title: "Labda Saves Her Baby"

For the diminutive παιδίον, see
Word Building, Chapter 25, page 124.

Translation

Lines 1–9

When Labda gave birth, the Bacchi-
adae send ten men to the village in
which Eetion lived, to kill the baby.
These men, having arrived and having
entered the courtyard, asked Labda for
the baby. She did not know why they had
come and, thinking that they were
friends of her husband, she brought the
baby and gave it to one of them. They
had decided (it had been planned by
them) on the way that the first of them to
receive (having taken) the baby would
kill it. And so Labda brought the baby
and gave it, but the baby by divine
chance smiled at the man (the one of the
men) who took it. And he was overcome
by pity (pitying) and could not kill it but
handed it over to the second, and he to the
third; and so it passed through all (their
hands) being handed over, since none
wanted to do the deed.

Lines 10–19

And so returning the baby to its
mother they went out, and standing at the
door they accused each other and
especially the man who had first received it, because he had not acted according to what had been decided, until
after a long time they decided to go in
again and all share in the murder. But
Labda heard all this, standing at the
very door; and fearing that if they got the
baby a second time they would kill it, she
takes it and hides it in a chest, knowing
that if they came back, they were going to
search everything. And this indeed is
what happened. They came in and
searched, and when the baby did not appear, they decided to go away and tell the
men who had sent them that they had

done everything that they had ordered.
And so they went away and said this.
And after this the baby grew up and because it had escaped this danger, it was
called Cypselus after the chest in which
it was hidden.

[ἑστῶτες (10) and ἑστῶσα (13): these
forms are from the second perfect of
ἵστημι (infinitive ἑ-στά-ναι, participle
ἑ-στα-ώς > ἑστώς, ἑστῶσα, ἑστός).

ὃ δὴ καὶ ἐγένετο (15–16): "which
thing indeed also happened"; ὅ is the
connecting relative.

ἐσελθοῦσι . . . καὶ ἐρευνήσασι (16):
datives with ἔδοξεν ("it seemed best to
them," "they decided").

Κύψελος (19): the story explains
Cypselus' name; the Greeks were very
fond of such etiological stories, especially in myth. In this case the story is
told about an important historical figure. Cypselus was the first of the Greek
tyrants and ruled Corinth with great
success until about 625 B.C. when he was
succeeded by his son Periander.

Compound verb to be deduced: δια-
φυγών (19).]

Exercise 27h

1. ὁ Κῦρος ἤδη ἐς Σάρδῑς ἀφῖκται· δεῖ
    ἡμᾶς παρασκευάζεθαι ὡς μαχ-
    ουμένους.

2. ἡ τῶν πολεμίων στρατιὰ τῷ
    Κύρῳ/ὑπὸ τοῦ Κύρου τεταγμένη ἐν
    τῷ πεδίῳ τῷ πρὸ τοῦ ἄστεως μένει.

3. αἱ κάμηλοι πρὸ τῆς ἄλλης στρατιᾶς
    τεταγμέναι εἰσίν. διὰ τί
    πεποίηται/πέπρᾱκται τοῦτο τοῖς
    Πέρσαις/ ὑπὸ τῶν Περσῶν;

4. οἱ ἵπποι τὰς καμήλους φοβούμενοι
    φεύγουσιν. δεῖ ἡμᾶς, καίπερ
    ἐμπείρους ὄντας τοῦ ἱππεύειν,
    πεζοὺς μάχεσθαι.

5. ἀνδρείως μὲν μεμαχήμεθα, τῷ δὲ
    σοφίσματι τοῦ Κύρου νενῑκήμεθα.

In no. 3, help as necessary with "the
rest of the army," cf. passage 27β:13; do
not penalize students if they use the Ionic
form στρατιῆς. "Before" in the English
sentence = "in front of " = πρό.

28
Ο ΑΠΟΛΛΩΝ
ΤΟΝ ΚΡΟΙΣΟΝ ΣΩΙΖΕΙ
(α)

Title: "Apollo Saves Croesus"

The purposes of this chapter are:

1. Reading: (α, β, and end reading) to give an adapted version of Herodotus' story of the fall of Sardis, Croesus on the pyre, and Croesus' recognition of his mistake; in an additional reading, to provide Bacchylides' account of Croesus on the pyre
2. Grammar: (α) to present the first and second perfect and pluperfect active; (β) to present verbs found most commonly in the perfect tense and a summary of the uses of ὡς
3. Background: to provide an account of various religious currents in ancient Greece

Vocabulary

ἁλίσκομαι: the stems are ἁλ- (for ϝαλ-) and ἁλο-. The digamma explains the augmented forms ἑάλων (from ἐϝάλων) and ἑάλωκα (from ἐϝάλωκα); remind students about the suffix (ί)σκω (see principal parts after passage 24β, pages 109–110). The verb is passive in meaning in all tenses, including the perfect.

The noun ἱππεύς is declined like βασιλεύς.

New usage of preposition: κατά (+ acc.) = after: κατ᾽ αὐτόν (11). Compare the use of this preposition in line 6 where it means "at," in line 9 where it means "down," in line 14 where it means "with regard to," and in line 24 where it means "according to."

Translation

Lines 1–13

Sardis was taken in the following way: when the fourteenth day of the siege of Croesus (for Croesus being besieged) came, Cyrus sent horsemen through his own army and announced that he would give gifts to the man who first climbed (set foot on) the wall. After this the army tried, but when there was no success, then, after the others had stopped (trying), a certain man called (by name) Hyroeades made an attempt approaching at that part of the acropolis where no guard was (had been) posted; for the acropolis was sheer and impregnable at this point. But this Hyroeades, having seen on the previous day one of the Lydians climbing down at this (part) of the acropolis for his helmet, which had rolled down from above, and picking it up, he thought about (it) and laid it to heart. Next thing, he himself had climbed up, and others of the Persians were climbing up after him. When many had got up there (had approached), Sardis was taken in this way and all the city was being sacked.

[ἐτέτακτο (7): note the pluperfect passive.

τότε δὲ δή (11): we follow Herodotus' text closely here; it is disconcertingly abbreviated; one moment Hyroeades is thinking about what he saw, the next moment he has already climbed the acropolis. Study of the tenses used in this paragraph offers useful insights into aspect.]

Lines 14–21

With regard to Croesus himself, this is what happened. He had a son (who was) in other respects capable, but mute. And when the wall was being taken, one of the Persians was advancing (going) to kill Croesus; and Croesus, seeing him coming against (him), because of his present misfortune, paid no heed (had got into a state of heedlessness), nor did it make any difference to him at all whether he died (to die). But this boy, the mute one, when he saw the Persian advancing, through fear broke into speech (broke his voice) and said, "Man, do not kill Croesus." This was the first thing this (boy) spoke, but after this he then

(now) continued speaking throughout
his whole life (for the whole time of his
life).

[ἄφωνος (15): cf. κωφός (26α:5).

τί (17): note that this is not the inter-
rogative τί (which always has an acute
accent), but rather the indefinite, which
is here accented because of the following
enclitic pronoun οἱ. The pronoun τι is
here accusative of respect, "with respect
to anything," "in any way," "at all."

Help as necessary with the infinitive ἀποθανεῖν (18), which is the subject
of διέφερε (17); literally, "nor did dying
make any difference to him," better
English, "nor did it matter to him
whether he died."]

Lines 22–30

The Persians held Sardis and took
Croesus himself alive, after he had
ruled for fourteen years and been besieged for fourteen days, and when he
had put an end to his own great empire
according to the oracle. After taking
him, the Persians brought him to Cyrus.
And he made a great pyre and put up on
it Croesus bound in shackles and twice
seven children of the Lydians, whether
intending to sacrifice them to some god,
or learning that Croesus was a god-
fearing man, he put him on the pyre for
this reason, wanting to learn whether
(if) one of the gods would save him from
being (so that he would not be) burned
alive.

[τεσσερεσκαίδεκα . . . τεσσερεσκαίδεκα
(23): these Ionic forms are accusative,
although they appear to have nominative
case endings (τεσσερεσ-). Coincidences
in the number of years and the number
of days of this sort struck the Greeks as
divinely ordained.]

Principal Parts

There is no difference in meaning
between the first and the second aorist of
φέρω. Note the Attic reduplication in the
perfect (see the principal parts after 29β,
page 187, and the note there in this
teacher's handbook for an explanation

of Attic reduplication and other examples). You may wish to mention Attic
reduplication in conjunction with the
grammar sections on the perfect and
pluperfect active in this chapter.

Other verbs from Book I with parts
from different stems are:

ἐρωτάω, ἐρωτήσω, ἠρόμην, ἠρώτηκα
I ask. The future and perfect are based
on the present, but the aorist is based on
ἔρομαι/εἴρομαι, ἐρήσομαι.

ζάω (*infinitive* ζῆν), (*imperfect*)
ἔζων, ζήσω or βιώσομαι (*from* βιόω),
(*second aorist*) ἐβίων, βεβίωκα I live.

σκοπέω, σκέψομαι, ἐσκεψάμην,
ἔσκεμμαι I look at, examine, consider.
Attic uses only the present and imperfect
of σκοπέω. The other tenses are supplied
by σκέπτομαι (stem σκεπ-).

Word Study

1. *gynecologist*: ἡ γυνή, τῆς γυναικός
    + ὁ λόγος, -λογία, -λογιστής = one
    who specializes in the study of the
    diseases of women (coined, 1847).

2. *pharmacologist*: τὸ φάρμακον =
    drug + ὁ λογιστής = one who spe-
    cializes in the use of medical drugs
    (coined, 1721).

3. *physiotherapist*: ἡ φύσις = nature
    + θεραπ- (as in θεραπεύω = I treat
    medically) + -ιστης = one who
    treats ailments by natural methods
    (coined recently).

4. *pediatrician*: ὁ παῖς + ἰᾱτρ-ός,
    ἰᾱτρ-εύω = one who specializes in
    treating children's ailments
    (coined recently).

5. *gerontologist*: ὁ γέρων, τοῦ γέροντ-
    ος + ὁ λογιστής = one who special-
    izes in the study of the diseases of
    the old (coined recently).

6. *anesthetist*: ἀναίσθητος, -ον =
    without feeling or sensation (ἀν-
    + αἰσθάνομαι = I perceive, feel)
    + -ιστης = one who specializes in
    making patients insensitive to
    pain (coined, 1848). Note that ἀν-
    is ἀ-privative before a vowel.

Grammar 1

Note that the accent of the perfect infinitive is not recessive.

Grammar 2

Notes:

Grammar 3

Notes:

Exercise 28a

1. λελύκᾱσι
2. λελυκότες
3. μεμαθηκέναι
4. πέπομφας
5. τέθνηκε
6. ἤχατε
7. δεδηλώκαμεν
8. νενῑκηκότες
9. δεδείχᾱσι
10. λελοιπέναι
11. γεγραφυῖα
12. πεπείκαμεν

1. ἐλελύκεμεν
2. ἐτετῑμήκει
3. ἤχεσαν
4. ἐπεπείκης
5. ἐπεπόμφεσαν
6. ἐδεδηλώκη

Exercise 28b

1. Have you done all that father has ordered?
2. Has your mother persuaded you to stay at home?
3. The Athenians have got into (are in) the greatest danger.
4. The hoplites have been defeated by the enemy, and the general himself is dead.
5. Those who had died in the battle have been honored by the people.
6. The slaves had loosed the oxen before the sun set.

7. Why have you left the plow in the field?
8. Being a young man then, I had not yet learned geometry.
9. But now a sophist has taught me all mathematics.
10. Archimedes, sitting in his bath, suddenly shouted (said shouting), "I've found (it)."

In nos. 8 and 9 students are to deduce γεωμετρίᾱν and μαθηματικά.

No 10: Archimedes is reputed to have shouted εὕρηκα when he discovered a method of determining the purity of the gold in the crown of Hiero, tyrant of Syracuse.

The California state motto ηὕρηκα is the only one in Greek.

Exercise 28c

1. οἱ δοῦλοι τοὺς βοῦς λελύκᾱσι καὶ/λελυκότες οἴκαδε ἤχᾱσιν.
2. τάς τε γυναῖκας καὶ τοὺς παῖδας ἐς τὰς νήσους πεπόμφαμεν.
3. ἡ γυνὴ πρὸς τῇ θύρᾳ ἕστηκε τὸν ἄνδρα μένουσα.
4. διὰ τί τοῦτο πεποίηκας; ὁ γὰρ διδάσκαλός σοι δεδήλωκε/δέδειχε τί δεῖ /χρῆ ποιεῖν/ποιῆσαι.
5. ἄμεινόν ἐστι τεθηκέναι/τεθνάναι ἢ αἰσχρῶς ζῆν.

Rationalism and Mysticism

For further reading, see *The Oxford History of the Classical World*, pp. 113–123 and 267–269, and *The World of Athens*, pp. 124–126.

Ο ΑΠΟΛΛΩΝ ΤΟΝ ΚΡΟΙΣΟΝ ΣΩΙΖΕΙ (β)

Vocabulary

Note that Attic uses the compound forms ἀναμιμνῄσκω, ἀναμνήσω, and ἀνέμνησα with the transitive meaning

"I remind someone" and that it uses the uncompounded forms μέμνημαι, ἐμνήσθην, and μνησθήσομαι to mean "I remember," "I remembered," and "I will remember."

Translation

Lines 1–9
That is what Cyrus did, but Croesus standing on the pyre, although he was in such great trouble, remembered the word(s) of Solon, that none of the living is happy. When he remembered this, he groaned aloud, and three times from the deep silence he called the name "Solon." And Cyrus hearing this told his interpreters to ask Croesus who this was he was calling on. And at first when Croesus was asked he kept silence, but finally when he was forced, he said that Solon (being) an Athenian had come to him and after seeing all his wealth had considered it worthless (of no importance), and that everything had turned out for him as he (Solon) had said.
[ἀποβεβήκοι (9): the optative is here used in indirect speech to represent a perfect indicative of the direct words in secondary sequence. In this passage we follow Herodotus in using ἦλθε (7, indicative) and ἀποβεβήκοι (9, optative) in the same sentence of indirect speech; it is often hard to see any reason for the writer's preference in this matter; in this instance it is hardly convincing to say that the writer uses the indicative because he wishes his words to be "more vivid."]

Lines 10–17
Croesus told this story (related these things), and the pyre had already been lit, and the furthest parts were burning. And Cyrus, hearing from his interpreters what Croesus had said, changed his mind and, pondering that he who was (being) himself a man was giving another man, who had been no less than himself in his good fortune, alive to the fire, and knowing that in human affairs

(of the things among men) nothing was safe, told (his men) to put out the burning fire as quickly as possible and to bring down Croesus and those with Croesus. And those who tried could not any longer get control over the fire.
[οὐκ . . . ἔτι (17): note the splitting of the word students are familiar with as the single word, οὐκέτι.]

Lines 18–33
Then it is said by the Lydians that Croesus, learning of Cyrus' change of mind, shouted for Apollo, calling him to stand by him and save him from his present trouble. Croesus called the god in tears, and, from a clear sky and windless calm, clouds suddenly gathered, and a storm broke out and much rain, and the pyre was put out. So Cyrus learned that Croesus was both dear to the gods and a good man, and he asked him this, "Croesus, what man (which of men) persuaded you to march against my land and become my enemy instead of my friend?" And he said, "O king, I did this to your good luck and to my bad luck; and the god of the Greeks is responsible for these things, who urged me to wage war. For no one is so foolish that he (who) chooses war in preference to peace; for in peace sons bury their fathers, but in war fathers bury their sons. But it was god's will (it was dear to a god) that this should happen, I suppose." So he spoke, and Cyrus freed him and made him sit down near him and honored him greatly.
[The first half of this paragraph is in continuous indirect speech, reporting what the Lydians say; hence the accusatives and infinitives.

συνδραμεῖν (21): compound verb to be deduced; make sure that students know that συν- in compounds means "together."

τῇ σῇ μὲν εὐδαιμονίῃ, τῇ δὲ ἐμαυτοῦ κακοδαιμονίῃ (26–27): dative of accompanying circumstance.

οὐδεὶς . . . οὕτω ἀνόητός ἐστι ὅστις . . . αἱρέεται (28–29): this would more commonly be expressed: οὐδεὶς οὕτω ἀνόητός ἐστι ὥστε . . . αἱρεῖσθαι. We keep Herodotus' text (notice that he does not use movable ν, e.g., ἐστι ὅστις).]

Principal Parts

Knowledge of the fact that the stem is extended with an ε will help students understand the apparent irregularities of these verbs.

Word Building

1. δω-/δο-: giving; gift; traitor; treachery
2. θη-/θε-: placing, laying down, thesis (*philosophical term*); law-giver (compare νόμον τίθεμαι = I make a law); proposal, assumption, hypothesis
3. στη-/στα-: standing, position, po-litical party, faction (the latter is by far the most common meaning of στάσις); one who stands before, a leader; leadership
4. γεν-/γον-: family, race; origin, creation; ancestor
5. γνω-/γνο-: opinion, judgment; knowledge; known, knowable
6. μνη-/μνα-: memory; memorial; memorial (the suffix -εῖον denotes either the means of action or the place of action, and τὸ μνημεῖον means either a record or a monu-ment); ever remembered

Grammar 4

Notes:

Grammar 5

Notes:

Exercise 28d

1. This woman, (as) it seems, is

most prudent by nature (has a very wise character).
2. I don't know a more prudent woman; and so I want to marry her.
3. But I'm afraid her father may refuse to give her to me (in mar-riage).
4. The young men, being (by nature) very brave, were not afraid.
5. The boys are accustomed to go to school every day.
6. But they do not always remember all that the teacher says.
7. Croesus remembered all that Solon had said.
8. The majority of the Athenians were accustomed to living in the country.
9. When we arrived at the Piraeus, we at once hurried to the agora.
10. There we heard someone saying that the ships had already arrived at the harbor.
11. And so let us go to the harbor to watch the ships.
12. How beautiful the ships are! How quickly they are sailing in!
13. This sailor says that two ships have not yet arrived.
14. Now it is possible to see the ships sailing as quickly as possible to-ward Salamis.
15. Listen! The admiral has got into a rage, (as) it seems, and blames the rowers for rowing (as rowing) slowly.

In no. 3, the compound verb ἐκδοῦναι is to be deduced.
In no. 12, the compound verb ἐσπλέουσιν is to be deduced.

Exercise 28e

1. ὡς οἴκαδε ἐπανήλθομεν/οἴκαδε ἐπανελθόντες τὴν μητέρα εἴδομεν πρὸς τῇ θύρᾳ ἑστηκυῖαν.
2. καίπερ εὐμενὴς πεφυκυῖα, ὠργίζετο/ὠργίσθη καὶ ἡμᾶς ἐμέμφετο ὡς ὀψὲ ἐπανελθόντας.

3. "πᾶσαν τὴν ἡμέραν μεμένηκα,"
    ἔφη, "φοβουμένη μὴ τεθνήκητε."
4. "ὡς τάχιστα ἐληλύθαμεν," ἔφην,
    "καὶ οὐκ εἰώθαμεν ὀψὲ ἐπανιέναι."

Ο ΚΡΟΙΣΟΣ ΓΙΓΝΩΣΚΕΙ ΤΗΝ ΕΑΥΤΟΥ ΑΜΑΡΤΙΑΝ

Title: "Croesus Learns (of) His Mistake"

Students will deduce the noun from their knowledge of the verb ἁμαρτάνω.

Translation

Lines 1–8
Cyrus, admiring Croesus for his wisdom, told him to ask for whatever gift he wanted. And Croesus said, "Master, you will show me the greatest favor, if you allow me to ask the god of the Greeks, whom I honored exceedingly, whether (if) it is his custom (the custom for him) to deceive those who do him well." And Cyrus asked why he asked for this. And Croesus told him the whole story (related all things), going through in detail the answers of the oracles and the offerings that he had sent to Delphi and how, induced by the oracle, he had waged war against the Persians. And Cyrus laughed and said, "You will get this from me and anything else you want."
[χαριῇ (2): help as necessary with this second person singular future indicative of χαρίζομαι.
δέῃ (8): help as necessary with this second person singular of δέομαι (+ gen.) "I want."]

Lines 9–11
When he heard this, Croesus sent messengers to Delphi and told them to put the shackles down in the temple and ask the god whether he was not at all (τι) ashamed (at) having induced Croesus by his oracles to wage war against the Persians.

Lines 12–19
And when the Lydians arrived and said what they had been commanded to

say, the Pythia spoke as follows: "It is impossible even for a god to escape his fated lot. With regard to the oracle that he was given (the having happened oracle) Croesus does not rightly blame (me); for Apollo said that if he waged war against the Persians, he would destroy a great empire. And any man who was going to take sound counsel (deliberate well) should have asked in addition whether he (Apollo) meant his own or Cyrus' empire." So the Pythia answered the Lydians, and they returned to Sardis and announced this to Croesus. And when he heard it, he acknowledged that the mistake was his, not the god's.
[συνέγνω (18): συγγιγνώσκω means "I know or think something with someone," hence, e.g., "share a secret"; ἐμαυτῷ συγγιγνώσκω = "I am conscious of something," "I admit," "I confess an error." Herodotus here omits ἐμαυτῷ.]

Exercise 28f

1. ὁ Κροῖσος ἀγγέλους πρὸς τοὺς Δελφοὺς πέπομφεν ὡς τὸν θεὸν ἐρωτήσοντας διὰ τί ὁ θεὸς ἑαυτὸν προδέδωκεν.
2. οἱ ἄγγελοι ἐς τοὺς Δελφοὺς ἀφῖγμένοι εἰσὶ καὶ ἐν τῷ ἱερῷ ἑστηκότες τῷ μαντείῳ κέχρηνται.
3. ἡ Πῡθίᾱ ἐξήγηται τὸν τοῦ Ἀπόλλωνος χρησμόν· ὁ θεὸς τὸν Κροῖσον μέμφεται ὡς οὐ σώφρονα γενόμενον/πεφῡκότα.
4. ὁ Κροῖσος τὸν χρησμὸν ἀκηκοὼς γιγνώσκει αὐτὸς ἁμαρτών.
5. "φεῦ, φεῦ," φησίν· "ὡς ἀνόητος ἦν αὐτός, ὡς ἔοικε, τὴν ἐμαυτοῦ ἀρχὴν καταλέλυκα."

We supply ἑαυτόν in no. 1; indirect reflexives will be touched on in Chapter 29, Grammar 3, pages 183–184.

ΑΛΛΟΣ ΛΟΓΟΣ ΠΕΡΙ ΤΟΥ ΚΡΟΙΣΟΥ

Title: "Another Story about Croesus"

Illustration

Belly amphora by the Myson Painter, ca. 500 B.C. (Paris, Louvre).

Caption under Illustration

"Croesus having mounted the funeral pyre is making a libation": the perfect participle is used because Croesus' past act of mounting results in his being set on the pyre (a present state of affairs).

Text

The text we follow for the extract from Bacchylides is that of Bruno Snell, Teubner, 1961. Lines 19–21 of our extract are particularly fragmentary in the papyrus, with only μῦρίων (19), ν (end of 20), and ἄστυ (21) preserved.

Translation

For once, when Zeus having fulfilled his fated judgment, Sardis was being taken by the army of the Persians, Apollo of the golden sword guarded even the ruler of horse-taming Lydia, Croesus; he, having come to the day he had never expected to see (the unexpected day), was not going to/did not intend to wait for tearful slavery; but he heaped up a pyre before his bronze-walled courtyard, and there he mounted with his dear wife and with his fair-haired daughters weeping inconsolably; and he raised his hands to the high air and calls aloud: "Mighty spirit, where is the gratitude of the gods? And where is the lord, son of Leto? The house of Alyattes has vanished, and what return from Pytho now appears for my countless gifts? The Medes are sacking the city taken by the spear; the Pactolus eddying with gold is reddened with blood; the women are led shamefully from their well-built palaces. What was hateful before (is now) dear; it is sweetest to die." So much he said and told the delicately-stepping (servant) to light the wooden pyre. And the maidens shrieked and threw up their own hands to their mother; for death foreseen is the most hateful death for mortals. But when the bright strength of the terrible fire was rushing through (the pyre), Zeus set a black-covering cloud above it and quenched the yellow flame. Nothing is incredible, whatever the care of the gods brings to pass; then Apollo born in Delos carried the old man (i.e., Croesus) to the Hyperboreans and settled him there with the maidens of the slender ankles (i.e., his daughters), because of his piety, because he had sent to holy Pytho the greatest (gifts) of (all) mortals.

[φίλᾱς (28): "their own," a common Homeric meaning.]

29
ΜΕΓΑ ΤΟ ΤΗΣ ΘΑΛΑΣΣΗΣ ΚΡΑΤΟΣ
(α)

Title: "Sea Power Is a Great Thing"

This is quoted from the speech Pericles made to the Assembly just before the outbreak of the war (see Chapter 21β:23–24).

The purposes of this chapter are:

1. Reading: (α and β) to present a slightly adapted version of the first of a pair of naval battle narratives from Thucydides; in the tail reading to give an adapted version of Thucydides' account of preparations for a second naval battle
2. Grammar: (α) to present the verb οἶδα; clauses of result with ὥστε; and the pronouns οὗ and σφῶν; (β) to present the potential use of the optative in main clauses
3. Background: to provide background information on Thucydides

Vocabulary

The word for "dawn" is declined ἕως, ἕω, ἕῳ, ἕω (no plural); cf. the declension of ὁ λαγώς, "hare," given in the first teacher's handbook, page 22. This is the so-called Attic declension.

Translation

Lines 1–4

The following winter the Athenians sent twenty ships around the Peloponnesus with (and) Phormio as general, who, based on Naupactus, kept guard so that no one should sail out of Corinth and the Crisaean Gulf (the Gulf of Corinth) or sail in.
[Κρισαίου κόλπου (4): Crisa was a city in Phocis near Delphi; the term refers to the Gulf of Corinth.
If the Athenians had been able to blockade the Gulf of Corinth effectively,

they might have been able to starve Corinth into submission, since she had to import nearly all her grain. It was very difficult, however, to make a complete blockade with triremes, which did not normally sail at night, and a squadron of twenty ships would have been too small to keep up a continuous blockade. They could, however, intercept fleets trying to get out of the gulf. Naupactus was at a strategic point, near the narrowest part of the gulf; it had been seized by Athens at the beginning of the First Peloponnesian War, and Messenians who left the Peloponnesus after the capture of Ithome by the Spartans were settled there by the Athenians in 459 B.C.]

Lines 5–9

The Corinthians and their allies were compelled to fight a sea battle about this time (around the same days) against Phormio and the twenty Athenian ships (ships of the Athenians) that were on guard at Naupactus. For Phormio was watching them as they were sailing along outside the gulf, wanting to attack them in open waters. [The map on page 178 shows Phormio's tactics. He thought, quite rightly, that the superior Athenian seamanship would be more effective in open waters, and so he let the Corinthian fleet sail unmolested until it was through the narrows.]

Lines 10–17

The Corinthians and their allies were sailing, prepared not for battle but more for carrying troops to Acarnania, and they did not think (not thinking) that the Athenians would dare start (make) a naval battle. But sailing past their own land, they saw the Athenians sailing along opposite, and when they were crossing from Patrae in Achaea toward the mainland opposite, they saw the Athenians sailing toward them from Chalcis. So they are compelled to fight in the middle of the straits.
[Ἀκαρνανίαν (11): locate Acarnania for

students on a wall map of Greece.

Acarnania and northwest Greece were one of the main theaters of war; both sides were trying to control the northwest coast of Greece, which was the route followed by grain ships sailing to and from Sicily, the main source of grain for the cities of the Peloponnesus.

ἂν τολμῆσαι (12): a potential optative in indirect statement with the infinitive substituted for the optative and the particle ἂν retained.]

Lines 18–26

And the Peloponnesians formed a circle of their ships, as large as they were able, the prows (facing) outward and the sterns inward, and they put the light boats, which were sailing with them, inside. And the Athenians, drawn up in single file, sailed around them in a circle and compressed them into a small (space), always sailing by within a hair's breadth; an order had been given to them by Phormio beforehand that they were not to attack until he gave the signal. For he expected that their formation would not hold but that their ships would crash into each other and that the boats would cause confusion; and if the breeze blew out of the gulf, which usually happened toward dawn, they would not stay still for any time (they would stay still, i.e., keep their formation, for no time).

[The Peloponnesian tactics were foolish and resulted from their fear of the superior Athenian seamanship. Phormio's tactics were extraordinarily bold and could not have been carried out except by extremely skillful crews.

Compound verbs to be deduced: ξυνέπλει (20), περιέπλεον (21).

προείρητο . . . σημήνῃ (22–23) and ἤλπιζε . . . αὐτούς (23–26): for the treatment of complex sentences in indirect speech, see Chapter 30, Grammar 2, pages 200–202. The sentence in lines 22–23 is analyzed on page 202 (iii). Full discussion should be left until Chapter 30, Grammar 2.]

Principal Parts

See Appendix for further discussion of these forms.

Word Study

The definitions given below are those of the Greek words and not of the English words as currently used.

1. *theology*: ἡ θεολογίᾱ (ὁ θεός + -λογίᾱ) = the study of God.
2. *Bible*: ἡ βύβλος/βίβλος, τὸ βιβλίον = The Book.
3. *dogma*: τὸ δόγμα = belief.
4. *orthodoxy*: ἡ ὀρθοδοξίᾱ (ὀρθός, -ή, -όν + ἡ δόξα) = right belief.
5. *heresy*: ἡ αἵρεσις (αἱρέομαι = I take for myself, choose) = choice, system of beliefs, religious or philosophical sect.
6. *ecclesiastical*: ἐκκλησιαστικός, -ή, -όν = concerned with the ἐκκλησίᾱ, the name given to the church by early Christians.

Grammar 1

Notes:

Exercise 29a

1. Do you know where the foreigners have come from?
2. No one knew where the merchants had sailed to.
3. I have never seen such an uproar. Do you know what has happened?
4. The farmer, not knowing what the foreigner wanted, was at a loss as to what he should do.
5. These men neither know when the Assembly will take place, nor do they want to know.
6. Wicked man, know well that you will suffer terribly (for) having done such terrible things.
7. The citizens did not know that the ambassador had lied.

8. The messengers went away before they knew whether we would receive their proposals or not.
9. Wait until you know what we want.
10. The women, knowing that their husbands had got into danger, were very afraid.

Exercise 29b

1. εὖ ἴσθι τὸν βασιλέα ὀργιζόμενον.
2. ἆρ' οἶσθα ποῖ ἐληλύθᾱσιν οἱ παῖδες;
3. βούλομαι εἰδέναι διὰ τί τοῦτο ἐποίησας.
4. ἡ γυνὴ εὖ εἰδυῖα τί ἐγένετο τῷ ἀνδρὶ τὸ ἀληθὲς εἶπεν.
5. οὐκ εἰδότες πότε ἀφίξεται ἡ ναῦς, πᾶσαν τὴν ἡμέρᾱν ἐν τῷ λιμένι ἔμενον.
6. ὅταν εἰδῶμεν τίς τοῦτο ἐποίησεν, εὐθύς σοι/εὐθὺς ὑμῖν λέξομεν/ἐροῦμεν.
7. ὁ δῆμος δι' ὀλίγου ᾔδει τὸν ῥήτορα οὐ τὰ ἀληθῆ λέγοντα.
8. ὁ γέρων ἀπῆλθε πρὶν ἀκοῦσαι πάντα ὅσα ἴσμεν.
9. δι' ὀλίγου εἰσόμεθα διὰ τί οὐκ ἔμεινεν.
10. οἱ τοῦ παιδὸς τεκόντες ᾔδεσαν αὐτὸν οὐ λέγοντα τὰ ἀληθῆ.

Grammar 2

Notes:

Exercise 29c

1. The Corinthians had so many ships that they did not think that the Athenians would start (make) a naval battle.
2. Phormio was so confident that he attacked (was confident enough to attack) the Corinthians although they had so many ships.
3. The wind was so strong that the ships crashed into each other.
4. τὸν πατέρα τοσοῦτον χρόνον ἐν τῇ ἀγορᾷ ἐμένομεν ὥστε μάλα κάμνομεν.

5. πάντα ἐθέλω πράσσειν ὥστε οἴκαδε ἐπανιέναι.
6. ἰδού· τέλος ὁ πατὴρ προσχωρεῖ, ὥστε ἡμῖν οἴκαδε σπεύδειν ἔξεστιν.
7. οἴκαδε ἐπανελθόντες οἱ παῖδες οὕτω ἔκαμνον ὥστε καθεύδειν.

Grammar 3

Notes:

Exercise 29d

1. The slaves were afraid that their master would become angry with them.
2. The Corinthians did not know that the Athenians had seen them.
3. The woman hoped that her husband would help her.
4. The ambassadors said that the king had sent them.
5. The Athenians became angry seeing their property destroyed.

Thucydides

For further reading, see *Ancient Writers*, Vol. I, pp. 267–289; *Cambridge History of Classical Literature*, Vol. I, pp. 441–456; and *The Oxford History of the Classical World*, pp. 193–197.

ΜΕΓΑ ΤΟ ΤΗΣ ΘΑΛΑΣΣΗΣ ΚΡΑΤΟΣ (β)

Vocabulary

καταδύω: the uncompounded forms of the second aorist are as follows: (*indicative*) ἔδῡν, ἔδῡς, ἔδῡ, ἔδῡμεν, ἔδῡτε, ἔδῡσαν; (*subjunctive*) δύω, δύῃς, δύῃ, δύωμεν, δύητε, δύωσι; (*imperative*) δῦθι, δύτω, δῦτε, δύντων; (*infinitive*) δῦναι, (*participle*) δύς, δῦσα, δύν.

Translation

Lines 1–11

When the breeze came down, and the ships, which were (being) already in a confined (little) space, were thrown into confusion at once by the wind and by the boats, and ship fell against ship, and the sailors shouting and abusing each other (using shouts and abuse) heard none (nothing) of the orders that were being passed along, then Phormio gives the signal; and the Athenians falling on them first sink one of the flagships and then destroyed the others wherever they went, and put them into a panic, so that they flee to Patrae and Dyme in Achaea. And the Athenians chased them and took twelve ships and picked up most of the men from them; then they sailed away toward Moly-crion, and after setting up a trophy at Rhion they withdrew to Naupactus.

[ἧ χωρήσειαν διέφθειρον (6): ἧ χωρή-σειαν is an indefinite clause with the optative in secondary sequence; see Chapter 25, Grammar 2b, page 117.

τῷ 'Ρίῳ (10): this is the headland (ῥίον) on the north shore of the Gulf of Corinth, referred to in the tail reading (line 4) as τὸ 'Ρίον τὸ Μολυκρικόν and now known as Antirrhium Promontory. The headland opposite on the south shore was known as τὸ 'Ρίον τὸ 'Αχαϊκόν (see tail reading, line 5) and is now known as Rhium Promontory.]

Lines 12–21

The Peloponnesians sailed along with the rest of their ships straight from Dyme and Patrae to Cyllene. And Cnemus and the ships of the Leucadians arrive at Cyllene from Leucas. And the Spartans also send advisers for Cnemus to the fleet (the ships), telling him to pre-pare another and more successful (better) sea battle and not to be shut out from the sea by a few ships. For they did not think that their fleet was deficient but that some cowardice had occurred; and so they sent off the advisers in anger. And those who had come with

Cnemus sent for other ships, summon-ing their allies to help, and they fitted out the ships already there (as) for battle.

[εὐθύς (12): previously this word has been used in the sense of "immedi-ately"; here and elsewhere in the readings from Thucydides it means "straight" (from one place to another, here from Dyme and Patrae to Cyllene.

Κυλλήνην . . . Λευκάδος (13): locate Cyllene and Leucas for students on a wall map of Greece.

Κνῆμος (14): Cnemus was the Spar-tan commander in chief in this theater of operations, based on Leucas, an is-land allied to the Peloponnesians; he sails to Cyllene with the ships of the Leu-cadian navy; this is clear in the Greek, since ἐκείνων (14) follows ἀπὸ Λευκάδος (13).]

Lines 22–28

And Phormio also sends messen-gers to Athens, to announce their (the enemy's) preparations and to tell of the battle that they had won, and telling them to send off to him as many ships as possible quickly, as he expected every day to fight a naval battle (the expecta-tion every day being that he would fight a naval battle). And the Athenians send him twenty ships and instructed the commander of the squadron (the man bringing them) in addition to go to Crete first to help some allies there.

Principal Parts

These verbs show a form of redupli-cation in the perfect tense known as Attic reduplication, although it occurs also outside the Attic dialect. The initial vowel and consonant of the stem on which the perfect is based are repeated, and what was originally the initial vowel is lengthened, thus ἐλα- > ἐλ-ήλα-κα. Other Attic reduplicated per-fects already given are ἀπόλ-ωλ-α (Vocabulary 26α, page 128), ἐλ-ήλυθ-α (Principal Parts 27α, page 146), and ἐν-ήνοχ-α, ἐν-ήνεγ-μαι (Principal Parts 28α, page 162).

The form ἐλαύνω comes from the stem ἐλα- + the nasal infix -υν- (see the lists of principal parts after passages 23β and 24α for other verbs with nasal infixes.

Word Building

1. custom, justice, right, lawsuit, penalty
2. just
3. I judge
4. a judge (at Athens a member of the jury panel, a juror)
5. concerned with law or trials
6. unjust

Here is a similar set based on σχολή:

  ἡ σχολή: leisure, study
  σχολαῖος, -ᾱ, -ον: leisurely
  σχολάζω: I am at leisure, I study
  ὁ σχολαστής: a man of leisure (this word only occurs in late Greek)
  σχολαστικός, -ή, -όν: inclined to leisure, inclined to study, scholarly
  ἄσχολος, -ον: without leisure, busy
  ἡ ἀσχολίᾱ: want (or lack) of leisure, business

Note that σχολαῖος, ἄσχολος, and ἀσχολίᾱ have the connotations of only the first meaning of σχολή.

Grammar 4

Notes:

Note that the negative with the potential optative is οὐ instead of μή, which is used with the optative of wish (see Chapter 25, Grammar 1, page 116). In future less vivid conditions, the main clause (which resembles a potential optative) also uses οὐ as the negative (see Chapter 30, page 194).

Exercise 29e

1. I wouldn't want to harm the child.
2. I couldn't do this.
3. I would gladly hear/I should like to hear what the young man wants.

4. Perhaps the king would give us some money.
5. We would scarcely obey the general if he gives such orders (giving such orders).
6. Would you tell me what has happened?
7. Who would trust this man, who has often lied to us?
8. You wouldn't escape the notice of the gods doing wrong (you would be seen by the gods if you should do wrong).
9. As they are hostile they would not want to help us.
10. You couldn't step into the same river twice. (This is quoted by Plato, *Cratylus* 402a, from the philosopher Heraclitus, who maintained that everything is in a state of flux—πάντα ῥεῖ, and so the river you step into tomorrow will be different from the one you step into today).

Exercise 29f

1. βουλοίμην ἂν τὸν ἰᾱτρὸν εὐθὺς ἰδεῖν.
2. ἴσως ἂν οὐκ ὠφελοίη με.
3. ἡδέως ἂν ἴοιμι ἐς τὴν Ἐπίδαυρον.
4. ὁ θεὸς δύναιτο ἄν με ἰᾱτρεύειν.
5. λέγοις ἄν μοι πότε μέλλει πλεύσεσθαι ἡ ναῦς;

ΑΜΦΟΤΕΡΟΙ ΠΑΡΑΣΚΕΥΑΖΟΝΤΑΙ ΩΣ ΑΥΘΙΣ ΝΑΥΜΑΧΗΣΟΝΤΕΣ

Title: "Both Sides Prepare for Another Naval Battle"

Translation

Lines 1–7
  The Peloponnesians in Cyllene, while the Athenians were detained (held back) around Crete, sailed ready (having been prepared) (as) for battle to Panormus in Achaea (of Achaea), where the land force of the Peloponnesians had come to their aid. And Phormio also

sailed along to Molycrian Rhion and anchored beyond (outside) it with the twenty ships, with which he had (already) fought. The Peloponnesians themselves also came to anchor at Rhion in Achaea, not far from Panormus, with seventy-seven ships, when they actually saw the Athenians.

[ὡρμίσαντο (6): the aorist followed by the "when" clause suggests that just as the Peloponnesians dropped anchor they saw the Athenian squadron; the distance between the two headlands is less than a mile and a quarter.

ὡρμίσαντο καὶ αὐτοί . . . ἐπειδὴ καὶ τοὺς Ἀθηναίους εἶδον (6–7): two uses of adverbial καί are illustrated here. The first καί emphasizes the single word αὐτοί = "they themselves also." The second καί gives emphasis to its whole clause, e.g., "when they actually saw. . . . "]

Lines 8–15

And for six or seven days they were lying at anchor opposite each other, practicing and preparing for battle, the Peloponnesians determined (having the intention) not to sail outside the Rhions into the broad waters, afraid of their former misfortune, and the Athenians (determined) not to sail into the narrows, thinking that battle in a little space was in their (the enemy's) favor. Then Cnemus and the other generals of the Peloponnesians, wanting to have the engagement quickly, before any aid came from Athens, called together the

troops and, seeing that the majority of them were afraid because of their former defeat and that their morale was low (they were not eager), exhorted them. [Words glossed earlier in chapter: ἐν ὀλίγῳ in a little (space).

Compound verb to be deduced: ξυνεκάλεσαν (14).

Thucydides proceeds to quote the speeches, first of the Peloponnesian commanders, then of Phormio to his troops.]

Exercise 29g

1. τοσαῦται νῆες ἦσαν τοῖς Κορινθίοις ὥστε μὴ φοβεῖσθαι τοὺς Ἀθηναίους ὀλίγους ὄντας. (Or ὥστε οὐκ ἐφοβοῦντο might be acceptable, but the sense suggests a "natural" rather than an "actual" consequence.)

2. ᾤοντο γὰρ τοὺς Ἀθηναίους οὐκ ἂν τολμῆσαι σφίσι προσβαλεῖν. (Or οὐ τολμήσειν σφίσι προσβαλεῖν could be used.)

3. ὡς δὲ ἐς τὴν εὐρυχωρίᾱν ἀφίκοντο, εἶδον τοὺς Ἀθηναίους σφίσι προσπλέοντας.

4. οὕτως οὖν ἐφοβοῦντο/ἐφοβήθησαν ὥστε ταξάμενοι κύκλον τῶν νεῶν παρεσκευάζοντο ὡς ἀμῡνούμενοι.

5. ὡς δὲ οἱ Κορίνθιοι τῷ πνεύματι/τῷ ἀνέμῳ ἐταράσσοντο, οἱ Ἀθηναῖοι αὐτοῖς προσπεσόντες ἐς φόβον κατέστησαν ὥστε ἔφυγον ἐς τὰς Πάτρᾱς.

30
ΜΕΓΑ ΤΟ ΤΗΣ
ΘΑΛΑΣΣΗΣ ΚΡΑΤΟΣ
(γ)

Title: "Sea Power Is a Great Thing"

The purposes of this chapter are:

1. Reading: (α and β) to present a slightly adapted version of the second of a pair of naval battle narratives from Thucydides; in the final reading to give an adapted version of Thucydides' account of a planned Peloponnesian attack on the Piraeus, which was diverted to an attack on Salamis instead
2. Grammar: (α) to present the various types of conditional sentences; (β) to show how complex sentences, including conditionals, are handled in indirect speech
3. Background: to carry the account of the Peloponnesian War through to its conclusion with the defeat of Athens

Vocabulary

The declension of κέρας, "wing" (of an army or of a naval fleet) is: κέρας, κέρως, κέρᾳ, κέρας; κέρᾱ, κερῶν, κέρᾱσι(ν), κέρᾱ.

New usage of preposition: περί (+ *dat.*) = concerning: περὶ τῷ χωρίῳ (9–10).

New usage of preposition: παρά (+ *acc.*) = along, past: παρὰ τὴν γῆν (11).

Translation

Lines 1–8

The Peloponnesians, when the Athenians did not sail into the gulf against them, wanting to lead them in (into the gulf) against their will, put out to sea at dawn and sailed in the direction of the gulf, arranging their ships four deep, with the right wing leading, just as they had been at anchor (as they

were also anchoring); and on this wing they posted their twenty fastest sailing ships, so that, if Phormio thought that they were sailing against Naupactus and sailed there to help (helping sailed along there), the Athenians would not escape their attack, but these ships would shut (them) in.

[The map and diagram of the battle on page 190 make these maneuvers clear.

δεξιῷ κέρᾳ ἡγουμένῳ (4): dative of instrument or accompaniment; see Chapter 26, Grammar 3d and e, page 138.]

Lines 9–16

And Phormio, as (which thing) they were expecting, frightened for (concerning) his base (the place) which was deserted, when he saw them putting out to sea, reluctantly (unwillingly) and hastily embarked and sailed along the land, and at the same time the infantry (foot army) of the Messenians came to (their) aid. And the Peloponnesians, seeing them sailing along in single file and already (being) inside the gulf and close to land, which they had wanted most, at one signal immediately turned their ships and sailed in close line with all speed against the Athenians, and hoped to cut off all the ships.

[προσεδέχοντο (9): students may need help with the meaning of the verb here; it was given in Chapter 22, page 80, with four meanings, "I receive, admit, await, expect."

Lines 17–24

But eleven of the Athenian ships, which were leading, escape the wing of the Peloponnesians; but the others the Peloponnesians caught and pushed out toward the land as they (tried to) escape and disabled (*note this meaning of the verb, which recurs in these passages*) them. And they killed all the Athenians who did not swim to shore. And they took in tow some of the ships and pulled them empty (and one they had already taken with its crew), but the Messenians, who came to help and went into the sea in full armor (with their weapons), boarded and, fighting from the decks, saved some when they were already being towed away.

[ὅσοι μὴ ἐξένευσαν (20): the negative is μή because the clause has a conditional force, "if they did not swim to shore."

αὐτοῖς ἀνδράσιν (21–22): dative of accompaniment; see Chapter 26, Grammar 3e, page 138; "with the men themselves" = "with its crew."

εἷλον ἤδη (22): note that the aorist with ἤδη is translated "had."]

Principal Parts

Earlier lists of principal parts following the reading passages have been restricted largely to verbs that students met in Book I, where they were given only the present and aorist tenses. In this and the final two sets of principal parts we repeat verbs that have already been given with complete sets of principal parts in the vocabulary lists in Book II but that deserve special attention.

Note that Attic uses the compound forms ἀναμιμνῄσκω, ἀναμνήσω, and ἀνέμνησα with the transitive meaning "I remind someone" and that it uses the uncompounded forms μέμνημαι, ἐμνή-σθην, and μνησθήσομαι to mean "I remember," "I remembered," and "I will remember."

The first principal part (ἀνα-μιμνῄσκω) shows both present reduplication (see the principal parts after reading 26α, page 130) and -(ί)σκω (see the principal parts after reading 24β, pages 109–110).

Word Study

1. *philosopher*: ὁ φιλόσοφος.
2. *analyze*: ἀναλύω = I break up, break into constituent parts, analyze (cf. ἡ ἀνάλυσις).
3. *political*: πολῑτικός, -ή, -όν.
4. *logically*: λογικός, -ή, -όν. τὰ λογικά = logic.
5. *hypothesis*: ἡ ὑπόθεσις. ὑποτίθημι = I set before, propose. ὑποτίθεμαι =

I set before myself, assume.
6. *ideal*: ἡ ἰδέα = form, shape (Platonic "form," "idea"); via Latin *idealis*.
7. *problem*: τὸ πρόβλημα (προβάλλω) = anything thrown forward, something put forward for discussion.
8. *politician*: πολῑτικός, -ή, -όν.
9. *agonizes*: ἀγωνίζομαι = I contend, struggle.
10. *sphere*: ἡ σφαῖρα = ball, sphere (English word *sphere* first used in sense of "sphere of action" in 1606).
11. *practical*: πρᾱκτικός, -ή, -όν = fit for action.
12. *cycle*: ὁ κύκλος = circle, wheel, cycle.
13. *crisis*: ἡ κρίσις = judgment, event, issue; (medical) the turning point in a disease, sudden change.
14. *therapy*: ἡ θεραπείᾱ = service; (medical) treatment.
15. *empirical*: ἐμπειρικός, -ή, -όν = concerned with experience (ἡ ἐμπειρίᾱ).
16. *ideology*: τὸ εἶδος/ἡ ἰδέᾱ + -λογίᾱ (coined 1796, via French *idéologie* = a system of ideas).
17. *dogma*: τὸ δόγμα = opinion, belief.
18. *theoretical*: θεωρητικός, -ή, -όν = contemplative, speculative (θεωρέω, I look at, inspect, contemplate with the mind).
19. *analysis*: ἡ ἀνάλυσις.
20. *pragmatic*: πρᾱγματικός, -ή, -όν = fit for action.

It is hard to see how this passage could be rewritten to give the same meaning without using the words derived from Greek. The attempt to rewrite it will demonstrate to students that some things cannot be expressed adequately without using words derived from Greek.

Grammar 1

Rarely, past contrary to fact conditions are found with the pluperfect instead of the aorist indicative.

In discussing contrary to fact and future less vivid conditions, which use the potential particle ἄν, it may be useful to compare the potential optative (Chapter 29, Grammar 4, pages 187–188), which may sometimes be thought of as the main clause of a future less vivid condition.

Exercise 30a

1. If you do not discuss (talk about) peace, I will not listen to you. (open, future more vivid)
2. If we had conquered the barbarians, all would have honored us. (past contrary to fact)
3. If we should hurry home, perhaps we would arrive in time. (remote, future less vivid)
4. If you told everything to the king, you were foolish. (open, past particular)
5. If you had stayed at home, you would not have got into such danger. (past contrary to fact)
6. If the allies were here, they would be helping us. (present contrary to fact)
7. If we summon the allies, they will come to help us. (open, future more vivid)
8. If you do this, I will kill you. (open future particular or minatory)
9. If we had set out immediately, we would already have arrived at the city. (past contrary to fact)
10. If you should speak the truth, I would believe you. (remote, future less vivid)
11. If ever you do this, I praise you. (present general)
12. If ever this dog saw a wolf, it used to run away. (past general)

Exercise 30b

1. If we should hurry straight to the city, perhaps we would arrive before evening falls.
   εἴ μοι ἡγοῖο, ἡδέως ἂν ἐποίμην.
2. If we had not met the shepherd, we

would have missed the way.
εἰ μὴ ἐσπεύσαμεν, ὀψὲ ἂν οἴκαδε ἀφῑκόμεθα.

3. If you listen to me, you will soon learn everything.
ἐάν μοι ταχέως ἔπησθε, ἀφιξόμεθα πρὶν γενέσθαι τὴν νύκτα.
4. If the children had obeyed their father, they would not have got into such danger.
εἰ οἴκοι ἐμείναμεν, τοὺς ἀγῶνας οὐκ ἂν ἐθεώμεθα.
5. Unless I trusted you, I would not be telling you this.
εἰ παρῆν ὁ πατήρ, ἡμῖν ἂν ἐβοήθει.
6. If the god had not quenched the fire, Croesus would have been burned alive.
εἰ μὴ ἐκάλεσε τὸν θεὸν ὁ Κροῖσος, οὐκ ἂν ἐσώθη.
7. If you see mother in the agora, ask her to hurry home.
ἐὰν μὴ δι᾽ ὀλίγου οἴκαδε ἐπανέλθῃ ἡ μήτηρ, ἐγὼ αὐτὸς εἶμι ὡς ζητήσων αὐτήν.
8. If my brother were not suffering so (suffering bad things), I would not be so sad.
εἰ παρῆν ἡ μήτηρ, ἠπίστατο ἄν/ᾔδει ἂν τί δεῖ ἡμᾶς ποιεῖν.
9. If ever the enemy invades the land, the farmers remove to the city.
ἐὰν οἱ Κορίνθιοι τῷ τοῦ Φορμίωνος ναυτικῷ προσβάλωσι, νῑκῶνται.
10. If ever the Athenians attacked, the enemy retired.
εἰ ἀναχωρήσαιεν/ἀναχωρήσειαν οἱ Ἀθηναῖοι, οἱ πολέμιοι προσέβαλλον αὐτοῖς.

Note that in no. 1, εὐθύς means "straight."

The Downfall of Athens

Illustration (page 197)

This relief and inscription are in the Acropolis Museum, Athens. The decree inscribed below the relief was passed in 405 B.C., but it was engraved on this relief and set up on the Acropolis in 403/402 B.C., when Cephisophon was secretary to the Council. It is worth quoting the opening lines:

Κηφισοφῶν Παιανιεὺς ἐγραμμάτευε. Σαμίοις ὅσοι μετὰ τοῦ δήμου τοῦ Ἀθηναίων ἐγένοντο. ἔδοξεν τῆι βουλῆι καὶ τῶι δήμωι· Κεκροπὶς ἐπρυτάνευε, Πόλυμνις Εὐωνυμεὺς ἐγραμμάτευε, Ἀλεξίας ἦρχε, Νικοφῶν Ἀθμονεὺς ἐπεστάτει. Γνώμη Κλεισόφου καὶ συμπρυτάνεων· ἐπαινέσαι τοῖς πρέσβεσι τοῖς Σαμίοις τοῖς τε προτέροις ἥκουσι καὶ τοῖς νῦν καὶ τῆι βουλῆι καὶ τοῖς στρατηγοῖς καὶ τοῖς ἄλλοις Σαμίοις ὅτι εἰσὶν ἄνδρες ἀγαθοί καὶ πρόθυμοι ποιεῖν ὅ τι δύνανται ἀγαθόν . . .· καὶ ἀντὶ ὧν εὖ πεποιήκασιν Ἀθηναίους, . . . δεδόχθαι τῆι βουλῆι καὶ τῶι δήμωι· Σαμίους Ἀθηναίους εἶναι, πολιτευομένους ὅπως ἂν αὐτοὶ βούλωνται.

Cephisophon of Paeania was secretary (to the Council). To all the Samians who stood by the Athenian people. The Council and people resolved; (the tribe of) Cecropis formed the prytany, Polymnis of (the deme) Euonymus was secretary, Alexias was archon, Nicophon of (the deme) Athmonia was chairman. The proposal of Cleisophus and his fellow prytaneis: to commend the Samian ambassadors of both the present and the previous embassies, and the (Samian) Council and generals and the rest of the Samians, because they are good men and eager to do what good they can . . . ; and in return for the benefits they have done the Athenians, . . . it has been resolved by the Council and people that the Samians should be Athenians (i.e., Athenian citizens), while keeping whatever constitution they themselves want. . . .

The first two lines form an introduction; the original decree begins at line 3, with the usual formal introduction (see essay, Chapter 22, page 78); your students could be reminded of how the constitution functioned. To grant

Athenian citizenship to individuals for the benefits they had conferred on Athens was not uncommon, but to enfranchise a whole state is quite exceptional.

For further reading, see *The World of Athens*, pp. 34–41.

ΜΕΓΑ ΤΟ ΤΗΣ ΘΑΛΑΣΣΗΣ ΚΡΑΤΟΣ (δ)

Vocabulary

ἔφθην: conjugated like ἔστην.

τρόπαιον: see note to line 27 of the translation.

New usage of preposition: ὑπό (+ *acc.*) = at (of time): ὑπὸ νύκτα (29).

Translation

Lines 1–10

And so here the Peloponnesians were prevailing and disabled the Athenian ships; but their twenty ships on (from) the right wing were pursuing the eleven ships of the Athenians that had escaped their turning movement. And except for one ship they escaped safely to Naupactus before the Peloponnesians could catch them, and facing with prows toward the enemy they prepared to defend themselves, if the Peloponnesians sailed to land against them. And they (the Peloponnesians) arrived and raised the victory song, as though they had already won (as being in a state of victory); but a Leucadian ship was pursuing the one remaining Athenian ship, alone (one) far in front of the others. And there happened to be a merchant ship moored out at sea; and the Athenian ship sailing around it strikes the pursuing Leucadian ship amidships (in the middle) and sinks it.

[ἐὰν . . . πλέωσιν (6): this is virtual indirect speech; the Athenians said, "We shall defend ourselves, if the Peloponnesians sail against us." In indi-

rect speech the original moods and
tenses may be retained, as here.

ἐμβάλλει . . . καταδύει (10): Thucydides, like Herodotus and indeed all
Greek authors, tends to use historic presents at dramatic moments.]

Lines 11–17

At this unexpected event (this unexpected thing having happened) the Peloponnesians panic (fear falls on the
Peloponnesians), and pursuing in disorder, some of the ships dropping their
oars stopped sailing, wishing to wait for
the others, and others ran aground onto
the shallows. And when the Athenians
saw this happening, they became confident, and with a shout (shouting) they
rushed at them. And because of their
present disorder they did not stand firm
for long (waited for a little time), and
then they turned toward Panormus,
from where they had put out.
[ἐθάρσουν (15): we retain Thucydides'
spelling (the regular Attic would be
ἐθάρρουν).]

Lines 18–23

And the Athenians pursued them
and took the six nearest ships (the six
ships being near) and rescued (saved)
their own ships, which the Peloponnesians had disabled near the land and
taken in tow; and of the men, they killed
some and took others prisoner. On the
Leucadian ship, which sank around the
merchant ship, was sailing the Spartan
Timocrates, and when his ship was destroyed, he slew himself and was cast
ashore into the harbor of Naupactus (of
the Naupactians).

Lines 24–30

And the Athenians withdrew (to
base) and set up a trophy and took up the
corpses and wrecks which (as many as)
were on their shore, and they gave back
to the enemy their dead (the things of
them) under truce. And the Peloponnesians also set up a trophy as victors
(as having conquered) for the rout of the
(Athenian) ships that they had disabled
near the land. And after this, fearing

that reinforcements would come from
Athens (the help from the Athenians),
they sailed at night into the Crisaean
Gulf (the Gulf of Corinth) to (and)
Corinth, all except the Leucadians.
[τροπαῖον (27): note Thucydides' Old
Attic accentuation of this word; the word
is derived from ἡ τροπή, turning, rout of
an enemy. Victors regularly set up a
trophy on or near the site of their victory;
for a land battle, this consisted in a
stake on which a full set of captured armor was fixed; for a naval victory it was
often a captured prow or stern. The
Peloponnesians on this occasion dedicated a whole captured Athenian ship,
setting it near their trophy. This Athenian victory was decisive; the Peloponnesians never again in the first ten
years of the war risked a naval engagement, and the Athenians were left
in total control of the seas both east and
west.]

Principal Parts

For the use of these verbs and of
φαίνομαι with supplementary participles, see Chapter 20, Grammar 3, page
55. For φαίνομαι, see the principal parts
after reading 22α, page 73.

Note that λανθάνω (stem λαθ-) and
τυγχάνω (stem τυχ-) have two nasal
elements, the ν and γ inserted before the
θ and χ respectively and the -αν-.

Word Building

1. ὁ/ἡ παῖς: child, boy (the nomina-
    tive is formed by adding ς to the
    stem παιδ-, and the δ drops out)
2. diminutive suffix -ιον = little child
3. adjectival suffix -ικός = of a child,
    playful
4. verbal suffix -ίζω = I play
5. compound word: εὖ + παῖς =
    blessed with good children
6. compound word: ἀ -privative + παῖς
    = without children, childless
7. verbal suffix -εύω = I educate
8. noun suffix -σις added to stem
    παιδευ- = education

9. compound word: παιδ- + ἀγωγ-
    (ἄγω) = a child leader, tutor
10. compound word: adjectival suffix
    -ικός added to stem παιδαγωγ- = of a
    tutor, teacher

1. λέγ-ω: primitive verb = I count, tell,
    say
2. λεγ-σις: stem + noun suffix =
    speech
3. λεγ-τικός: stem + adjectival suffix
    -τικός = good at speaking
4. λόγ-ος: primitive noun (change
    from ε to ο is regular) = word,
    speech, reasoning, etc.
5. λογ-ικός: stem + adjectival suffix
    -ικός = of speaking, reasoning,
    logical
6. λογ-ίζομαι: stem + verbal suffix
    -ίζομαι = I count, reckon
7. λογιστής: verbal stem λογιζ- +
    noun suffix -ιστής = calculator, au-
    ditor
8. ἄλογος: compound word: ἀ-priva-
    tive + λογ-ος = speechless, irra-
    tional
9. εὐλογίᾱ: compound word: εὐ +
    -λογίᾱ = eulogy
10. λογογράφος: compound word: λόγος
    + γραφ-(ω) = speech writer

Also:.λογοδιάρροια: compound
word: λόγος + δια-ρέω (ῥοίᾱ) (I
flow through) = verbal diarrhea

Grammar 2

In addition to the new grammar in
this section (subordinate clauses in
indirect speech) there is review of the
three types of indirect statement (ὅτι, infinitive, and participle; see Chapters 22
and 23) and review of some of the types of
conditional sentences from Grammar
1.
   Note also that potential ἄν is often
found with the infinitive in indirect
statement, e.g., οὐκ οἰόμενοι τοὺς ᾿Αθη-
ναίους ἄν τολμῆσαι, "not thinking that
the Athenians would dare" (29α:12; see
also 30 tail:4). The actual thought was οἱ
᾿Αθηναῖοι οὐκ ἄν τολμήσαιεν. Students

will be asked to produce this construction in Exercise 30d, no. 2.

Exercise 30c

1. ἡ Πῡθίη ἔφη ἐὰν στρατεύηται (εἰ
    στρατεύοιτο) Κροῖσος ἐπὶ Πέρσᾱς,
    μεγάλην ἀρχὴν καταλύσειν.
2. ὁ πατὴρ ᾔδει τοὺς παῖδας οὐκ ἄν
    καταστάντας εἰς κίνδῡνον, εἰ οἴκοι
    ἔμειναν.
3. ὁ Κροῖσος τοὺς ἀγγέλους ἐκέλευε
    ὅσ᾿ ἄν λέγῃ (ὅσα λέγοι) τὰ
    χρηστήρια γράψαντας ἀναφέρειν
    παρ᾿ ἑαυτόν.
4. οἱ Λῡδοὶ ἔφασαν τὸν Κροῖσον
    πρῶτον μὲν σῑγὴν ἔχειν, τέλος δέ,
    ὡς ἠναγκάζετο, πάντα εἰπεῖν.
5. οἱ ἄνδρες πρὸς τοὺς πέμψαντας
    εἶπον ὅτι πάντα ἐποίησαν
    (ποιήσειαν) ἃ ἐκεῖνοι ἐκέλευσαν.

ΟΙ ΠΕΛΟΠΟΝΝΗΣΙΟΙ
ΒΟΥΛΕΥΟΥΣΙΝ
ΑΠΟΠΕΙΡΑΣΑΙ
ΤΟΥ ΠΕΙΡΑΙΩΣ

Title: "The Peloponnesians Plan to
Make an Attempt on the Piraeus"

   Students are to deduce the compound
verb.

Translation

Lines 1–7
   Before dispersing the fleet that had
returned to Corinth, Cnemus and the
other generals of the Peloponnesians at
the beginning of winter wanted to make
an attempt on the Piraeus, the port of the
Athenians; for the harbor was un-
guarded. For the Athenians did not
think that the enemy would dare to attack it. They decided that each of the
sailors should take his oar and go on foot
from Corinth to the sea toward Athens,
and when they reached Megara and had
launched forty ships, which happened to
be there, they should sail straight
against the Piraeus.
Lines 8–13
   When they had made this decision,

they went immediately. They arrived at
night and launched the ships but sailed
not against the Piraeus, afraid of the
risk, but toward the promontory of
Salamis that looks toward Megara.
There was an Athenian garrison there
and a squadron (garrison) of three
ships. And so the Peloponnesians attacked the garrison and dragged off the
ships empty (i.e., without crews) and
ravaged the rest of Salamis.

Lines 14–20

Beacons were raised (with signals)
to Athens, warning of an enemy attack,
and there was great consternation; for
those in the city thought that the Peloponnesians had already sailed into the Piraeus, and those in the Piraeus thought
that Salamis had been taken and that
now the enemy (they) were sailing
against them. At daybreak the Athenians, coming in full force to the Piraeus
to help, launched ships and boarding
(them) hastily sailed with their ships
against Salamis, and with their infantry they set up guard posts
(garrisons) for the Piraeus. But when
the Peloponnesians perceived (that) help
(was coming), they sailed away
quickly.

[The Peloponnesian plan was bold and
well conceived; they might have done
the Athenians serious damage if they
had carried it out instead of panicking

at the last minute and attacking the
easier target of Salamis.

ἡρῆσθαι (16): help as necessary
with this perfect passive infinitive of
αἱρέω.

καθίσταντο (19): note the force of the
middle voice—"they set up (guards) *for
their own protection.*"]

Exercise 30d

1. εἰ οἱ Κορίνθιοι εὐθὺς ἐπὶ τὸν
    Πειραιᾶ ἔπλευσαν, ῥᾳδίως ἂν εἷλον
    αὐτόν.
2. οὐδὲν γὰρ ἦν ναυτικὸν τὸν λιμένα
    φύλασσον, διότι οἱ Ἀθηναῖοι
    ᾤοντο τοὺς πολεμίους οὐδέποτε ἂν
    ἐπιπλεῦσαι αὐτῷ.
3. οἱ δὲ Κορίνθιοι τὸν κίνδυνον οὕτως
    ἐφοβοῦντο ὥστε οὐκέτι ἐπὶ τὸν
    Πειραιᾶ ἔπλεον ἀλλ' ἐπὶ τὴν
    Σαλαμῖνα.
4. φρούριον ἦν ἐκεῖ τριῶν τριηρῶν,
    ὥστε μήτε εἰς τὰ Μέγαρα ἐσπλεῖν
    μηδένα μήτε ἐκπλεῖν.
5. οἱ οὖν Κορίνθιοι ταύτᾱς τὰς
    τριήρεις ἑλόντες τὴν ἄλλην
    Σαλαμῖνα ἐπόρθουν· τῇ δὲ
    ὑστεραίᾳ πρὶν βοηθῆσαι τοὺς
    Ἀθηναίους, κατὰ τάχος/ταχέως
    ἀπέπλευσαν.

Help students as necessary with
ἄν + the infinitive in no. 2 (= a potential
optative in indirect statement); see note
with Grammar 2 above.

31
ΑΧΑΡΝΗΣ
(α)

Title: "Acharnians"

The purposes of this chapter are:

1. Reading: to present selections from Aristophanes' *Acharnians* to round out the readings in the course by returning to the Athenian farmer, Dicaeopolis, and his family with which the course began (for further information on the readings, see below)
2: Grammar: to present matters of orthography that students will encounter in Aristophanes (crasis, elision, and prodelision or aphaeresis), to present verbal adjectives in -τέος (and -τός; note in teacher's handbook, Grammar 4), to present summaries of uses of participles and negatives, and to present third person imperatives
3. Background: to present information on Aristophanes and Old Comedy

Aristophanes and Old Comedy

For further reading, see *Ancient Writers*, Vol. I, pp. 291–312; *Cambridge History of Classical Literature*, Vol. I, pp. 370–398; and *The Oxford History of the Classical World*, pp. 174–180.

The Reading Selections

The selections contain 160 lines taken from the first 279 lines of the play. The selections comprise the following lines of the original: (α) 1–3, 17–33, and 37–42; (β) 43–47a, 51b–54, 56–64a, 65–67, 73–78, 80–94, 98–109, 123–125, and 128–133; (γ) 175–193a, 194–196, and 198–203; (δ) 204–210a, 234–255a, 257–262, and 263–279 (with some deletions, which do not allow retention of the meter).

The first passage (α) has been kept short, since students are likely to find the poetry of Aristophanes more difficult than (or at least different from) the prose that they have been reading. We have omitted a number of lines (and parts of lines) that might prove unusually difficult to students at this stage or that contain allusions that would require tedious explanation. Even so, some of the passages may be difficult for some students, in particular lines 11, 13–14, 25, 55–64, 66–67, 69, and 136–141. We have provided extra help in the notes, and we urge that teachers be generous in helping students with these passages and throughout these selections from the *Acharnians* to make sure that the students' first exposure to a substantial reading of Greek poetry is a positive one. We think that the selections as we have chosen and presented them will be both manageable and enjoyable.

The selections offered here in Greek cover only part of the plot of the entire play, but they offer a clear beginning, middle, and end.

They begin (α) with Dicaeopolis sitting on the Pnyx, waiting for the Assembly to begin; he longs for peace and is prepared to disrupt the proceedings if anyone talks about anything other than peace. This scene continues (β) with the beginning of the Assembly and the arrival of the immortal Amphitheus, who claims that the gods have allowed him to make peace with Sparta. Amphitheus is shunted aside, however, and ambassadors are introduced who have returned from the king of Persia, to whom they were sent by the Athenians to seek aid in the war against Sparta. They bring envoys dressed in Oriental splendor as peacocks. The whole scene is a travesty of responsible politics, and Aristophanes mocks both the ambassadors and the envoys with scatological language that is typical of the poet and that will delight students. Dicaeopolis is so disgusted that he confers with Amphitheus and sends him off to Sparta to conclude a private peace with the

Lacedaemonians for himself, his children, and his wife.

The midpoint (γ) of the plot that is contained in our Greek selections has Amphitheus returning from Sparta bearing three alternative truces, from which Dicaeopolis is allowed to choose. On the last part of Amphitheus' return journey he was met by hardened old Acharnians who want no truce as long as their farms are being devastated by the enemy and who pursue him and threaten to stone him. Amphitheus has outrun the Acharnians, however, and Dicaeopolis scorns their threats. He chooses one of the truces with Sparta and exits, delighted to be rid of the war and determined to celebrate his private peace by enacting his own Rural Dionysia.

In the final scene presented here (δ) the Acharnians enter in hot pursuit of Amphitheus, but they withdraw when Dicaeopolis calls for holy silence and emerges from his house with his wife, his daughter (who carries a sacred basket), and his slave Xanthias and a second unnamed slave (who carry a phallus-pole). A sacrifice is made, and Dicaeopolis arranges a Dionysiac procession to celebrate a mock Rural Dionysia and sets the procession in motion. He then sings a joyous song to Phales, the Dionysiac god of the phallus, in honor of the peace he has accepted with Sparta.

This is by no means the end of Aristophanes' play, which continues with the Acharnians attacking and disrupting Dicaeopolis's procession, but it is an appropriate conclusion to the story of Dicaeopolis as told in *Athenaze*. The processional scene reassembles the characters of Dicaeopolis, his wife, daughter, and slave from the earlier chapters (only Philip and his grandfather are absent); it shows the rituals and organization of a Dionysiac procession such as students read about in Chapter 9β; and it shows the joy that farmers such as Dicaeopolis would have felt if

the war had ended and they had been allowed to return to their beloved farms and resume their accustomed country life.

Teachers may wish to have their students read the entire play in translation to see how the complication of the plot produced by the Acharnians' disruption of Dicaeopolis's procession is finally resolved, but the selections given here will provide in themselves a satisfying story with its own beginning, middle, and end.

Style

The passages illustrate a number of features typical of Aristophanes' style. The teacher might mention these to students before beginning the readings and then have students locate examples as they procede through the text:

> Compound words and comic coinages: e.g. 3, 62, 77, 96, 123, and 143.
> Clusters or series of verbs or adjectives: e.g., 17–18, 19–20, 22, 95–96.
> Puns: 30–31, 63–64, 77/79, and 105.
> Scatological language: 55–58.
> Direct attack on individuals by name: 62.
> Breaking of dramatic illusion: e.g., 120–121 and 146.
> Alliteration: e.g., 123, 142.

Vocabulary

Notes:

Translation:

Lines 1–26

Dic: How (much) I've been stung in my heart, and had few pleasures, very few, four (to be exact), and what pains I've suffered—sand-hundred-heaps. But never yet . . . was I so stung as now, when there's a regular meeting of the Assembly at dawn and the Pnyx here is deserted, and they (the people) chatter in the agora and run up and down avoiding the red rope (flee the red rope). Not even the prytaneis have come, but they'll come too late and then push each other when they get here (having come) like mad (how do you think?) for the front seat, all streaming down in a bunch (together); but as for peace (how peace shall be), they don't care a bit; o city, city! And I always come back first to the Assembly and sit; and then, when I'm alone, I groan, I yawn, I stretch, I fart, I'm at a loss, I doodle, I pluck out my hairs, I count, staring toward the country, loving peace, hating the city and longing for my deme. And so now I've come absolutely ready to shout, interrupt, abuse the speakers, if anyone speaks about anything except peace. But look, (for) the prytaneis are here at midday. Didn't I tell you? That's just what I said; every man is jostling for the front seat.

[τὴν ... καρδίαν (1): accusative of respect.

ἀλλήλοισι (12): note the Ionic dative pl. ending; see the notes on the Ionic dialect at the beginning of Chapter 27.

ὅπως (13): see Chapter 24, Grammar 4, page 104.

εἰς (15): Aristophanes uses both εἰς and ἐς (19).

Compound verb to be deduced: ἀποβλέπων (19).]

Grammar 1

Notes:

Grammar 2

Notes:

Grammar 3

Notes:

ΑΧΑΡΝΗΣ (β)

Vocabulary

ἀλαζών: see lines 43 and 61.

The declension of μήν is μήν, μηνός, μηνί, μῆνα; μῆνες, μηνῶν, μησί(ν), μῆνας.

The declension of ὄρνῑς is: ὄρνῑς, ὄρνῑθος, ὄρνῑθι, ὄρνῑν; ὄρνῑθες, ὀρνίθων, ὄρνῑσι(ν), ὄρνῑθας.

The declension of the contract adjective χρῡσοῦς is as follows: χρῡσοῦς, χρῡσῆ, χρῡσοῦν; χρῡσοῦ, χρῡσῆς, χρῡσοῦ; χρῡσῷ, χρῡσῇ, χρῡσῷ; χρῡσοῦν, χρῡσῆν, χρῡσοῦν; χρῡσοῖ, χρῡσαῖ, χρῡσᾶ; χρῡσῶν, χρῡσῶν, χρῡσῶν; χρῡσοῖς, χρῡσαῖς, χρῡσοῖς; χρῡσοῦς, χρῡσᾶς, χρῡσᾶ.

For the preposition παρά (+ gen.) = "from," see line 41. Students met this use in Chapter 26, tail reading, line 11; it is introduced in a vocabulary list for the first time here in Chapter 31.

Translation

Lines 27–89
Her.: Come forward!
    Come on, so that you may be inside the purified area.
Amph.: Has anyone spoken yet? Her.: Who wishes to speak?
Amph.: I do. Her.: Who are you? (being who?) Amph.: Amphitheus.
    Her.: Not a man (= human being)? Amph.: No,
but an immortal . . .
    . . . and the gods have commissioned (entrusted to) me
to make a truce with the Spartans on my own (alone).
But as I'm an immortal, gentlemen, I haven't got any travel allowance (journey money).

For the prytaneis won't (don't) give
    me any. Her.: Archers!
Dic.: Prytaneis, you are wronging the
    Assembly
  in ejecting the man who wanted
  to make a truce for us and to hang up
    our shields.
Her.: Sit down, be quiet. Dic.: No, by
    God, I won't,
  unless you (if you don't) introduce a
    motion about peace for me.
Her.: The ambassadors from the King.
Dic.: What king? I'm fed up with am-
    bassadors
  and peacocks and imposters
    (impostures).
Her.: Be quiet. . . .
Amb.: You sent us to the great King
  on a salary (receiving as pay) of two
    drachmas a day
  when Euthymenes was archon.
    Dic.: Oh my, (those) drachmas!
Amb.: We were entertained perforce
    and drank
  from crystal goblets and golden
    vessels
  sweet wine undiluted. Dic.: O Cra-
    nian city,
  do you see how the ambassadors
    mock you?
Amb.: For the barbarians consider only
  those who can eat and drink the
    most (to be really) men.
  In the fourth year we arrived at the
    palace.
  But he (the King) had taken his
    army and gone off to the la-
    trine,
  and he was shitting on the Golden
    Mountains for eight months.
Dic.: And when (within what time) did
    he close his ass?
Amb.: At the full moon. Then he went
    off home.
  Then he entertained (us); he served
    us
  whole oxen, oven-baked (from the
    oven). DIC.: And who ever saw
  baked oxen? What humbug!
Amb.: And yes, by Zeus, he set before us

a bird three times as big as
    Cleonymus;
  it was called a cheatiebird.
Dic.: This (as it seems) is how you
    cheated us, taking the two
    drachmas.
Amb.: And now we have come, bringing
    Pseudartabas,
  the King's Eye. Dic.: May a raven
    strike it (the King's Eye)
  and knock it out—and yours too, the
    ambassador's!
Her.: The King's Eye! Dic.: O lord
    Heracles!
Amb.: Come on then, (you) tell what the
    King sent you
  to say to the Athenians, Pseu-
    dartabas.
Pseud.: Iartaman exarxan apissona
    satra.
Amb.: Did you understand what he is
    saying? Dic.: No, I didn't by
    Apollo.
Amb.: He says the King will send you
    gold.
  (You) tell (us) about the gold louder
    and clearly.
Pseud.: No getty goldy, wide-assed Ioni.
Dic.: Oh misery, how clear that is!
    Amb.: What's he saying
    again?
Dic.: What (does he say)? He calls the
    Ionians wide-assed,
  if they expect gold from the barbar-
    ians.
Amb.: No (he doesn't); but this man
    says bushels of gold.
Dic.: Bushels indeed! You're a great
    imposter.
Her.: Be quiet! Sit down!
    The Council invites the King's Eye
  to the Town Hall. Dic.: Well, isn't
    this enough to make you hang
    yourself?
  But I shall do some terrible and
    mighty deed.
  But where's my Amphitheus?
    Amph.: Here I am.
Dic.: (You) take these eight drachmas
    for me

and make a truce with the Spartans
for me alone,
and for my young children and
wife.
And (you) go on with your embassies and gape like fools!
[Compound verb to be deduced: ἀπά-
γοντες (37).

κάθησο (39): like the imperative of
δύναμαι.

τῆς ἡμέρας (46): genitive of time
with a distributive sense, "each day."

Line 51: note the accent of
κατάγελων, καταγέλωτος, ὁ mockery.

Compound verb to be deduced:
παρετίθει (59).

'Αθηναίοισιν (70): Ionic dative pl.
ending.

Line 71: although this utterance is
complete nonsense, the sounds do suggest Greek words, e.g., ἐξάρξαν =
ἔξηρξα "I began"; σάτρα = σάθρα
"rotten things."

Line 75 = οὐ λήψῃ χρῡσόν,
χαυνόπρωκτοι "Ιωνες "you won't get
gold, you wide-assed Ionians." The
only words that are correct Greek are οὐ
and the obscene χαυνόπρωκτ'.

The ambassadors, both Greek and
Persian, are repeatedly referred to as
ἀλάζονες "imposters," and in a passage
we have omitted, where Dicaeopolis
himself questions the Persian ambassadors, he reveals them as Athenians
dressed up to look like Persian
grandees (a revelation quite neglected
by the herald, who immediately after
this invites them to the Town Hall).

τοῖσι παιδίοισι (88): Ionic dative pl.
endings.]

Illustration (page 210)

Attic red figure plate signed by
Epictetus, ca. 500 B.C. (London, British
Museum).

Principal Parts

For these verbs, see Chapter 18,
Grammar 1, pages 22–24, and Chapter
20, Grammar 1, pages 48–50. For fur-

ther information, see Appendix.

Grammar 4

Note that the exercises to accompany
Grammar 4 are on page 228. Note also
the one example of a verbal adjective in
-τέος in the reading (line 147). We
recommend that Exercise 31d be de-
layed until completion of the readings
from Aristophanes. It is a good exercise
with which to end the course.

Another set of verbal adjectives has
endings in -τός, -τή, -τόν. Students
have met a number of these in the Word
Building exercises, e.g., γνωστός (p.
170), γραπτός (p. 136), ποιητός (p. 136),
τακτός (p. 82), and χρηστός (p. 136). See
the note in this teacher's handbook on
the Word Building exercise in Chapter
17. These adjectives are formed by
adding the suffix -τός to the verb stem,
and they are either passive in meaning,
e.g., γραπτός, -ή, -όν = "written," or
they denote possibility, e.g., γνωστός,
-ή, -όν = "known" or "knowable."
They may be used with a dative of agent,
e.g., τοῖς οἴκοι ζηλωτός "envied by those
at home," Xenophon, *Anabasis* 1.7.4.

Grammar 5

Notes:

Exercise 31a

1. Dicaeopolis got to the Pnyx before
    all the citizens (anticipated the cit-
    izens arriving . . .).
2. When he's alone, he sighs, loving
    peace, hating the city and longing
    for his own deme.
3. He has come prepared to abuse the
    speakers, if they don't speak of
    peace.
4. Dicaeopolis was angry with the
    prytaneis for not honoring peace.
5. The ambassador from the King
    happened to be present, having ar-
    rived from Asia.

6. Dicaeopolis loathes the Athenians'
   ambassadors because he thinks
   they are imposters (as being imposters).
7. He was angry with them because
   they had received two drachmas a
   day.
8. The ambassadors are clearly
   telling lies.
9. We all know that the King will
   send us no gold.
10. The barbarians only consider
    those who can drink the most (to be
    really) men.
11. Dicaeopolis says that the Atheni-
    ans are fools, if they expect gold
    from the barbarians.
12. Amphitheus ran into the Assembly
    unseen by the archers.
13. Although I am a god, I cannot jour-
    ney to Sparta, unless the prytaneis
    give me journey money.
14. Dicaeopolis sent Amphitheus to
    make a truce with the Spartans.
15. He is rejoicing as if the peace had
    already been concluded.

ΑΧΑΡΝΗΣ (γ)

Vocabulary

Notes:

Translation

Lines 90–117
Dic.: But, (look, for) here's Amphitheus
      (back) from Sparta.
   Hello, Amphitheus. Amph.: Don't
      (greet me) yet, until I stop run-
      ning.
   For I must flee and escape the
      Acharnians.
Dic.: What's the matter? Amph.: I was
      hurrying here bringing you
   the truces; but some old men
      smelled them out;
   Acharnians, tough old men, oaken,

unsoftened Marathon-fighters,
   tough as maple.
And then they all began to shout,
   "Villain,
are you bringing truces, when our
   grapevines are cut down?"
And they began to gather stones into
   their cloaks.
But I began to flee; and they began to
   pursue and shout.
Dic.: Well, let them shout. But do you
      bring the truces?
Amph.: I certainly do (I say I do), these
      three samples.
   This one is for five years. Take it
      and taste.
   Dic.: Ugh! Amph.: What's the mat-
      ter? Dic.: I don't like this one
      because
   it smells of pitch and the prepara-
      tion of ships.
Amph.: Well, take this one, for ten
      years, and taste it.
Dic.: This smells, too, very sharply, of
      ambassadors (going) to the ci-
      ties. . . .
Amph.: But this truce is for thirty years
      by both land and sea. Dic.: O
      Festival of Dionysus!
   this one smells of ambrosia and
      nectar.
   And it says in my mouth, "Go where
      you wish!"
   This I accept and I pour it out (as a
      libation) and I will drain it off,
   bidding a long farewell to the
      Acharnians.
   And rid of war and troubles,
   I'll go in and celebrate the Rural
      Dionysia.
Amph.: But I'll flee the Acharnians.
['Αχαρνέᾱς (92): the noun 'Αχαρνεύς,
"an Acharnian," is declined exactly
like the noun βασιλεύς.

   πρεσβῦται (94): this noun is from ὁ
πρεσβύτης, an alternate form of ὁ
πρέσβυς used in the sense "old man."]

Grammar 6

Notes:

Exercise 31b

1. I was never so stung as now, because the citizens are not here at the Assembly.
2. Let's not stay any longer on the Pnyx; for not even the prytaneis have come.
3. If the prytaneis don't arrive soon/unless the prytaneis arrive soon, the citizens will not wait any longer.
4. Unless you spoke about peace, I wouldn't keep silent.
5. The herald ordered Dicaeopolis not to abuse the speakers and not to interrupt.
6. The barbarians do not consider those (the sort of people) who cannot drink a lot (to be really) men.
7. Dicaeopolis knew clearly that the King would never send gold.
8. I wish the ambassadors would stop lying (may the ambassadors no longer lie).
9. For neither of them can deceive the people.
10. For everyone knows they are not saying a word of truth (are saying nothing true).
11. Since both the prytaneis and the people refused to make a truce (neither the prytaneis nor the people being willing to . . .), Dicaeopolis decided not to despair but to do a mighty deed.
12. Fearing that he would never get peace (peace would never happen) any other way, he sent Amphitheus to Sparta.
13. For he hoped that the Spartans would not throw Amphitheus out, as he was an immortal, but would make a truce.
14. For whoever does not listen to an immortal, soon gets it in the neck (fares badly).
15. Although Amphitheus has not yet returned, Dicaeopolis rejoices as if he were no longer involved in (using, experiencing) war.

In no. 8 students are to deduce the meaning of the verb ψεύδοιντο.

Grammar 7

Notes:

Exercise 31c

1. Let the slaves loosen the oxen and return home, but let the boy hurry with me.
2. Let the girls not be afraid but stay quiet in the house.
3. Let all those present be silent and watch the procession.
4. Let the master not be angry but listen to the words of the slave.
5. Let the young men not fight but sit in the marketplace.

ΑΧΑΡΝΗΣ (δ)

Vocabulary

Notes:

Translation

Lines 118–160
Chor.: This way, follow everyone; chase him; and ask about the man from all the passers-by. For it is worth the city's while to catch this man. But inform me, if anyone knows where in the world the man bringing the truces has gone (turned).
He has fled; he has gone, vanished. But it's necessary to seek the man and to look Peltingward and to pursue him from land to land, until at last (sometime) he's found; I could never have my fill of pelting him with stones.
Dic.: Keep holy silence, keep holy silence!

Chor.: Quiet everyone, did you hear his
        call for holy silence, men?
    This is the very man we're looking
        for. But everyone (come) here,
    out of the way. For the man is
        coming out to sacrifice, it
        seems.
Dic.: Keep holy silence! Keep holy si-
        lence! Let the basket-bearer go
        forward a little!
    Let Xanthias stand the phallus-pole
        up straight!
    Put down the basket, daughter, so
        that we may begin.
Daugh.: Mother, hand me up the soup-
        ladle here,
    so that I can pour the soup over this
        broad, flat cake.
Dic.: And indeed it's a fine thing! Lord
        Dionysus,
    (grant) that I, conducting this pro-
        cession in a manner pleasing
    to you and sacrificing with my
        household,
    may lead the Rural Dionysia with
        good fortune,
    rid of (service in) the army; (grant)
        that my thirty-years'
    truce may turn out well.
    Come on, daughter, pretty girl, (see
        to it) that you carry the basket
        prettily,
    looking as if you had eaten savory.
        How happy
    whoever marries you. . . .
    Advance, and take care
    that no one in the crowd slyly nib-
        bles away at your golden jew-
        elry.
    Xanthias, the phallus-pole must be
        held straight up
    by the two of you behind the basket-
        bearer;
    and I, following, will sing the
        phallic song;
    and you, wife, watch me from the
        roof. Forward!
    Phales, companion of Bacchus,
    after five years (in the sixth year) I
        address you

going happily off to my deme,
having made a truce for myself,
rid of troubles
and battles.
O Phales, Phales,
If you will drink with me, in (from)
    a drinking-bout
from earliest dawn you will drain
    dry the cup of peace;
and my shield will be hung beside
    the fireplace (in the chimney).

[Compound verb to be deduced: ξυλ-
λαβεῖν (120).
    προίτω (131) and στησάτω (132):
help students as necessary with these
third person imperatives (see Grammar
6). Compare them with the second person imperative κατάθου in line 133.
    ἀνάδος (134): compound verb to be
deduced; help students as necessary
with this aorist imperative of ἀναδίδωμι.
    σφῷν (147): dual dative of the second
person pronoun, thus "by the two of you";
this is the only indication that a second
slave accompanies Xanthias.
    ἐκτέος (147): the verbal adjective is
treated formally in Grammar 7.
    τὸ φαλλικόν (149): students are to
deduce this ("phallic song") from the
noun τὸν φαλλόν (132).
    θεῶ (150): help as needed with this
imperative of θεάομαι.
    Lines 151–160: some words and
lines have been cut here, but we have not
marked them with ellipsis points in the
printed text.
    ἕκτῳ . . . ἔτει (152): Dicaeopolis
speaks as if only now after five years of
war, cooped up in the city, has he
returned to his beloved deme; in fact, the
farmers returned to the country each
year when the invasion ended.
    προσεῖπον (152): occasionally in di-
alogue the aorist is used of an action
immediately past, where we must use
the present.
    ἡ . . . ἀσπὶς . . . κρεμήσεται ((160):
cf. κρεμάσαι τὰς ἀσπίδας (line 38).]

Illustration (page 224)

Attic red figure cup, ca 470–460 B.C. (Boston, Museum of Fine Arts).

Illustrations (pages 226 and 227)

We include these illustrations at this point as reminders of Athens' enemies in the Peloponnesian War, an end to which Dicaeopolis celebrates in his joyful procession.

Illustration (page 228)

Detail of the cup by Douris, ca. 480 B.C. (London, British Museum), shown at the beginning of Chapter 25.

Acknkowledgments

The text of the extracts from Aristophanes is based on the second edition of the Oxford Classical Text of Aristophanes, edited by F. W. Hall and W. M. Geldart. The edition of C. E. Graves, *Aristophanes: The Acharnians*, Cambridge University Press, 1967, was consulted in preparing the facing notes in the student's book and some of the material in the teacher's handbook.

Exercise 31d

1. Then shall we not begin their education with music before gymnastics? There are two sorts of stories (a double type of stories), the one true, the other false (a lie). Should we educate them in both?
   ("Music" includes literature—see Chapter 24; early education in music will consist largely of storytelling; the false stories are myths representing gods and heroes as having human faults and vices. In Plato's state, literature is severely censored; Homer and Hesiod are excluded.)
2. These stories are not to be told in our city.
3. And after music the young must be trained in gymnastics.
4. We must select from the other guardians the sort of men who most seem to do with all enthusiasm whatever they consider to benefit the state.
5. If we are going to use women for the same purposes as the men, we must teach them the same things.

Plato's views may be reconstructed as follows:

Plato adopts the traditional division of education into music and gymnastics. Education will begin with music, the telling of stories to the very young. These stories will be censored, and all "false" stories, such as myths which do not represent the gods and heroes in a true and noble light, will be excluded.

In gymnastics Plato seems to be concerned with physical health and self-discipline as much as with exercise.

Women are to have the same education as men, including gymnastics, and will play their part in war.

APPENDIX:
PRINCIPAL PARTS

The principal parts of selected verbs (usually those introduced in Book I) are given after most of the main reading passages in the student's book; it is intended that students should learn these carefully. In the notes to each chapter in this handbook we provide essential information that the teacher will find useful in explaining the groupings of principal parts and pointing out noteworthy features. In this appendix, we amplify that information, and we provide additional examples of other verbs used in this course and numerous cross-references. We do not suggest that all of the linguistic information in this appendix should be conveyed to students; teachers must decide how much their students will be helped by such information.

Numbers in parentheses refer to the chapters in which the verbs that are so marked first appear in the readings or appear in vocabulary lists; when the numbers are followed by Greek letters, they refer to the lists of principal parts following the reading passages in the designated chapters and/or to the notes associated with them in this appendix. Asterisks indicate hypothetical forms.

Chapter 17α

Principal Parts: Stems in -υ- and -αυ-

Other verbs of these types occurring in the course are:

ἐξαρτύω (29), θύω (21), καταδύω (29), μηνύω (31), and φύω (28)

Note in particular:

καταδύω, καταδύσω, κατέδῡσα, καταδέδυκα, καταδέδυμαι, κατεδύθην (*transitive*) I sink
  Second aorist κατέδῡν (*intransitive*) I sank; (*of the sun*) set

φύω, φύσω, ἔφῡσα (*transitive*) I produce
  Second aorist ἔφῡν (*intransitive*) I grew
  Perfect πέφῡκα (*intransitive*) I am by nature, am

Both of these verbs have first aorists (transitive) and second aorists (intransitive); compare ἔστησα = I made to stand, and ἔστην = I stood.

Note that καίω (καυ-/και-) (9), καύσω, ἔκαυσα, κέκαυκα, κέκαυμαι, ἐκαύθην is entirely regular except for the change in stem; this is accounted for by the disappearance of digamma: καίϝω. We include it here because it does not fit in any other group.

Chapter 17β

Principal Parts: Stems in -ευ-

Other verbs with stems in -ευ-, all following the regular pattern of πιστεύω, are:

ἀγορεύω (21), ἀροτρεύω (3), βασιλεύω (6), βουλεύω (21), γεύομαι (31), ἱππεύω (27), κινδῡνεύω (23), νυκτερεύω (20), παιδεύω (24), στρατεύω (16), and φονεύω (26).

The verb λούω (22) follows the same pattern but has a contracted imperfect ἔλουν.

For ἀκούω, ἀκούσομαι, ἤκουσα, ἀκήκοα, ἠκούσθην, see 29β.

Chapter 18α

Principal Parts: -ε- and -α- Contract Verbs

Contract verbs in -ε- constitute the most common type of Greek verb. The following occur in this course; all are regular like φιλέω (with exceptions as noted):

ἀγνοέω (19)
ἀδικέω (31)
αἰτέω (11)
ἀκολουθέω (18)
ἀποδημέω (25)
ἀπορέω (12)
αὐλέω (24)
βοηθέω (2)
δειπνέω (3)
ἐνθῡμέομαι (28)*
ἐπιμελέομαι (24)**
ἐπιχειρέω (29)
εὐφημέω (31)
ζητέω (5)
ἡγέομαι (6)
θαρρέω (17)
θεωρέω (16)
κῑνέω (18)
κρατέω (18)
λαλέω (31)
λοιδορέω (31)
λῡπέω (16)
ναυμαχέω (15)
νοσέω (11)
νοστέω (19)
οἰκέω (1)
ὁρμέω (30)
ποθέω (31)
ποιέω (4)
πολεμέω (21)
πολιορκέω (16)
πονέω (1)
πορθέω (28)
στυγέω (31)
φοβέομαι (6)
φρονέω (17)
φρουρέω (29)
φωνέω (27)
χωρέω (3, 29)
ὠφελέω (11)

*aorist ἐνεθῡμήθην
**aorist ἐπεμελήθην

The verb παραινέω has ε instead of η in all parts except the perfect passive.
Other verbs in -ε showing variations in quantity of the stem vowel are:

ἀκέομαι (17), ἀκοῦμαι (Attic future), ἠκεσάμην
δέομαι (δεε-) (26), δεήσομαι, ἐδεήθην
δέω (28), δήσω, ἔδησα, δέδεκα, δέδεμαι, ἐδέθην

For δοκέω (δοκ-), see 20β (guttural stems). For σκοπέω (σκεπ-), see 19α (labial stems).

ἐκπνέω (πνευ-) (29), ἐκπνεύσομαι or ἐκπνευσοῦμαι, ἐξέπνευσα, ἐκπέπνευκα
πλέω (πλευ-) (6, 17), πλεύσομαι or πλευσοῦμαι, ἔπλευσα, πέπλευκα, πέπλευσμαι

Note the alternative contracted future forms (Doric future) in the verbs above. Note also that monosyllabic stems in -ε- (like πνέω) only make ει contractions, e.g.: πλέω, πλεῖς, πλεῖ, πλέομεν, πλεῖτε, πλέουσι(ν).

Other verbs following the regular pattern of τῑμάω are:

βοάω (5), μελετάω (24), νῑκάω (10), ὁρμάω (7), σῑγάω (9), τελευτάω (16), τολμάω (18), and φοιτάω (24).

Chapter 18β

Principal Parts: -α- and -o- Contract Verbs

Also:

ἐάω (23), ἐάσω, εἴᾱσα, εἴᾱκα, εἴᾱμαι, εἰάθην (for the irregular augment, see 25β)

Irregular:

ἐράω (31), (imperfect ἤρων), ἐρασθήσομαι, ἠράσθην (only present and imperfect active; the future and aorist come properly from ἔραμαι and are deponent; ἠράσθην = I fell in love with)
ἐρωτάω (12), ἐρωτήσω, ἠρόμην, ἠρώτηκα (regular except for the second aorist, which is supplied from ἔρομαι/εἴρομαι)
ζάω (24), ζήσω has η where regular contraction is ᾱ, e.g., infinitive ζῆν. Other tenses are supplied by βιόω, βιώσομαι, ἐβίων, βεβίωκα (second aorist conjugates like ἔγνων)

Other verbs with stems in -o-, all following the pattern of δηλόω are:

δουλόω (15), ἐλευθερόω (15), and πληρόω (21)

ἀντιόομαι (27), ἀντιώσομαι, ἠντιώθην (note the deponent aorist, passive in form)

Chapter 19α

Principal Parts: Labial Stems (-β-, -π-)

1. Many verbs with labial stems add τ to the stem in the present tense; β, and φ before τ become π, e.g., *βλάβ-τω > βλάπτω, *θαφ-τω > θάπτω.
2. All verbs with labial stems have second perfect active, and many aspirate the preceding consonant, e.g., βλάπ-τω, *βέβλαβ-α > βέβλαφα.
3. In the perfect passive the final consonant of the stem becomes μ, e.g., *βέβλαβ-μαι > βέβλαμμαι.
4. Many (but not all) verbs in labial stems have second aorist passives, e.g., ἐβλάβ-ην.
5. In the perfect active a stem vowel ε often changes to o, e.g., πέμπω, πέπομφα, λείπω, λέλοιπα (for this pattern of vowel gradation, see the notes in this handbook on the principal parts after passage 23α, and see 26β); compare the similar change in nouns and adjectives formed from verbs, e.g., πέμπω, ἡ πομπή; λείπω, λοιπός, -ή, -όν (see Book I, Chapter 15, Word Building, page 191).

Other verbs with stems in -π- are:

βλέπω (2), βλέψομαι, ἔβλεψα
σκοπέω (σκεπ-) (11), σκέψομαι, ἐσκεψάμην, ἔσκεμμαι
τέρπομαι (9), τέρψομαι, ἐτερψάμην

Chapter 19β

Principal Parts: More Labial Stems (-π-, -φ-)

Other verbs in -φ-:

θάπ-τω (θαφ-) (25), θάψω, ἔθαψα, τέθαμμαι, ἐτάφην (note τ for θ, for the sake of euphony)
κρύπτω (κρυφ-) (20), κρύψω, ἔκρυψα, κέκρυμμαι, ἐκρύφθην
μέμφομαι (27), μέμψομαι, ἐμεμψάμην/ἐμέμφθην
στρέφω (27), στρέψω, ἔστρεψα, ἔστραμμαι, ἐστράφην/ἐστρέφθην (note change of ε to α; for this pattern of vowel gradation, see the notes in this handbook on the principal parts after passage 23α, and see 26β)

Chapter 20γ

Principal Parts: Guttural Stems (-γ-)

1. All verbs with stems in gutturals have second perfect active forms, and most aspirate the final consonant of the stem, e.g., διώκ-ω, δεδίωχ-α.
2. In the perfect passive, the last consonant of the stem becomes γ before μ.
3. In the aorist passive, the last consonant of the stem is aspirated before θ, e.g., διώκ-ω, ἐ-διώχ-θην.
4. Most verbs ending in -ττ-/-σσ- in the present tense have guttural stems and follow the pattern of πράττω.
5. ἄγω is regular except for the reduplicated second aorist.

Chapter 20δ

Principal Parts: More Guttural Stems (-κ-, -χ-)

Other regular verbs with stems in gutturals are:

ἀμέλγω (7), ἄρχω (21), δέχομαι (6), εἴκω (15), εὔχομαι (8), στενάζω (στεναγ-) (4), σφάζω (σφαγ-) (30) (present stem was spelled σφάττ- after Plato), ταράττω (ταραχ-) (29), τάττω (ταγ-) (23), and φυλάττω (φυλακ-) (5).

διαλέγομαι (8), διαλέξομαι *or* διαλεχθήσομαι, διείλεγμαι, διελέχθην (note the future middle and passive forms, the aorist passive form, and the prefix εἰ- instead of reduplication in the perfect) συλλέγω (19), συλλέξω, συνέλεξα, συνείλοχα, συνείλεγμαι, συνελέγην (note the prefix εἰ- instead of reduplication in both perfects; note also the vowel change from ε to ο in the perfect active; and note the second aorist passive)

The verb ἐρέσσω (ἐρετ-) (13), ἤρεσα does not have a guttural stem (see notes below on 21β).

For ἕλκω, see 25β.
For λέγω, see 27β.
For μάχομαι, see 28β.
For τρέχω, see 27α.

Verbs with inceptive suffix -(ί)σκω, e.g., θνή-σκω, εὑρ-ίσκω, do not have guttural stems (see 24β).

Chapter 21α

Principal Parts: Dental Stems (-δ-, -ζ-)

Nearly all dental stem verbs (except those in -ίζω) follow the same pattern:

1. The final consonant of the stem is dropped before -σ- in the future and the aorist active and before -κ- in the perfect active.
2. The final consonant becomes σ in the perfect passive and aorist passive.

Other verbs with stems in -δ- are:

ᾄδω (for ἀείδω) (13, 19, 31), ᾄσω, ᾖσα, ᾖσμαι, ᾔσθην
ἥδομαι (24), ἡσθήσομαι, ἥσθην (passive deponent)
σπένδομαι (31), σπείσομαι, ἐσπεισάμην, ἔσπεισμαι. The change in the spelling of the stem (σπενδ-, σπει-) is regular; when ντ, νδ, or νθ come before σ, the ν is dropped and the preceding vowel is lengthened: *σπένδ-σο-

μαι > *σπείδ-σομαι > σπείσομαι. Compare πάσχω (πενθ-), πείσομαι, and *λύοντσι > λύουσι. ψεύδομαι (31), ψεύσομαι, ἐψευσάμην, ἔψευσμαι, ἐψεύσθην

Other verbs in -άζω, all following the pattern of θαυμάζω, are:

ἀναγκάζω (15), ἐργάζομαι (8) (see 25β), ἡσυχάζω (13), and ὀνομάζω (26).

σῴζω (σω-/σῳ-) (6), σώσω, ἔσωσα, σέσωκα, σέσωσμαι, ἐσώθην (the iota subscript only appears where ζ follows ω, though some inscriptions have it throughout)

Chapter 21β

Principal Parts: More Dental Stems (-ιζ-, -θ-)

Other stems in -ίζω, all following the pattern of κομίζω, are:

ἀγωνίζομαι (27), ἀκοντίζω (26), βαδίζω (1), ἐλπίζω (14), θεσπίζω (27), and κιθαρίζω (24)

καθέζομαι (23) (*imperfect* ἐκαθεζόμην), καθεδοῦμαι
καθίζομαι (8), καθιζήσομαι, ἐκαθισάμην
καθίζω (1) (*imperfect* ἐκάθιζον)

The verb πείθω has a first perfect πέπεικα (I have persuaded) and a second perfect πέποιθα (I trust + *dat.*); note the change of the stem vowel from ε to ο.

Stems in -τ- are very few:

ἐρέσσω (ἐρετ-), ἤρεσα
πίπτω (πετ-) (see 26α)

Chapter 22α

Principal Parts: Liquid Stems (-λ-, -ν-)

Presents in -λλω are formed from stems in -λ-, to which the semivowel *y* is assimilated.
Verbs with stems in liquids do not show the infix σ in the future or the first aorist active; the future adds -ε- to the stem, resulting in contract forms, and

the first aorist lengthens the stem vowel
(see Chapter 17, page 9, for the future,
and Book I, Chapter 12, page 149, for the
aorist).

βάλλω: note the transposition of the
vowel and the consonant in the perfects
and the aorist passive: βαλ-/βλη-.
Compare καλε-/κλη- (18α), and θαν-/
θνη- (24β).

στέλλω (στελ-/σταλ-) (29), στελῶ,
ἔστειλα, ἔσταλκα, ἔσταλμαι, ἐστάλην.
Note the change in stem vowel from ε to
α in the first perfect active, the perfect
middle, and the second aorist passive;
this change usually occurs in verb stems
containing λ, μ, ν, or ρ. Compare:
σπείρω (σπερ-/σπαρ-) (3), σπερῶ, ἔσπει-
ρα, ἔσπαρμαι, ἐσπάρην.

βούλομαι, ἐθέλω, μέλει, and μέλλω
all have stems in ε- (see 28β).

For ἀπόλλυμι (ὀλ-), see 26β.

Chapter 22β

*Principal Parts: More Liquid Stems
(-ν-)*

> Others:
>
> ἀμΰνω (13), ἀμῡνῶ, ἤμῡνα
> νέμω (19), νεμῶ, ἔνειμα, νενέμηκα,
>   νενέμημαι, ἐνεμήθην
> σημαίνω (19), σημανῶ, ἐσήμηνα,
>   σεσήμασμαι, ἐσημάνθην

For verbs ending in -άνω in the
present, see 23β.

For βαίνω, ἐλαύνω, and τέμνω, see
24α.

For γίγνομαι, see 26α; for πίνω, see
24α; and for φθάνω, see 30δ.

Chapter 23α

*Principal Parts: More Liquid Stems
(-ρ-)*

> Others:
>
> ἀγείρω (27), ἤγειρα
> οἰκτΐρω (20), ᾤκτῑρα
> σπείρω (3), σπερῶ, ἔσπειρα,
>   ἔσπαρμαι, ἐσπάρην

For φέρω, see 28α.
For εὑρ-ίσκω, see 24β.

Chapter 23β

*Principal Parts: Verbs with Nasal Infix
(-αν-)*

Many verbs have a present stem that
is formed by adding an infix containing the nasal -ν-; note the following
types of nasal infixes (given with examples):

1.   -ν-: δάκ-ν-ω, τέμ-ν-ω, φθά-ν-ω
2.   -αν-: αἰσθ-άν-ομαι, ἁμαρτ-άν-ω,
       αὐξ-άν-ω
3.   -αν- added to the stem and μ, ν, or γ
       inserted in the stem: λα-μ-β-άν-ω
       (λαβ-), μα-ν-θ-άν-ω (μαθ-), πυ-ν-
       θ-άν-ομαι (πυθ-), τυ-γ-χ-άν-ω
       (τυχ-)
4.   -νε-: ἀφικ-νέ-ομαι (ἱκ-)
5.   -υν: ἐλα-ύν-ω
6.   -ιν: βα-ίν-ω
7.   -νῡ-: δείκ-νῡ-μι

We have put types 2 and 3 in this
chapter and the remainder in 24α.

> Others:
>
> λανθ-άν-ω (λαθ-/ληθ-) (20; see
>   30δ), λήσω, ἔλαθον, λέληθα
> πυνθ-άν-ομαι (πευθ-/πυθ-) (26),
>   πεύσομαι, ἐπυθόμην, πέπυσμαι
> τυγχ-άν-ω (τευχ-/τυχ-/τυχε-) (17;
>   see 30δ), τεύξομαι, ἔτυχον,
>   τετύχηκα

Note 1:

Note that many verbs with the infix
-αν- extend the stem with ε (lengthened
to η) to form the other tenses, except the
second aorist, e.g.:

> αἰσθ-άν-ομαι (αἰσθ-/αἰσθε-) (31),
>   αἰσθήσομαι, ᾐσθόμην, ᾔσθημαι
> ἁμαρτ-άν-ω (ἁμαρτ-/ἁμαρτε-) (18),
>   ἁμαρτήσομαι, ἥμαρτον,
>   ἡμάρτηκα, ἡμάρτημαι,
>   ἡμαρτήθην

Note 2:

λαμβάνω and λανθάνω lengthen the
stem vowel in all tenses except the
aorist.

Note 3:

The verb λαμβάνω in the perfect has
εἰ- prefixed to the stem instead of reduplication (εἴ-ληφ-α, εἴ-λημ-μαι); the
only other verbs in the course having
this peculiarity are συλ-λέγω, συνείλοχα
(see 20δ) and δια-λέγομαι, διείλεγμαι
(see 20δ). Only two other Greek verbs
have this: λαγχάνω, εἴ-ληχ-α, and
μείρομαι, εἵμαρται (it is fated).

Chapter 24α

*Principal Parts: More Verbs with Nasal
Infix (-ν-, -νε-, -ιν-, and -νῡ-/-νυ-)*

This group illustrates types 1, 4, 6,
and 7 (see notes above with 23β).

Note that τέμνω transposes the vowel
and the consonant of the stem in the perfect active and passive and in the aorist
passive; compare βάλλω, βέβληκα, and
καλέω, κέκληκα.

Other verbs:

Type 1:

δάκ-ν-ω (δακ-/δηκ-) (31), δήξομαι,
ἔδακον, δέδηγμαι, ἐδήχθην
πῑ-ν-ω (πι-/πο-/πω-) (9), πῐομαι,
ἔπιον, πέπωκα, πέπομαι, ἐπόθην
τέμ-ν-ω (τεμ-/ταμ-/τμη-) (23), τεμῶ,
ἔτεμον, τέτμηκα, τέτμημαι,
ἐτμήθην. Note the transposition
of the vowel and the consonant of
the stem in the last three parts.
φθά-ν-ω (φθα-) (see 30δ)

Type 4:

ἀφ-ικ-νέ-ομαι (6) only.

Type 5:

ἐλα-ύν-ω (ἐλα-) only; see 29β.

Type 6 (-νῡ-μι):

Most verbs of this class are like
δείκ-νῡ-μι (guttural stems):

ἀνοίγ-νῡ-μι (22), ἀνοίξω, ἀνέῳξα,
ἀνέῳχα, ἀνέῳγμαι (I stand open),
ἀνεῴχθην

ζεύγ-νῡ-μι (ζευγ-) (22), ζεύξω,
ἔζευξα, ἔζευγμαι, ἐζεύχθην
ῥήγ-νῡ-μι (ῥηγ-/ῥωγ-/ῥαγ-) (22),
ῥήξω, ἔρρηξα, ἔρρωγα (I am
broken), ἐρράγην.
But σβέν-νῡ-μι (σβε-), σβέσω,
ἔσβεσα, ἔσβηκα (I have gone out),
ἐσβέσθην

For ἀπ-όλλῡμι (= *ὄλ-νῡ-μι) see 26β.

Chapter 24β

Principal Parts: Verbs in -(ί)σκω

ἀποθνή-σκω (11): note the metathe-
sis θαν-/θνη-.
For ἀνα-μι-μνή-σκω (μνα-) see 30γ.
For δι-δά-σκω (δαχ-) see 26α.
For πά-σχω (παθ-) see 26β.

Other verbs of this class are:

ἀλ-ίσκομαι (ἀλ-/ἀλο-) (28),
ἁλώσομαι, ἑάλων or ἥλων,
ἑάλωκα or ἥλωκα. Aorist forms:
ἑάλων, ἁλῶ, ἁλοίην, ἁλῶναι,
ἁλούς (compare ἔγνων). The
stem was originally ϝαλ-, hence
the irregular augment. This
verb is used as the passive of
αἱρέω.
ἀρέ-σκω (ἀρε-) (20), ἀρέσω, ἤρεσα
(+ *dat.*). This verb is commonly
used impersonally, e.g., ἀρέσκει
μοι it pleases me.

Chapter 25α

Principal Parts: Three Deponent Verbs

Notes:

Chapter 25β

*Principal Parts: Verbs that Augment to
εἰ- in Imperfect*

A few verbs starting with a vowel
augment to εἰ- instead of following the
usual rules for temporal augment. This
irregularity is accounted for by the disappearance of an initial digamma or σ

(or both). Thus:

> ἐργάζομαι = *ϝεργάζομαι,
> (*imperfect*) *ἐϝεργαζόμην.
> When ϝ drops out, ει results.
> ἕπομαι = *σέπομαι, (*imperfect*)
> *ἐ(σ)επόμην > εἱπόμην. The pres-
> ence of an original σ is indicated
> by the aspiration (compare ἑπτά =
> Latin *septem*). The second aorist
> *ἐ-σ(ε)π-όμην > ἑσπόμην. Here
> the original σ of the stem is re-
> tained, but the ε is dropped
> (syncope).
> ἔχω = *σέχω, (*imperfect*) *ἔσεχον >
> εἶχον. In the future ἕξω, aspira-
> tion indicates the original σ. In
> the stems σχ- and σχε-, the σ is
> retained but the ε is dropped.

Other verbs with irregular augment
are:

> ἐάω (23) = *σεϝάω, (*imperfect*) εἴων,
> ἐάσω, εἴᾱσα, εἴᾱκα, εἴᾱμαι, εἰάθην
> (ἔθω) (28) = *σέθω, (*perfect*) εἴωθα
> ἕλκω (25) = *σέλκω, (*imperfect*)
> εἷλκον, ἕλξω. The other tenses
> are formed from the stem
> (σ)ελκυ-: εἵλκυσα, εἵλκυκα,
> εἵλκυσμαι, εἱλκύσθην.
> ἵ-η-μι (see Chapter 21, Grammar 4,
> pages 68–70) = *(σ)ί-(σ)η-μι,
> ἥσω, ἧκα, εἷκα, εἷμαι, εἵθην
> ἵ-στη-μι (see Chapter 20, Grammar
> 1, pages 48–50) = *(σ)ί-στη-μι,
> (*perfect active*) ἕ-στη-κα,
> (*pluperfect*) εἱ-στή-κη
> ὁράω (see 29α) = *ϝοράω (*imperfect*)
> ἑώρων, (*perfect active*) ἑόρᾱκα or
> ἑώρᾱκα, (*perfect passive*) ἑώρᾱμαι
> or ὦμμαι
> For εἶδον = *ἔϝιδ-ον and οἶδα =
> *ὄϝιδ-α, see 29α.

Chapter 26α

*Principal Parts: Verbs with Present
Reduplication*

Present reduplication consists of the
first letter of the stem + ι, e.g., γι-γνώ-
σκω (γνω-/γνο-), δί-δω-μι (δω-/δο-).

γί-γνομαι (γεν-/γενε-/γον-) = *γι-
γέν-ομαι
πί-πτω (πετ-/πτω-) = *πι-πέτ-ω

These two verbs follow regular patterns. In the second perfect of γίγνομαι,
the common change of stem vowel from ε
to ο occurs. In πίπτω (πετ-) the τ drops
when σ follows, in common with other
stems in dentals. In the perfect, the
vowel and consonant of the stem are re-
versed (metathesis).

> διδάσκω (διδαχ-) = *διδάκ-σκω

Here the χ drops out in the present
stem. The verb follows the regular pattern of a guttural stem but is irregular
in retaining the prefix δι- in all tenses.
The root of the verb is δα-, which is
found in the poetic verb δά-ω, δαήσομαι,
ἐδάην I learn; (*causative*) I cause to
learn, teach.

Chapter 26β

*Principal Parts: Verbs with Three Grades
of Stem Vowel*

For the terminology used to describe
the three grades of stem vowel, see the
note in this teacher's handbook with the
principal parts in Chapter 24α.

πάσχω (πενθ-/πονθ-/παθ-):

The root of this verb is πενθ-; compare τὸ πένθος grief.
The present is formed from παθ-:
*πάθ-σκω > πάσχω (the θ drops out be-
fore the σ, and the κ is aspirated).
The future is formed regularly from
πενθ-: *πένθ-σομαι > πείσομαι. The
-νθ- drops out before the σ and the pre-
ceeding vowel is lengthened; compare
σπένδομαι, σπείσομαι, ἐσπεισάμην.
The perfect is formed regularly with
a change in stem vowel from ε to ο: πέ-
πονθ-α.
The verb often has a quasi-passive
meaning, e.g., εὖ πάσχω = I am treated
well.

ἀπόλλῡμι from *ἀπ-όλ-νῡμι
(ὀλ-/ὀλε-/ὀλο-) (26), ἀπολῶ,

ἀπώλεσα I destroy, ruin, lose
ἀπολώλεκα I have ruined, ἀπόλωλα
    I am ruined
ἀπόλλυμαι, ἀπολοῦμαι, ἀπωλόμην I
    perish

Note the Attic reduplication (see 29β)
of both the first perfect and the second
perfect: ἀπ-ολ-ώλε-κα, ἀπ-όλ-ωλ-α.

Chapter 27α

Principal Parts: Verbs from Unrelated Stems

αἱρέω, (second aorist) *ἔ-ἑλον >
    εἷλον.

The other tenses of this verb are
formed regularly from the stem αἱρε-,
except for ε- in the aorist passive.

ἔρχομαι: for εἶμι see Chapter 17,
    Grammar 2, page 17.

From another stem (ἐλευθ-) related
to this verb is formed the epic and lyric
future ἐλεύσομαι. From the stem ἐλυθ-
is formed the epic and lyric second
aorist ἤλυθον = ἦλθον by syncope. Note
the Attic reduplication in the second perfect ἐλ-ήλυθ-α (see 29β).

Chapter 27β

Principal Parts: Another Verb from Un-related Stems

The parts formed from the stem λεγ-
are regular guttural formations.
The verb εἴρω in the present is found
only in the *Odyssey*. Stem: ἐρ-/ῥή-
(metathesis) for ϝερ-/ϝρη-, hence in the
perfects *ἔ-ϝρηκα > εἴρηκα and *ἔ-
ϝρη-μαι > εἴρη-μαι.
The second aorist is supplied from
the stem ϝεπ-: *ἔϝεπ-ον > εἶπον. Note
that the augment is retained in all
moods.

Chapter 28α

Principal Parts: Another Verb from Un-related Stems

Although the principal parts of φέρω
look idiosyncratic, they become more

intelligible if the principles of Attic
reduplication are understood (see 29β).
The perfect active and passive and the
aorist passive are formed from the stem
ἐνεκ- (ἐνοχ-). The strangest feature of
the verb is the appearance of first and
second aorists with the same stem and
no difference in meaning.

Chapter 28β

Principal Parts: Verbs Adding ε to Stem

Others:

κaθεύδω (2), (*imperfect*) ἐκάθευδον
    or κάθηυδον, καθευδήσω
μέλλω (7), μελλ-ήσω, ἐμέλλ-ησα
μέλει (26), μελήσει, ἐμέλησε,
    μεμέληκε
τύπ-τω (6), τυπτήσω
χαίρω (21), χαιρήσω, κεχάρηκα,
    ἐχάρην

Chapter 29α

Principal Parts: ὁράω and οἶδα, Seeing and Knowing

For the augment in ἑώρων, ἑόρᾱκα
or ἑώρᾱκα, ἑώρᾱμαι, see 25β (ἑώρων =
*ἐϝόρων, similarly εἶδον = *ἔϝιδον).

οἶδα (ἰδ-)

This verb is a second perfect in
form, with augment: *ἔϝιδ-α. In the
first, second, and third persons singular
of the perfect, the initial ε changes to ο,
giving οἶδ-α; in the plural, the augment
is dropped, and σ replaces δ. In the pluperfect, εἰδ- is augmented to ἠδ-, and in
the plural again σ replaces δ. The imperatives use the basic stem ἰδ- with σ
replacing δ. The subjunctive, optative,
infinitive, and participle are regular
perfect forms.

Chapter 29β

Principal Parts: Verbs with Attic Redu-plication

A small number of verbs beginning
with α, ε, or ο reduplicate by repeating
the initial vowel and consonant and by
lengthening α and ε to η and ο to ω.

ἀκούω (4), ἀκ-ήκο-α; ἐλαύνω
(ἐλα-) (2), ἐλ-ήλα-κα; ἐσθίω (ἐδο-)
(9), ἐδ-ήδο-κα.

ἐγείρω (ἐγερ-, ἐγορ-) (see 23α), ἐγ-
ρήγορ-α (for ἐγ-ήγορ-α), ἐγ-
ήγερ-μαι

ἔρχομαι (ἐλυθ-) (see 27α), ἐλ-ήλυθ-
α

ὄλλῡμι (ὀλ-) (see 26β), ὄλ-ωλ-α

φέρω (ἐνεκ-) (see 28α), ἐν-ήνοχ-α
(note the change in the stem
vowel from ε to ο and the aspirated second perfect), ἐν-ήνεγ-
μαι

Chapter 30γ

*Principal Parts: ἀναμιμνῄσκω and
μέμνημαι*

Notes:

Chapter 30δ

*Principal Parts: Verbs with -αν-/-ν-
That Take Supplementary Participles*

Notes:

Chapter 31β

Principal Parts: Verbs in -μι

All three of these verbs have present
reduplication: ῐ́-στη-μι = *σῐ́-στη-μι

(compare Latin *stāre*); the initial σ
drops out, and its original presence is
indicated by aspiration.

So also ῐ́-η-μι (see Chapter 21,
Grammar 4, pages 68–70), ἥσω, ἧκα,
εἷκα, εἷμαι, εἵθην. Originally *σῐ́-ση-
μι (ση-/σε-); the σ drops out, hence *ἕ-
σε-κα > εἷκα.

Other verbs in -μι:

ἀνοίγ-νῡμι, δείκ-νῡμι, ζεύγ-νῡμι,
ῥήγ-νῡμι (see Chapter 22, Grammar
3, pages 82–83 and 24α)

ἀπόλλῡμι (26)
δια-σκεδάν-νῡμι (σκεδα-) (27)
δύνα-μαι, ἐπίστα-μαι, κεί-μαι (see
25α)
εἰμί (ἐσ-): the σ drops out, and *ἐσμί
becomes εἰμί
εἶμι (εἰ-, ἰ-) (see Chapter 17, Grammar 2, page 17)
κρεμάν-νῡμι (κρεμα-) (19)
πί-μ-πλη-μι (πλη-/πλα-) (17)
σβέν-νῡμι (σβε-), σβέσω, ἔσβεσα,
ἔσβηκα (I have gone out),
ἐσβέσθην (see 24α). The original stem was σβεσ-; the σ drops
out and the nasal infix -νυ- is
added.
φημί (φη-/φα-) (see Chapter 23,
Grammar 5, pages 96–97)

SUBJECT INDEX

At the end of the Index is a separate listing of Greek words for grammatical and cultural reference.

WORD STUDY INDEX

The page references are to the Word Study sections in the student's book.

WORD BUILDING INDEX

The page references are to the Word Building sections in the student's book.